Hugh McManners was born in Oxford, the eldest son of Canon John McManners FBA, the Regius Professor of Ecclesiastical History, and latterly a Fellow of All Souls College. He was brought up in Australia, in Tasmania and New South Wales, and was educated at several schools including Sydney Church of England Grammar School and Magdalen College School, Oxford.

He joined the Army in 1972, went to Sandhurst and was commissioned into the Royal Artillery. His service has included six months as part of the United Nations peace-keeping forces in Cyprus immediately after the 1974 Turkish invasion.

In 1975 the Army sponsored him to read Geography at St Edmund Hall, Oxford University, where he gained a Boxing Blue, Half Blues for Modern Pentathlon and a degree.

He joined 148 Commando Forward Observation Battery in 1978. He was awarded a 'Mention in Despatches' for his part in the Falklands War.

He left the Army in 1989, and is now a writer and broadcaster. He was The Sunday Time's defence correspondent for five years, and has written books on outdoor activities, travel and military matters including *The Scars of War* and *Crowning the Dragon* (both published by HarperCollins). He is married with two sons.

# FALKLANDS COMMANDO

Hugh McManners

🏛 HarperCollins *Military History*

HarperCollins*Publishers*
77-85 Fulham Palace Road
Hammersmith
London
W6 8JB

The HarperCollins website address is:
www.fireandwater.com

First published in Great Britain by William Kimber & Co Ltd 1984
Second Edition published by Grafton Books 1987

This revised edition published by HarperCollins 2002

ISBN: 0 00 714175 0

Editor: Ian Tandy
Editorial Assistant: Samantha Ward
Drawings: Jan Suermondt
Design: Ray Barnett

Printed and bound in England by Clays

*Front cover photograph*: The Author during Operation Brewers Arms in May 1982.
*Rear cover photograph*: Forward Observation Team 1 awaiting transport after the
cessation of hostilities, June 1982.

To my mother Sarah, and to Deborah,
the mother of our two lovely boys, William and Joseph.

# Editor's Note

The first edition of Falklands Commando 'hit the streets' over eighteen years ago and even as a teenager I was struck by its frank and vivid portrayal of life at the 'sharp end' on a *modern* battlefield. I still enjoy reading it now; some twenty years after the Falklands War, it's still as fresh and relevant as it was then.

The experiences of soldiers like Hugh helped shape the training, equipment and operational methodology of today's British Army, and if that's not reason enough to re-publish this work, let me suggest another:

Hugh's description of the discomfort and stress for the modern-day soldier is little changed since 1982 and we should be errant if we fail to remember this when we consider the working environment of our young volunteers, both of 1982 and now. Another of Hugh's titles includes the excellent *The Scars of War*, which examines the issue in some uncomfortable detail of how our Armed Forces address, or fail to address, the problems combatants face on their return from the battlefield.

I deem it a privilege to have been able to have worked with Hugh on this revised edition. To the author's credit, he again decided to omit a number of episodes, unflattering accounts of individuals' behaviour which might adversely affect the reputations of more than one senior Officer.

Hugh has revisited the entire text, adding information not originally included; new maps, made clearer through using modern printing methods, have been added; additional photography from his and Colonel Keith Eve's personal collections, now in colour, adorn these pages. And finally, Hugh has provided a retrospective introduction, allowing a personal and professional reflection on his experiences over the last twenty years.

# CONTENTS

## List of Maps and Diagrams

# Acknowledgements

I owe a great deal to many people who helped me in the writing of this book, and I am glad to have the opportunity of expressing my thanks to them.

General Sir Thomas Morony, KCB, OBE, the Master Gunner St James's Park, read my first draft and gave encouragement and advice. My father reflected over the work with the jaundiced eye of a professional historian and the perceptions of a World War II soldier, and gave me counsel and the faith to persevere. My mother transformed herself into a military expert to draw the original maps and compile the index; I owe a lot to her painstaking toil. Dr Richard Fargher, a World War II gunner and Oxford academic, and Mary his wife, volunteered to do my proof reading; their exactitude and insight has saved me from many mistakes. Mr Roger Opie, a Cornish dairy farmer whose military knowledge would make him a formidable adversary if ever the Duchy declared itself independent, was the reader for whom I first imagined myself to be writing; to his encouragement, his wife Sue added the photographic expertise which contrived the flattering portrait that adorns the back wing of the jacket.

Captain Patrick Mason of the army Legal Corps was an invaluable confidant and discussed with me many aspects of my presentation (aspects by no means confined to his own profession) over glasses of German beer in sleepy Verden.

I am grateful also to Lt-Colonel Keith Eve, Captain Brown and Captain David L., Falklands comrades-at-arms, for refreshing and correcting my memories, and to Major Mickey Warrender of the Irish Guards, Dr Mark Ironmonger and Mr Mike Sims (the librarian of the Staff College) who read versions of my story and approved.

I have profited from a great deal of advice, and I am deeply grateful for it; I have not, however, always followed it, and any errors that remain are my own responsibility.

In addition to his other assistance, Lt-Colonel Eve provided me with darkroom work on my own.

It is only now that I have come to realize what a jungle of problems confronts the inexperienced author; for shrewd and friendly guidance through these complexities I must thank my publisher Mr William Kimber and his team.

A final word of gratitude should go to my colleagues in 148 Commando Forward Observation Battery, with whom I spent four happy years, culminating in Operation Corporate. This book is the story of only five members, but I hope it may give my readers an idea of the sort of tasks in which we were all engaged and the relevance of these tasks to the final victory.

# NEW INTRODUCTION

*Falklands Commando* was in many ways, the initiator of the "special forces book syndrome" which has plagued the MoD for the last decade. But it was published into a very different, and in some ways more rational world. Up until the SAS' Iranian Embassy siege rescue operation in 1980, there had been no more than half a dozen special forces books published. The publicity attending the televised hostage rescue established the current voracious journalistic appetite for all things SAS, and around 30 special forces books were published in the 1980's. Then after the Gulf War between 1991 and 1996, around 80 books were written about SAS operations, 15 of them in 1996 alone.

Like *Falklands Commando,* these books were autobiographical, written by members of the special forces while their memories of the campaign were fresh, and not by senior commanders – with the one exception. Critics say that SAS general Sir Peter de la Billière started the avalanche of damaging special forces (SF) literature, by revealing details of SAS operations in the Gulf War in his *"Desert Command"* memoir. The former SAS commanding officer Brigadier Andy Massey joined Sir Peter in the MoD doghouse after appearing in a BBC four part documentary series on the Gulf War, and indulging in a spot of newspaper article writing. Another officer, writing under the pen name of Captain James Rennie, upset the brass hats by publishing an interesting but comparatively sober book about undercover Intelligence Corps operations in Northern Ireland. And so a host of recently retired SAS men, aided and abetted by their ghost writers, agents and excited publishers, rushed into print claiming that the general had set a precedent. The MoD went into freefall, banning authors from seeing their mates at the SAS' base in Hereford – but running shy of extending castigation and bans to Gulf War hero Sir Peter and the other two renegade Army officers. The media had a field day, the books were published and their authors damned – as if they cared. US special forces joked that typing and world processing skill were a vital part of SAS Selection.

Since 1996, the MoD has tried to stamp out this unwelcome literary genre; through contracts and exclusion orders that seek to make SF authors *persona non grata*. The MoD make every member of UK Special Forces sign a gagging contract agreeing not to divulge anything about their work. If they subsequently write books, they can be sued for any money they might make as an author, as well as be prosecuted under Official Secrets legislation. If a book about special forces is published today, the Ministry of Defence would almost certainly slap on a High Court ban and sue the author for breach of contract. If the author is a serving Army officer, he would be court martialled; and face imprisonment, heavy fines, and the ruination of his military career. If the author goes through the proper channels and submits his manuscript for MoD clearance, as happened to a friend of mine writing responsibly and sensibly about the military aspect of news coverage of special forces activities, he or she would be slapped on the wrist for being so presumptuous (black marks being inserted into their confidential "P" file), and ordered not to show the hard-wrought manuscript to anybody else.

Meanwhile in the outside world, the public continue to soak up much-hyped books by "SAS authors". At best the public are reading books ghosted by professional thriller writers who know how to spin out a good yarn. At worst they are reading some very tall tales indeed, by people who were never badged members of the SAS, or indeed in the case of one particular best selling author, had invented both their SAS credentials and the extraordinarily damaging events they said they had been involved with.

## INTRODUCTION

*Falklands Commando* could never have been published today. It escaped the nightmare of civil service interference and military censure through the offices of the then director of army public relations, now recently retired Inspector of Her Majesties Prisons, General Sir David Ramsbotham. Immediately after the war, I was posted into Whitehall, to work as a staff captain in the outer office of the Chief of the General Staff. My family suggested I might write a book (my father is a well-known historian and author), so I asked Sir David if given the special forces content, such a book might be possible. His response was unequivocal: "If only you would. We'd love to see something by a soldier to counter all these books being rushed out by the journalists. What you did was history, so write about it. Give it to me and I'll get it cleared." I was also greatly encouraged by my immediate boss, General Sir Thomas Morony, a witty, razor-sharp Old Etonian who was then the Army's second-in-command, who read my first draft on one of his rare weekends off. (I predict incredulity from currently serving military officers.)

And that was that. Sir David told me he'd enjoyed reading it, but hoped I wouldn't mind making one amendment. On page XX I'd talked about political attitudes at home, and expressed concern at "Margaret Thatcher and the Conservatives pushing Galtieri into a corner from which like a wounded bull, he would have no choice but to fight." Sir David reckoned this might be considered overly political for an army officer, which would require him to pass the book on to the appropriate civil service branch for their clearance, which could involve red pencil work elsewhere, affecting parts of the book they would not understand. He advised substituting "Some people" for "Margaret Thatcher and the Conservatives". Done.

And so the book was published, with some surnames replaced by letters, but complete with photos of special forces people. The then head of the SBS told me the pics didn't need sexy black strips across the faces as since the war, they had all changed in appearance so as no longer to be recognisable. Common sense prevailed, and I had the daunting experience of having a book published whilst slogging away as a student on the Army Staff College course at Camberley, surrounded by the brightest of my peers, each one an expert who would not pull any critical punches. God bless 'em. They all bought copies and were very kind. And after a week one RAF officer came quietly up to me at coffee to ask where the Puma helicopters had come from. I stared blankly at him, knowing the nearest Pumas were being flown by the RAF at Ascension Island. He turned to a page in the Operation Brewers Arms chapter, where I described being extracted by a brace of Pumas. A classic proof-reading error which only I could have spotted – but hadn't. We were in fact picked up by Sea Kings, which to my untutored soldierly eye, look like Pumas…

As a serving major, I did get a phone call from an MoD official when I submitted one of my Falklands stories for publication in a magazine. He wanted to know if *Falklands Commando* had actually been cleared for publication, and was out to ban me from publishing all of the stories that appeared in the book, as they were "too sensitive". But those were gentler days. We had a conversation in which this official made the interesting comment: "Well even though all this is published world wide already, we wouldn't wish to repeat the damage by allowing you to publish it again in a magazine". But in the end, the piece was published, I wasn't drummed out of the regiment, and the public came to read what it was actually like as a member of special forces fighting in the Falklands war.

During the actual fighting of the Falklands war, the MoD's desire to control the public's understanding of events was far more intense. Their media campaign was flawed, many mistakes were made, and a number of lessons were learned in time for the Gulf War nine years later. But relationships between the media and the MoD (and the over-arching government media handling machine) have remained fraught with suspicion, dishonesty and anger. This is a serious, unnecessary and unworthy problem, which will seriously affect future military operations.

Even now, in 2002, twenty years and several large-scale operations further on, the Ministry of Defence' media handling department remains antagonistic to the media upon which it depends. In 1982, many UK journalists were strong supporters of the military, and we still had proper defence correspondents on our national newspapers, who had taken years learning about the armed forces in order to report military matters accurately for a readership that was interested. (Today, only Michael Evans on the Times can be described as a professional, long-term defence correspondent; and he is an endangered species.)

But rather than help these potentially co-operative journalists to acquire and file helpful stories, MoD civil servants tried to control the media, a fruitless effort fronted by the robotic-sounding Ian MacDonald, an unhelpful, deliberately pedantic spokesman. It was as though the MoD saw itself fighting two wars: one on the other side of the world against the Argentine forces, and the other closer to home. The MoD were just not understanding the reality of media life, that regardless of any other consideration, the pages and television time still had to be filled. One of the colonels I worked with in the MoD on my return from the war (now a senior general), described Falklands War press conferences as if they were football riots: "The press came swarming in here every day demanding to know what was going on – *like vermin.*" I know now, having degenerated into journalism myself, that many of the British 'vermin' were well aware of the need for security, and could have written stories that were less damaging than many of the ones that were printed – or even just photographs, had the MoD been less autocratic, and worked to establish some good working relationships with particular journalists.

But the MoD's media department had already abdicated responsibility by treating the media as an enemy to be thwarted – the easiest and safest option. The top defence journalists were all down south with the Task Force, being obstructed by ignorant and largely ineffective MoD media officers who controlled the only means of transmitting copy once written. It was left to severely pressurised military commanders to talk with journalists on the spot, and on various occasions to intervene to prevent their stories from being hacked to pieces by the MoD minders, before transmission back to London. The MoD's media department had no credibility with journalists, and so could do nothing to ameliorate the media coverage it was trying so hard to suppress.

Since the Falklands War, I've had the opportunity to see all this from the journalist's perspective, as the Sunday Times' defence correspondent. Between 1995 and 2000, I reported various British military operations: Bosnia, the bombing of Baghdad and the Kosovo campaign. Since the Falklands war, satellite communications and other technological innovations have made it possible for the media to report wars independently, without any official help, forcing the MoD to include television and press facilities as part of their operational plan. But the antagonism and mutual distrust remains the same.

However unlike the rest of Whitehall, where civil servants can obfuscate, prevaricate and mislead journalists with little direct danger to anybody else, the MoD's media department cannot afford to play the same game. A war is too important. The media *en masse* will drop everything to cover it; it's a real drama of life and death that affects every news consumer. Media coverage affects national morale very deeply, and can sway the electorate in their support for military action. Our fighting troops, whose WAP phones, radios and miniature television sets keep them in contact with CNN, the BBC and ITN hour by hour, are also deeply affected. In recent campaigns, every military HQ has had at least one television set showing CNN round the clock. All too often, CNN gets the news out faster than the military's own battlefield information systems; the troops learn what's going on in their war at the same time as everybody else in the world.

There is no doubt that the wars of the future will increasingly be determined by media–led public opinion. But without an enormous (and depressingly unlikely) change of attitude, culture and perception by the MoD's media organisation, the battle for this all-important public opinion mandate will become increasingly more difficult for military commanders to win.

In the span of modern campaigns, the Falklands War was basic and brutal. Despite a huge array of modern technology, the war was won by exhausted soldiers with soaking wet clothing and bad feet, who walked across East Falkland to use bomb and bayonet on their enemy. But now, in the dawning years of the 21$^{st}$ century, we are becoming used to wars being won from the air, by bombers and smart missiles, with only the odd, often accidental casualty – the consequence of battlefield mistaken identity, minefields or a post-combat mix-up. Technology spares us from the harrowing homecomings of body bags. But judging from the wars fought by the USA and its allies against Iraq and Serbia, this growing reliance upon technology, air power and a remote technological way of killing people, condemns innocent civilians in an almost totally one-sided battle. Our military theorists talk of "asymmetric warfare", by which they means they mean small, often poorly equipped forces like the Vietcong taking on massive, well equipped forces like the US Army. In that example, the flea won the war, but many military experts – particularly in the world's air forces - believe that technology can now enable wars to be fought remotely without mutually high levels of bloodshed. Asymmetric warfare is no longer the worrying spectre it was, its asymmetry referring now to a stark imbalance in casualty rates; the large numbers of low tech "baddies" plus innocent third world civilians on the receiving end, and a few accidental deaths on the high tech side.

But I write this postscript just a few weeks after the appalling terrorist attacks of 11<sup>th</sup> September. The "baddies" used craft knives with medieval barbarity, killing more "high tech" people than any previous terrorist attack in history. Predictably the US military relied yet again on its technology to bomb retribution upon Afghanistan; and they look lucky – in that as I write, the Afghan leaders seem bent upon creating a stable country which will no longer give safe haven to terrorists. It has become clear that behind all the President's Texas tough talk of "smokin' 'em out", the US military had just the one card up their sleeve – as ever the laser guided bombs, missiles, and World War Two high altitude carpet bombing from our old favourites – the B52s. Doubtless the campaign's success will again be attributed to air power. In reality however, air strikes can only be at best a catalyst for change. It was the local opposition to the Taliban, empowered by the activities of SAS and US special forces on the ground, who did the fighting and achieved the result.

We cannot rely upon technology to save us from having to fight and if necessary die for what we believe in. I fear that the 21<sup>st</sup> century will provide our military people with plenty of opportunities. Asymmetric warfare is now developing new and more terrifying ways of striking back at rich, high tech nations - of which the USA is prime target. The economic grievances of the less developed world must become the prime concern of prosperous nations, even if the solutions mean we have to give things up. Their grievances fuel the anger and hatred that creates international terrorism; and only when they are assuaged, can many-headed monsters like *Al Qaeda* and *Islamic Jihad*, be strangled in their nests. It would be cheaper to bring trade and prosperity to the rest of the world, than to create the forces, agencies, weapons and high tech solutions needed to fight an increasingly hopeless battle against fanatical enemies who are not going to go away.

# INTRODUCTION

Fighting a war against this ill-defined asymmetric enemy will be very hard for the democracies, whose lawyers argue bitterly over anti-terror laws restricting civil rights, whose electorates will not tolerate military campaigns in which the body count grows too large. As we have already seen in the USA, the pressures on politicians to take revenge are enormous, even though this will certainly lead to increased terrorism. As I write, I am hoping that the USA and its allies will bring military-delivered aid to Afghanistan as part of the short term 'revenge' mission to arrest bin Laden – but will continue with this aid as part of a long term, global strategy.

But the terrorists themselves are not going to evaporate just because we hand over billions of dollars in aid money. They will continue operating, and as we have seen in Northern Ireland, positioning themselves so they can benefit financially, as local contractors, or gangsters. Aid must be provided not as large cheques to line the pockets of government officials, but as well organised, closely supervised, long-term projects that will get the local economy creating wealth for itself and its people. And at the same time, the world's police, military and secret service agencies must use the widest range of techniques and tactics to root out terrorists. Technology has its part to play, but success can only be achieved by putting men and women onto the ground, and the risking of lives. And as is obvious, they must be properly equipped – with clothing and equipment that takes advantage of the most up-to-date technology.

Britain's armed forces are increasingly engaged in all manner of operations that are unpredictable and potentially very hazardous. They have also emerged from the most miserable period of money-saving cuts, with the prospect of further serious budgetary difficulties not far over the horizon. Our Armed Forces are slimmed to the bone, with none of the slack needed either for formation training, or the unforeseen reinforcement of units already on operations. Service men and women are over-worked and morale is fragile.

Politicians and even some senior officers, resorting to self-congratulation to paper over cracks in the much presumed upon morale of our armed forces, have correctly stated on various occasions, that our troops are the best in the world (a truth better left unsaid – at least by us, in my opinion...). But as they enjoy the reflected glory of hard-won military success, these same politicians, senior officers and civil servants ignore the bathos that could so easily overwhelm the people who actually have to do the work and take the risks. MoD officials will doubtless cite the various reorganisations and improvements that they would argue make my criticisms out dated. I have not however mentioned the state of the Forces' (particularly the Army's) medical services. We could not go to war and expect to cope with any predicted level of casualties without seriously affecting Britain's civilian National Health Service. General Sir Michael Rose, an SAS officer and Adjutant General (responsible for all personnel matters) who in Bosnia set much of the agenda for future military peace keeping operations, has already warned that though we assume our armed forces will continue to win wars, without radical changes (and more money), we must prepare ourselves for a serious military disaster; as our battle winning troops cannot be expected to do it on their own indefinitely.

The SA-80 (L85A1) rifle saga is a typical and disgraceful example. Apart from boots, a soldiers' rifle is his (or her) most important piece of equipment. Boots and rifle, the rock-bottom fundamentals of any armed force – or so you might think. (I will forego telling the equally disgraceful history of the British Army's useless DMS boot.)

In the 1980's, many British soldiers wanted to use US made M-16 rifles in preference to their heavy and mostly worn out SLR's, or the ineffective, old fashioned and often dangerous SMGs, that were British Army standard issue personal weapons. I used the Colt Commando AR-15 variation of the M-16 during the Falklands war. An off-the-shelf buy of M-16's from the USA would have given us what we needed, and saved millions of pounds.

But to keep British arms manufacturing in business, the UK developed its own new rifle known as the SA-80 (of the Nato standard 5.56mm calibre, matching the M-16) at great cost. This took a very long time, and after the new weapon entered service, serious flaws were very quickly discovered. But presumably because it was hoped other countries might buy the new weapon, these flaws, a combination of fundamental design faults and shoddy manufacture, were ignored – despite well-informed and extensive media coverage of the problems. Only when British troops went to war in the Gulf against Iraq and the media ran stories of SA-80 jamming in the desert sands, firing pins breaking and so on, was something done. At the same time, it was revealed that Britain's much-vaunted new Challenger tank (another putative British defence industry money spinner) could not cope with desert conditions; the MoD had not bothered to purchase sand filters to protect Challengers' engines.

Millions were spent investigating SA-80's faults. Then in 2001, two decades after the SA-80 had been designed, and extensive modifications, the MoD announced that "exhaustive trials" proved that SA-80 could finally be considered reliable. Fingers crossed chaps, while the MoD's procurement chiefs offer their most earnest thanks for the good fortune that kept British Army line regiments from being sent to war during all those years.

But despite this and many other procurement disasters, nothing much has actually changed. In the large-scale military exercise in Saudi Arabia in Autumn 2001, from which special forces troops were flown directly into the Taliban war in Afghanistan, many soldiers were not issued with proper desert uniforms and equipment. Their ordinary black combat boots for example, got so hot that people's feet were burned.

The problem is one of perception verging on ignorance. The MoD's army of civil servants is greater in number than Britain's actual Army and twice the size of the Royal Navy and the RAF. They have their own peculiar perceptions. They inhabit bureaucratic enclaves in places like Bath and Whitehall, with very little contact with real troops, who live scattered across Britain in military towns like Catterick, Aldershot, Colchester and Warminster, on remote airbases in the Fens, or near ports like Plymouth, Rosyth and Portsmouth. Maybe it's a peacetime thing too, in which the smooth functioning of the MoD as one of the highest spending Departments of State, is the over-riding consideration?

There are no short cuts here; if we really want a secure, peaceful world, we have to pay for it – not just in time, effort and money, but by using and sometimes losing, the lives of dedicated men and women brave enough for such a commitment. These unique people: armed forces, secret service, police, fire and ambulance services... must be supported, equipped, paid decently and respected. And when their time of service is over, they must be helped back into normal life – particularly if they have been injured or affected by what they have had to do.

This was not understood before, during or after the Falklands, when a peacetime army went to war. We fought wearing boots that gave us trench foot, water-proofs we had bought with our own money from climbing stores, and heavy, out dated, low-tech radio equipment. And when we got home, there was no attempt to find out whether we had been adversely affected by the experience.

As this book is published, from 1st March 2002, the MoD are to defend themselves in London's High Court, from being sued by some 1800 veterans of the Falklands, Northern Ireland, Bosnia and Gulf campaigns, all of whom have suffered psychological damage, but were not looked after as they should have been. This case has dragged on for years, with the MoD using every trick in the legal book to avoid addressing the very serious issues involved. The case will be a severe PR disaster for the MoD and the Treasury Solicitors, but nevertheless MoD insiders insist the alternatives as they see them are far worse. It's all about money. Having been forced to pay out millions to military females forced to leave the Services because of pregnancy, the potential for further MoD payouts are enormous, and the judgement will affect the veterans of other campaigns too.

The MoD has already attempted to subvert the arguments involved in this case by pouring scorn on a supposedly new "blame" culture that they argue has created what they say are unreasonable legal claims. Senior officers have talked in the past of serious combat-related psychological conditions like depression and PTSD as "compensationitis". But the March 2002 court case is nothing to do with whether or not soldiers should be compensated for being affected by combat. Many people, litigant Falkland veterans as well as the opposing MoD defence lawyers, agree that experiencing combat is a reasonable expectation of a military career. Indeed some of those litigants, plus others like me, would have been disappointed if their military careers had not included a few actual combat operations. At issue is not the adverse psychological effect of combat upon soldiers, which just like the more manifest physical injuries are well understood by the medical profession; but whether the MoD and more particularly the Army took proper and responsible care of the psychological well-being of its combat soldiers before and after the fighting.

In a book I wrote in 1993, "*The Scars of War*", I describe the way modern soldiers are affected by combat, and how despite the considerable body of medical knowledge in the area of post-combat psychology, many British war veterans are left to cope on their own with severe combat-related mental problems. The book created an inevitable flurry of knee-jerk outrage from some of the old-school military, highlighted by a strange, apoplectic (and wildly libellous) six page letter sent on open distribution to several very senior officers within the MoD. The bombast died away rapidly as people actually read the book, which subsequently appeared on the official reading lists of the Army Staff College and Royal Military Academy Sandhurst.

In particular, *"The Scars of War"* described how until the late 1980's and the Gulf War, the British Army's psychiatrists neglected both the education of troops into the likely psychological affects of combat, and the detection and consequent treatment of psychologically damaged soldiers. I ascribed this to the Army's overall lack of interest in what they then considered to be "sideshow" conflicts (like the Falklands – "not a proper war" as one senior armoured corps officer told us at Staff College in 1984), which diverted attention from the Cold War and the British Army's prime role in maintaining an armoured impasse between the NATO and the Warsaw Pact in Central Europe.

These hypothetical Cold War armoured battles would certainly produce large numbers of full-blown battle shock casualties, and were considered more worthy of medical staff attention than the more insidious PTSD symptoms exhibited by the psychological casualties of lower intensity operations. The then Professor of Military Psychiatry, who moved up to become Director of Army Psychiatry, Brigadier Peter Abraham, was a well-known expert on battle shock. As several more junior Royal Army Medical Corps psychiatrist officers explained to me with some frustration, battle shock was the priority, rather than the psychological injuries actually being suffered by our soldiers - in Northern Ireland particularly. Vietnam and other so-called "low intensity" wars had provided a huge amount of medical information that British

Army psychiatrists should have been using in preparing troops for battle and looking after them afterwards.

In the High Court, the war veterans' case is that they should have been told what to expect, then been trained to identify symptoms and take basic remedial actions, and received proper psychiatric assessment and treatment afterwards – just as they would expect for physical injuries. If this had been done, the damaging effects of their experiences would have been mitigated, and affected vets would now be able to function normally. Instead, lives have been ruined, families destroyed, tough, sane people have committed suicide, and many committed career Service men and women have quit when they actually wanted to stay.

This fundamental lack of care cannot be tolerated. In our terrible new, post 11th September world, we have only the people who risk their lives on our behalf to keep us all from the same darkness that engulfed the New York Trade Centre. If we do not insist that our people are properly treated, they will no longer come forward to do this work. And we will all be finished.

Canterbury
Kent
Christmas Day
2001

# 1984 INTRODUCTION

I write from a second-floor room (overlooking the cricket square) of the Staff College at Camberley, tucked away from the bustle of the Royal Military Academy, Sandhurst, behind green lawns and trees, with marbled halls lined with paintings of moustached generals and glass cases full of threadbare service uniforms worn by famous men in history-book battles. The columns around the central gallery are engraved with the names of the dead of half-forgotten wars in unpronounceable places – carefully annotated 'died of wounds', 'died of sickness' or 'killed in action'. These battles would have been long over by the time the news of their outcome (and indeed the news that they had ever happened at all) had reached the outside world.

Two years after the day when the Argentine 'Buzo Táctico' (a company of their marine commandos) landed at Mullet Creek in East Falkland (2 April 1982) my memories of the extraordinary four months that followed are fresh, some of them deeply etched. Yet the whole episode stands apart from anything else. My mind seems to be able to merge things into each other, putting them into context, but not so with the Falklands saga. I suspect that this phenomenon is widespread: an inability to associate the geographical isolation of those islands and the political problem they now represent with the national fervour generated over their occupation and recapture in 1982. Other nations shared in this excitement and yet today talk disparagingly about the wisdom of sending the Task Force for so little material gain. The question of principle seems to have been forgotten.

From the stability of day-to-day life, with its routines and mild excitements, in 1982 the world seemed suddenly to go mad. Then just as suddenly it was all over.

From the time the Argentine commandos threw phosphorus grenades into the Royal Marine Barracks at Moody Brook until, three days later, the Task Force set sail was a period of intense preparation and chaos. It was not clear what the Task Force was going to do – indeed some thought we would simply float around for a while and then come home. Once at sea the pace eased off into an expectant lethargy, time being occupied in training and listening to the World News. As with most other people's experience of war, it was boring and uncomfortable – but above all worrying.

Once hostilities began – with the capture of South Georgia on 25 April and then the naval battle (the sinking of the *Belgrano* on 2 May and the successful Exocet attack on HMS *Sheffield* on 4 May) a dreadful sort of momentum developed as we all concentrated on the tasks that we were going to have to perform. The lethargy had completely evaporated, everyone was screwed up with tension and events seemed to follow on rapidly.

As this is a real story, the exciting bits happen too suddenly (and sometimes too often) for a well-constructed plot. They are separated by periods of boredom made worse by the uncomfortable conditions and the continual gnawing worry. The end came with little real drama, as a tired and foregone conclusion which had been dragged out for several weeks. As far as we were concerned, once 3 Commando Brigade was safely ashore the outcome was decided. It was simply a question of when the 'Argies' would see sense and give up. The Argentine surrender was not a sudden relief either; it introduced a completely new set of problems and left us stuck eight thousand miles from home. In short, as a story it has disadvantages of timing and plot. When compared with the battles carved in marble around the balconied foyer of the staff College, there are many differences and some similarities. It all happened far from home – a part of the world that many people thought was nearer Scotland than South America. The distance was the maximum that could be imagined for an amphibious group to cover without a friendly port. The speed at which the operation was mounted is unparalleled and it was all over extraordinarily quickly. Modern communications meant that the commanders on the spot (Brigadier Thompson and Rear-Admiral Woodward then Major-General Moor) spoke daily to their masters at Northwood, who in turn were influenced daily by the War Cabinet. This is in contrast to the Boer War when the news took weeks to arrive and commanders simply got on with fighting their battles.

Although the media had less of an influence than in other recent wars (by virtue of the distance and the lack of independent means of transmitting the stories) the men of the Task Force were avid consumers of media conjecture – by means of out-of-date newspapers and the World Service of the BBC. Interest in the political manoeuvrings early on was keen and morale fluctuated according to how the media viewed the progress of diplomatic talks. When diplomacy failed and the war started, lurid headlines in some papers made us uncomfortable – and some made us angry. The armchair admirals and their sometimes wildly inaccurate pronouncements were amusing, but when they started to get it right (for instance discussion about the impending attack on Darwin and Goose Green on the very evening that the Paras were sweating through the bogs and tussock grass of Laguna Legna for a surprise night attack) it seemed insensitive and indiscreet. Of course they were guessing – just as the Argentinians could guess. Indeed their conjecture might have helped give an impression another diversionary raid (D Squadron SAS had raided Darwin on the night of the San Carlos Landings). However, that interpretation is really too charitable as that night the Argentine garrison at Goose Green was reinforced by helicopter.

This sort of thing made us feel very isolated and a little bitter that we could not rely on our own countrymen, in warm television studios, to be reticent on our behalf.

The men whose names are carved in marble in the galleried entrance hall at Staff College Camberley, died as much from sickness as from enemy action. Medical science was rudimentary. Men would more often die from wounds than recover. In the South Atlantic however the medical services were superb; no one died of sickness and astonishingly every man who made it alive to the Main Dressing Station at Ajax Bay (nicknamed the 'Red and green Life Machine) survived in spite of the horrible wounds that modern weapons inflict. The surgeons attributed this to the very high standard of physical fitness of the wounded soldiers and their will to survive. The superb skill and dedication of the medical staff, often dead tired, is the other half of the story.

Unlike in Vietnam, where soldiers were only minutes by helicopter from the most modern hospitals, Falklands wounded had to lie out, often for hours, before helicopters could get to them. Medical training on the voyage south enabled their mates to keep them alive during this waiting. Every man knew basic major-road-accident-type first aid – techniques for stopping massive bleeding, external heart massage, mouth-to-mouth resuscitation and putting up drips, either intravenous of intra-rectal, introducing a new cry on the modern battlefield: 'Medic, Medic…for god's sake shove it up my arse!'

Afterwards, in the comfort of normal surroundings with time to reflect, Operation Corporate (as the whole operation was termed) seems like a dream that happened to other people. It was like stepping through a looking glass – but once on the other side there was no guarantee of getting back. The first time I allowed myself to think realistically of getting back home was a few days before the Argentine surrender, but even then I did not count on it until I was in the comfort and warmth of HMS *Intrepid* watching video films of Wimbledon.

I have not felt inclined to philosophise – I don't think warfare lends itself to that. It is cruel, unfair and brutal. Human nature sadly makes wars inevitable and so, when forced to fight them, soldiers must be resolute and ruthless and the experts at their trade, to get them over with as fast as possible.

Exposure to violence has a deadening effect on emotions and as my story unfolds this becomes apparent. Loyalties within my own little group become more important than anything else. A sort of weariness envelops everyone, a phenomenon that can only truly be understood by those who have been involved in wars. Clear moral distinctions become blurred and people move with tired resolution through one sad and violent crisis to the next. Strangely there are also unique moments of clarity, of comradeship and joy of living, which can only exist in contrast with the discomfort and danger. It is a triumph of the human spirit that men are able to live through wars without becoming barbaric and losing their moral values. If only we did not have to go and fight them.

I wrote this book as a 'worm's eye view', without the benefit of hindsight. My aim is to convey the flavour of life below decks and in the mountains, and my impressions of a small slice of the war. I hope that my comrades at arms will find the variations between their memories of events described and mine interesting rather than irritating. (No two people ever remember the same thing in the same way.)

For several months after I got back from the South Atlantic I was somewhat of an oddity. It took time to readjust to normal life. New acquaintances (such was the interest in the campaign) were unable to resist asking the question 'What was it like?' A brief answer to that simple question would take at least an hour. Military people kept telling me how lucky I was to have gone south and been a part of it all. Some of the Operation Corporate was boring. For much of the time I did not know exactly what was going on and everything had a backdrop of worry and discomfort. There is a fair amount in the story that has to be explained to the reader in preparation for when the action starts. In addition I have tried to show how we enlivened the boredom and coped with the anxiety, fear and sadness.

Although primarily for the friends who were perceptive and kind enough not to ask, this book is also an answer to the question 'What was it like?' Operation Corporate was like nothing else at all. Furthermore, I do not count myself lucky to have gone south, but lucky to have come home afterwards when so many did not. Now I am home safely I would not exchange my 1982 April 'break' with anyone. The book is also for Nick Allin, Des Nixon, Steve Hoyland and Tim Bedford who are in the story throughout, even though I do not manage to work them in as often as they deserve. They kept me on the rails and I very much enjoyed being with them – in spite of the terrible world outside.

The Staff College
Camberley
February 1984

# Chapter 1
# The Calm Before the Storm

On 2nd April I went down to Cornwall for two weeks' Easter leave. I had conspired to get there a few days early, using the excuse that I was reconnoitring a number of parachute-dropping zones for an exercise to be held in the summer. I travelled from my base at the Royal Marines Poole in Dorset in a blue RAF Ford Escort driven by Flight Lieutenant Jeff Diggle – of the Special Forces Flight – who was as keen as I was to get out of the office.

We spent the day tramping the wet tussocks and sand dunes around Perranporth and chatting about approach headings for aircraft and hazards for paratroopers – like the mineshafts for the unwary to drop into – and estimating the extent of the tides.

The day was extraordinarily bright, the way it is in Cornwall when the rain stops. We could see the church in Cubert (far larger than Cubert itself) and across green –capped dunes, the wind-worn granite of Perran Cross and its companion mound and large white cross (a mysterious looking hillock that is a monument to modern vandalism as it protects the remains of the sixth century church of Saint Piran which has been reburied to save it for a future generation that might respect the past on which our culture is founded).

The now empty shanties of the ghastly Perranporth caravan site litter the dunes. Appropriately, under these dunes is said to lie the storm-ruined city of Langarrow – a Cornish Sodom which perished, to be overlaid by the oldest Christian church in the country and then a caravan site.

The flat-topped hill, with the small cruciform of houses that form the hamlet of Rose, was a slightly misty pastel green, blurred by the vivid blue of the sea, the white of the choppy clouds and merged into the soft green of the land. Seagulls wheeled and squawked and the chunter of a tractor carried a long way in the constant buffet of the wind.

The temperature was certainly fresh, but as April begins there is a mellowing of the sort that is not strictly to do with a few extra degrees on the thermometer. The long, wet haul of the winter was ending and everything was relaxing in preparation for the hectic activity of the summer. Quietly in the birth of the new spring, the harsh, natural beauty of the North Cornwall coast is softened and the true gentleness emerges.

Jeff and I had a pastie and a cup of tea in a large formica, seaside café in Perranporth. The shopkeepers, hoteliers and café owners spend the first month or two before Easter wondering about opening up again after the long winter, trying to remember where everything was put – back in September or October last year. At that time they had no desire to organise for the summer to come as they watched the last holidaymaker strap his suitcase ton the roof rack and start off up the Budnick Hill on the log flog home to the Midlands.

When they do open their summer businesses it is on a trial basis to sort out all the problems, find the utensils and get back into the routine before the hordes descend yet again. Then comes the worry time (like waiting for the monsoon rains), never sure if they will come this year because of petrol price increases or Sir Freddie Laker being back in business again.

Personally I can never see the point of going abroad when England is so lovely – especially in the summer. Even in bad weather there is always something interesting to do. As a philosophical proposition, the good only exists when in contrast with the bad but this is probably the projection of my lifestyle, in which bad weather has to be endured, cannot be avoided and so must be accepted.

The beach café was slowly opening up, the waitresses were staring blankly through the misted-up plate glass windows and feeling bored.

## THE CALM BEFORE THE STORM

We sat, intruders amid deserted tables, out of place in our camouflage smocks and high-calved parachute boots. The café was empty but all systems were ready to go.

It was the calm before the storm.

St Agnes village is timeless, the same whenever I return. I own a stone house in the main street that was once the residence of the Mine Captain. Each mine had a manager who was styled the 'captain' and was a man of local importance. The house had then been a printing works with the machines in the garage, a shop in half of the house and the family living in the rest. The back garden is overlooked by the chimney of what was once the beam engine house for one of the many shafts in the area.

The road to St Agnes is confusing, going down the hill and into the hollow of Peterville, which is often mistaken for the main village; then past the group of cottages at the top of the road leading down to the Trevaunance Cove. Today, peace and tranquillity cloak the same buildings, which were once a busy port and mining complex. The houses are small, with thick granite walls and slate roofs; the woodwork is painted either white or green and the front doors are sometimes of brighter, even vivid, colours. The slightly higher temperature caused by the maritime influence and the more southerly latitude lead to the odd palm tree which catches the eye.

In winter it generally rains and then the colours are grey and dull and the roofs shiny with water. When there is clear sunshine the transformation is dramatic – Easter time is interspersed with good and bad weather and I was lucky to return to glorious sunshine, the washing lines billowing with bed sheets.

I was very much looking forward to the delightful prospect of the two weeks' leave owed to me. I'd be able to tinker with a few of the many improvements necessary in the old house, go down to the rugby club on Saturday night, risk all in the surf trying to ride a six foot board and run for miles every day along the cliffs, alone with the gulls and the ocean.

Jeff pushed off in the Escort, having noted two useable drop zones, including one on Perranporth beach, which would, when used, interest the holidaymakers. I spent my first evening amongst friends at the St Agnes Hotel, which is a few yards down the main street from my house. This pub has been a hotel since the turn of the century and still has a good restaurant, sitting rooms and bedrooms upstairs. The front bar is dark and cosy and the walls are covered with model ships, photos of life-boat crews both old and new, and of the port in its heyday, with ore being loaded on to sailing ships down chutes from horse drawn carts.

I had made arrangements to meet people there next evening. However at six o'clock in the morning Maurice, the local policeman, knocked on the door. I was to report back to Royal Marines Poole at once, no reason given. He packed me into his panda car and we drove to Truro station for the next train going up country.

I was returning to Royal Marines Poole, a modern military camp at the edge of Poole harbour and next door to Rockley Sands holiday camp. The full name of my military unit was '148 Commando Forward Observation Battery Royal Artillery' and it had been based at Poole under several different names almost since the camp was created – in the grounds of a shooting lodge owned by Lord Wimborne.

Our unit cipher was the red-on-blue Combined Operations flash – with interlinked Thompson sub-machine gun, and eagle upon an anchor, signifying the combination of expertise involved. This device had been worn by the first commandos in the Second World War – when the Royal Navy had provided the coxswains for the boats, and the Army the soldiers to form the raiding parties that caused mayhem along the coast of occupied France. 148 Battery is directly descended from the Dundonald Bombardment Units formed at the same time and still recruits from both the Army and the Royal Navy. It is the only commando unit surviving that combines the expertise of the two services in the way that it did in those early days.

Each member of the 148 Battery has survived an arduous selection process. Each man has first to pass a preparatory 'beat up' and then the Commando Course at the Commando Training Centre at Lympstone. (As you travel on the train from Exeter to Plymouth you can see it on the far side of the River Exe estuary. Its modern buildings and grass banks belie the nature of its purpose, although you may be lucky enough to see small figures with weapons and packs trying to run in the mud at low tide or going around the assault course endlessly).

Those that succeed go on to Aldershot, to the Depot of the Parachute Regiment, and undertake the notorious 'P' company. This is a very severe physical test lasting four weeks and involving carrying heavy weights on long runs and marches, with assault courses, log races and field exercises designed to test determination, fitness and sense of humour. The parachute course itself, run in a gentlemanly fashion by the RAF, is sedate and relaxing by contrast with what has gone on before. The embryo 'Nigsfo' (as the Naval Gunfire Support Forward Observation is abbreviated) then starts his six month communications, tactics and observation course. Not everyone who gets this far succeeds, because the mental aptitude to pass this course is not tested in the hard and often brutal process of the commando and parachute selection.

The main purpose of the Commando Forward Observation Unit is to control the fire of the guns of the Royal Navy, from the ground, and the unit is equipped and trained to be put ashore in every way imaginable so as to be able to do this job. The unit is divided into a number of forward observation teams (FO teams), each of five men.

Each FO team is led by a captain from the Royal Artillery, who has a bombardier (the artillery equivalent of a Corporal) as his assistant. If the team splits in two on operations, the bombardier will take charge of one of the two teams created. The other three are a LRO (leading radio operator) or RO1 (radio operator class one) from the Royal Navy, a lance bombardier and a gunner. Each team member is able to control the fire from a naval gunship and ordinary field artillery. The officer and bombardier are also trained to call in strike aircraft to bomb targets. The teams are normally well forward in battle, being put ashore by boat, parachute or helicopter many days before the main force. Thus they are part of the special forces network of eyes and ears that send information back to UK and the ships at sea.

Royal Marines Poole is very well equipped for the specialized training that is necessary to prepare for this demanding role. The dock area, known as the 'Hard', is the home of the Landing Craft Company Royal Marines, who are experts in larger scale assault craft-work. The Special Boat Squadron also has their home in Poole and 148 Battery has very close links with them, for the specific purpose of working together in war. This close relationship turned up trumps in the Falklands. At this time it was my responsibility to organize the teams allocated to working with the SBS and to lead one of the teams, FO1 (which is short for Forward Observation Team Number One).

It is hard to get into 148 Battery, and once you have passed all the courses you have to be accepted as a reliable member of the team, which can take some time. The odd combination of hardness, fitness, technical expertise and intelligence produces an out-of-the-ordinary sort of soldier who prefers to do things his own way.

Personal relationships within the FO teams are very close. The teams remain together for long periods and travel the world as a tightly knit little group. The officer is "the boss" and the soldiers are referred to by their nicknames, in a very relaxed, informal style that can be relied upon to irritate senior officers from outside the unit. On the rare occasion when the teams are in barracks everyone makes great efforts to behave with due military deference, avoiding embarrassing cries like 'Hey, Topsy, have you packed your container yet?' or 'Oi, boss, what the hell have you done with my magazine?'. Such slips across the parade ground rather give the game away.

When away, the teams will go out on the town together and become gratifyingly unmilitary. There is more contact with the Royal Navy and the Royal Air Force than the Army, and this creates a 'cosmopolitan' attitude, which does not always gain approval in the Army proper. The trick of avoiding upsetting people is achieved by being as quiet and as anonymous as possible.

As the prime role of the 148 Battery is to find and engage enemy targets with naval gunfire, the nature and effect of the naval gun systems needs a little explanation.

Naval gunfire support (NGS for short) is very similar to field artillery, only it operates from the sea and not from the land. However, it delivers a very much heavier shell than the 105mm Light Gun with which the gunners in the Falklands were equipped and is generally more accurate than artillery. (In many instances this greater accuracy is a disadvantage – for instance when trying to stop the advance of troops spread out over a large area or when shelling a defensive area which would be spread out over a large area of ground.)

The older ships (such as HMS *Antrim* and HMS *Plymouth*) fire a 55lb high explosive shell 18,000 yards at a rate of more than one every two seconds – using the twin barrels on a single turret. (A field artillery gun fires a 35lb shell at up to four or five per minute, depending on the fitness and skill of the crew.) This fire is very accurate and puts down about a ton of high explosive every minute. Some of these older ships have twin turrets, which doubles their fire power.

The newer ships (Type 21's and Type 42's) with digital computers and fully automatic loading systems are even more accurate with each single barrel firing a 46lb shell 24,000 yards at the rate of 24 shells every minute. The response time is very fast (the time from when the ship receives the coordinates of the target over the radio from us, to when the round lands) and with the one gun, two targets can be engaged at the same time with one of them being illuminated with starshell (which is loaded automatically and fired to burst above the target). Targets can be stored in the computer and fired upon immediately if needed in a hurry.

The accuracy of the gun does not spread the shells around like the widely spaced guns of an artillery battery. This is ideal for seriously damaging (even destroying) buildings and bridges and wrecking trench positions, killing and wounding enemy whose overhead cover and fortifications would have withstood a field-artillery bombardment.

NGS has many peculiarities that make it seem a bit of a black art to those familiar only with artillery. The shells sometimes don't seem to do what they should and there are seemingly inexplicable delays. All these things are in the nature of the system and it is only with experience and training that this very powerful weapon system can be made to unleash its full potential. And that is the job of 148 Commando Forward Observation Battery.

For January, February and most of March, 148 Battery had been away in Norway with 3 Commando Brigade doing and mountain-warfare training. This had finished with a week of parachuting – using special techniques involving sledges, on to frozen fjords, remote, wooded hillsides and into the sea – and finally a large NATO exercise into which most of the unit parachuted in 5-man groups at night. This three months in the ice and snow was a regular commitment and many of the battery spent every winter there. One NCO had a total of sixteen winters in Norway under his belt.

I had been in hospital for two weeks in January 1982 and had gone out to Norway late to join the unit for the last part of the deployment, which was the parachuting and the final large exercise. I was not allowed to jump because of the back problems that had put me in hospital, so I was handling all the administration – which was not really my style at all.

In April, thanks to our stint in Norway, we were already acclimatised and prepared for war in the cold. The Falkland Islands (if that was where I was to be sent) would certainly be much wetter, but this was not a problem as our traditional training areas in the UK (Dartmoor, Okehampton, Cape Wrath, etc) were, it seemed, specially selected for rain, wind and cold. The malevolent being responsible for designating those parts of the British Isles as suitable for us to freeze and shiver our way through training exercises certainly did us a favour, because we had been through it all many times before and knew exactly how to cope.

Bad conditions force you to get to your procedures absolutely right away because you find that you have to devote more time to surviving than doing the job. Training under atrocious conditions means that you are less likely to be found lacking on the day, when things may actually be easier. At least the training had been realistic. The maxim 'Train hard, fight easy' is very true.

As the Inter-City 125 flashed smoothly through the beautiful countryside, across the Tamar with a glimpse of gleaming, grey warships at anchor off Plymouth, then through the lush green of

Devon and alongside the red sandstone cliff path (with the ocean on the right hand side) by Dawlish golf course, I wondered whether I was being recalled to do something about the Argentine scrap-metal men on South Georgia.

In fact the day after returning from Norway, I had a little amusement with Captain Kevin Arnold, our battery second-in-command. I concocted a message about 'Operation Penguin', which set him telephoning the usual people whom we contact when sudden moves are afoot. Kevin was easily fooled because in our line of business you tend to look on world affairs with a jaundiced eye and half a mind to possible participation. A panic move to Antarctica having just returned from Norway and the Arctic was not so surprising. April Fool's Day had been a few days ago and now the joke had backfired on me. A god with such a sense of humour would be hard to handle. So, I reasoned on the train, it was probably the Falklands.

# FALKLANDS COMMANDO

# Chapter 2
# Preparation and Departure

When I got back to the playing-fields and grey, modern buildings of RM Poole, the camp was in turmoil. The Argentinians were believed to be poised to invade the Falklands and so Landing Craft Company, the Special Boat Squadron and ourselves were getting ready to go.

The Falkland Island Garrison force, a company of Royal Marines known as Naval Party 8901, were changing over and the majority had left RM Poole a week earlier. The last few troops to go were still in the camp, after completing six months' training and preparation at Poole.

We had come to know them well, so we would all have a deep personal involvement in this crisis if the Falklands were to be invaded. There was much Falklands experience at Poole. Several ex-NP 8901 worked here and now produced maps, photos and even cine film taken during their tours of duty in the South Atlantic. Above all we had Major Ewen Southby-Tailyour, who had commanded NP-8901 in the past and had painstakingly mapped the Falklands coastline, charting its coves and inlets. Ewen, an irascible, amusing, and a good friend, was to become an invaluable source of information for the higher command in the forthcoming campaign….but this is to anticipate events.

Watching television news in the anteroom of the officers' mess, drinking tea and munching toast, it became clear that the Argentine invasion had taken place. We watched with disbelief as the story unfolded – like every other viewer but with a little more bated breath

41

and a lot more personal interest. When the first TV pictures were broadcast, the ex-NP8901 hands were able to point out exactly what we were seeing in valuable detail. We saw shots of our friends spread-eagled on roads being searched at gun-point by Argentine Special Force soldiers.

NP8901 was a token force and not intended to fight, although it did until, very visibly; the Governor ordered surrender because the overwhelming odds made further resistance and loss of life pointless. We were very relieved when later we heard that they had all returned safely to the UK. [We were later to see many of them going back again in *Canberra* as an extra company in 42 Commando (J Coy) led by another friend, their ebullient OC (Officer Commanding) Major Mike Norman.]

The next few days were chaotic, spent telephoning round Britain for equipment that we had either not been permitted to have or that we were due to have at some undetermined time in the future. The floodgates were open and there were no problems. Storemen, dug out of their beds at 4 a.m., were not only polite and extremely helpful, but asked if there was anything else that we might need - and even arranged transportation! Captain Bob Harmes our admin officer, lied furiously for days on end and turned up things of which we had only dreamed.

We watched the news with astonishment as the pictures of armoured cars in Port Stanley were shown and the story of the brave effort by NP8901 unfolded. It was chilling to see the armoured vehicles that might end up shooting at us, and the soldiers that soon might become our 'enemy'.

It was a simple matter to get 148 Battery ready to go. The Duty NCO had phoned everybody up and we all came in, from wherever we had managed to get on our own leave. (Captain Willie McCracken and his team were in New Zealand on an exercise and were back a few days later.) Our equipment, the Bergen rucksacks and webbing belt fighting order, was placed in our parachute training hangar in rows according to which team we were in.

Once this was done the confusion started, generated by a stream of contradictory instructions. What vehicles should we take if any? We still had the over-snow BVs (bandwagons) that we'd been using in Norway. Did we need to take skis and full arctic equipment, and would we need the boats? The only way to avoid the confusion was to take everything – which we did.

The battery never had a send-off as such; we simply rushed away to join various ships and aircraft – usually with very little warning. I do remember however a gathering at which we were all told - by our boss of all people, an unpopular and somewhat miscast major called Mike Morgan - that we were off for at least three months and this would be spent getting bored at sea. He urged us not to get the idea into out heads that we were going to fire bullets at Argentinians. Mike's final prophetic remark was, that if any of us fired any 4.5inch naval shells into Port Stanley he would eat his boots!

I was due to be the first off the mark with my second-in-command Nick Allin and an *ad hoc* team. FO1, had been together for some time, but this strong and experienced group was split up in what I thought was a misplaced attempt to spread expertise throughout the battery. Nick Allin and I were cross about this; in particular we lost my 'sailor' Stan Hardy, who was our medic, at just the time we were most likely to need a medic. I'd sent Stan to get hands-on experience in the casualty department at Poole General Hospital, and he'd also handled gunshot wounds and other injuries and illnesses during a stint with me running jungle warfare training in Belize, Central America.

However, Bombardier Nick Allin remained my second-in-command. We had been working together a lot and we knew each other very well. In fact, his marriage was the first social event I had attended in the battery when I first joined five years earlier, and we had spent plenty of time with each other, on exercises and socially. Nick is a cheerful and quite noisy bloke with a very sharp sense of humour that gets people working and keeps them amused. He comes from Okehampton and as a result gets quite a lot of stick about his 'janner' accent and the shortcomings of being a country boy. He replies to such sallies very sharply and with the appropriate references to the place of origin of the critic. Nick was also a Royal Navy lightweight boxing champion.

My new sailor was RO1 Steve Hoyland, a very bright and cheerful Northerner from Middlesborough ('Burra' as he used to call it) who had the alarming habit of removing his front teeth and grinning through the gap. He had been a radio operator on several big RN ships before coming to us; he had just completed all the courses and FO1 was his first FO team. He delighted in wishing himself back on board these ships when we were particularly cold, wet and miserable. He would paint pictures of the dogwatch lounging about in the warmth, making cups of coffee and then sauntering off to their nice warm "pits" - bunks. We used to say, 'Come on, you'd much rather be here with us, in spite of everything'; and he'd say 'No, give me a nice warm radio room any day.' Then he'd say, 'Ah well, boss, I'd miss you, so I suppose I really prefer it here.'

Gunner 'Des' Nixon was a Yorkshireman, older than the average gunner, having left the Army and then come back in. He is a very experienced soldier who had been in 7 Regiment Royal Horse Artillery when that regiment was part of the Parachute Brigade. The whole regiment were paratroopers and, with the light 105mm pack howitzers with which they were equipped, were parachuted into battle. Des had been a gun 'Number One', in charge of a gun and its detachment. He had left the Army and after several adventures and time spent working on building sites decided to come back. To do so he had to relinquish his former rank and start again. He was a sharp as nails and absolutely uncrackable, with a direct and sometimes very gentle sense of humour. His shortness and fair hair gave the wrong impression to anyone who was looking for trouble, and when pressed the Nixon reaction was swift and absolute. The rest of the team referred to him as the 'Old Man' or 'Des the Shovel' (after an unfortunate evening in Norway when a group of Royal Marines made the mistake of taking him on), and more often than not the 'Old Man' showed them the way home.

The fifth member of FO1 was also the youngest, Gunner Tim

Bedford. Like Steve and Des he had just completed the technical course at the end of all the selection. He had been in the forces less time than any of us, having come to 148 Battery virtually from Basic Training. He was inclined to be the quietest of the five of us, tall, straight-backed and rather serious-looking. Initially he, more than the other two, was worried about his lack of expertise. As time went on his self-confidence increased and he was more forthcoming.

Faced with putting a new team together at such a time, the overall lack of expertise was rather a worry for us all - but it did actually turn out to be a good thing. We used the weeks we were to spend on board ship going through everything we knew, talking about it and practising until we were perfect. There was also stacks of chat, wit and repartee which in my view is the best sign of all. They were great fun to be with.

The chaotic week of preparation was tiring. We worked away on the phones in the battery offices, we were summoned for briefings at strange times and went down into Poole for boozy dinners and hilarity in wine bars. We were summoned from our beds in the early hours of the morning to check equipment that had just arrived, and, when I finally received the word to pack our gear on to a four-ton truck and prepare to go, it was a relief.

Initially we were told to drive up to Arbroath, near Dundee in Scotland, to join 45 Commando. Then 45 were told they would have to sail to Marchwood in Hampshire to load some vehicles, so we decided to wait. Finally 45 were told to load everything into their trucks, drive south to Marchwood, take over their vehicles and load into a Royal Fleet Auxiliary ship (RFA) at the military port. This was the best solution for us, as Marchwood was only an hour down the road.

On the morning of 4th April, with a four-ton truck full of kit, and ourselves in a Land Rover, we set off for Marchwood to load onto the Royal Fleet Auxiliary *Sir Percivale*. We had 5 full sets of arctic gear, for South Georgia and in case the Falklands operation lasted into the winter. We had two inflatable rubber boats (Gemini) and four outboard motors and spares to match. In large wicker-work hampers, carefully padded, were our radio sets, one for each of us and several spares, with two hand 'wankers' (hand generators to charge up the batteries) and spare batteries. Bayonets had been issued, more as a declaration of intent as they fitted only one of the two sorts of rifles that we used. We took the 7.62-mm Self Loading Rifle (the SLR) and 9-mm pistols. However we found a lighter 5.56mm Armalite a better weapon for our purposes and so swapped, keeping the automatic pistols as well for a concealed 'last resort' weapon.

We were ready to parachute, if required, so we had chutes, the special fuel bags needed when parachuting with a Gemini boat and outboard motors, para helmets, CSPEP's (carrying straps personal equipment parachutist), heavy duty zip-up, waterproof bags, and so on. There was talk of us being parachuted on to the gunships that were already at sea in order to save time and get us there quickly.

I collected a huge pile of stationery from our chief clerk: notebooks, plastic film to waterproof the maps, sellotape, pens and pencils, A4 lined paper, exercise books, rulers, scissors and anything else I could purloin.

Later, after a few days boredom at sea, I was stricken with regret at my failure to bring my guitar with me from Cornwall. I had left it there as a sort of talisman to ensure my return. It did not seem somehow to be 'proper' to take such a frivolous thing to war and it would certainly have been lost in the chaos that ensued once we actually went into action. But I really should have brought it along. You need all the frivolity that you can conjure up when life gets too serious.

Our REME (Royal Electrical and Mechanical Engineers), Corporal Bob Summers, was furious at being left out of the orbat (order of battle). Not all the battery were due to go and, in his case, it was common sense that he should remain in Poole and use our absence to get the vehicles serviced and in good order. That was precisely what he did not want to do. He ran a very good MT (motor transport section) but also took every opportunity to do the military things, like parachuting. He came on as many exercises as he could to carry the mountains of kit and help with radio work. He had been told that he could not come and he was not at all happy about it. As his part of the war effort he drove our 4-tonner down to Marchwood like a dervish, swerving in a fearful U-turn when we took the wrong exit off a roundabout, as highly supportive civilian drivers, giving us the thumbs up and waves through their wind screens, pulled over out of our way.

We stopped off at Des Nixon's house (in a compound of Army houses) en route to pick him up – and enacted the same scene that occurred every time a team went away. On this occasion we had no idea how long we might be gone or what we might have to do (the diplomats might sort it out next week!). There were worried wives being cheerful and puzzled children who had seen Dad going off like this many times but realised that the atmosphere this time was different.

The Royal Fleet Auxiliary ship *Sir Percivale* was moored at Marchwood Military Port with her stern ramp lowered and a progression of forklift trucks picking pallets up from the quayside, running them down an incline onto a floating pontoon and across the lowered ramp into the ship's hold. The bow also had a ramp so that vehicles could if required run right through the ship and into succession of further ships linked together like a chain of very large caves. Three gangplanks were in use and two cranes were lifting stores in large nets, and loading Land Rovers, trailers and 105-mm Light Guns using special chain harnesses. The other side of the narrow jetty was similarly occupied with the loading of RFA *Sir Lancelot*.

Lines of Land Rovers were parked along the dock, their trailers bulging with camouflage nets and wooden poles, up-ended Bergen rucksacks, wickerwork hampers full of radio sets, black plastic jerry-cans and petrol cans, all emptied and vented according to regulations, ready for the voyage. Much of this equipment had come straight from Norway without having been unpacked, to be rapidly re-serviced then drawn again from the Q stores. Troops, in camouflage windproof smocks, dark green 'OG' trousers (Olive Green) and boots, wearing their webbing equipment and carrying personal weapons (a rifle or a submachine gun) lounged against the vehicles and chatted. Some were sitting in the cabs, others rooted about in the backs of trailers checking that nothing had been forgotten and rearranging their kit. The RCT dockers (Royal Corps of Transport) with white construction helmets, loaded the ships and we waited until the loading schedule got to us. There was no rush or impatience, as we knew we'd be on board for three months at least. In due course, when our time came, we went quietly up the gang plank and selected our bunks, staking the claim with a pile of kit. I noticed a name on a cabin door that I recognised, so I plonked my stuff on one of the spare bunks in that cabin.

We whiled away the afternoon with a chaotic lunch in the main galley – where cooks overwhelmed with the extra numbers, had their larder stripped bare as if by locusts, and knowing we had hours of waiting to fill, I wandered away from the dock, up through the camp to the picturesque officer's mess to read the newspapers.

Loading continued until 4:30 pm as we filtered off and onto the ship. Tea and 'stickies' were served on board but no one was hungry, having by that time ransacked the main cookhouse ashore. I made a last few phone calls from the call box on the quay, the gangplanks were drawn up and the deck parties coiled ropes and prepared to sail. The loyal wife of one of the helicopter pilots had driven all the way down from Scotland (he had flown in his Gazelle) to see him off and stood waving on the quay wearing deliciously tight red jeans.

There were farewells taking place on board as the wives of the RFA officers took their leave. Some had been living on board in their husband's palatial double cabins, travelling with the ship on an extended holiday. Operation Corporate entailed a rude curtailment of this nautical idyll, their sudden eviction on the eve of the ship's previously scheduled sailing for the delights of tourist Rotterdam, adding to the general confusion.

We put to sea two days before the rest of the Task Force, being pulled out from the jetty by dirty, cheerful tugs into the centre of the Solent just opposite the *QE2*'s berth (which was quiet). We got under way slowly as the dusk grew and the streetlights were lit on a blue-green, misty, spring evening. We nosed carefully down the channel past the river opening and Beaulieu and the old Army mental hospital at Netley. *Sir Lancelot* our sister ship, was astern, hooters sounded, echoing around the deserted shipyards and jetties, and we were as fine a convoy as you could wish. A Ford Transit van and a small saloon car parked up on a hard, hooted and flashed headlights to us. We waved back as the twilight deepened.

When the darkness made it impossible to see anything but the lights of the other ships and the lines of the quaysides, we melted away from the upper decks and went below to think about the open-ended sentence that we were starting. It sounds melodramatic to say, but for some of those on that deck watching England slip away into the night, it was their last glimpse of home.

# Chapter 3
# At Sea

For our first two days at sea we could still receive TV broadcasts from home. Reception was very good, which was not surprising for *Sir Percivale* had sailed from Marchwood around the back of Isle of Wight where she stayed. On the TV screens we watched the animated preparations in Portsmouth and Plymouth, the loading of the LPD HMS *Fearless* (standing for Landing Platform Dock - describing the large flight-deck on the stern and the rear-entry internal dock, which takes four large landing-craft). *Fearless* was to be the amphibious operations centre from which all the war planning would emanate. The two aircraft carriers, HMS *Hermes* and the new HMS *Invincible*, were crawling with chains of ant-like matelots passing stores hand to hand up the gang-planks; everything from boxes of baked beans and barrels of beer to Sea Dart missiles.

As *Sir Percivale* jerked and rolled in the swell, we saw on TV the emotional farewell given by the City of Plymouth to HMS *Fearless*, the whole ship's company lining the rails, the embarked commandos on parade, the helicopters lined up on the deck and the landing-craft following in the wake like ducklings chasing after their mother. The wives gathered at the best vantage points to catch the last glimpses and hold small children up for a farewell wave.

Only a few weeks earlier I had been on *Fearless*, sailing back from Norway into Plymouth Sound to be greeted by HM Customs on a go-slow and no one else. The purple blue hills were the same, the slate-grey houses and strange drowsy bustle, but the colour and slightly desperate carnival atmosphere today reminded me more of leaving Grand Harbour, Valetta (in Malta) than departing from Plymouth in the spring.

These farewells (on the wardroom telly) differed from those we were to see later (on video cassettes dropped by parachute) of the departure of 5 Brigade in the *QE2*. By then, three weeks later, it seemed that we were going to have to fight. When *Sir Percivale* sailed, the Task Force represented merely a floating threat, the back up for political negotiations and a diplomatic lever, lending weight to the measured formulae of negotiation. Our departure also seemed to brighten the clouds of the economic recession. Later the more sombre implications had become more apparent and so the mood was different.

HMS *Fearless*, from her homeport of Plymouth, HMS *Hermes*, HMS *Invincible, and* SS *Canberra,* from Southampton, sailed with a blaze of media glory, carefully stage managed as part of a process of being seen to react to the Argentine invasion. The entire crew and complement of these ships lined the decks, shoulder to shoulder, waving and cheering with various Royal Marine Bands playing jaunty regimental marches, pop tunes and the strangely haunting Rod Stewart song 'I Am Sailing'. The fire tugs sent sprays of water high into the air and the bunting fluttered. But for us already at sea, the weather was taking a turn for the worse and the sea mist had obscured even the south coast of the Isle of Wight.

Most of us were accustomed to life on board ship. We slipped into our own curious routines – essential to retain privacy under crowded conditions and to prevent frustration turning to friction. For the officers, the focal point of the ship was the wardroom. With the ship's officers, we ate in the small dining room and drank at the bar. They, however, with their huge double-cabins and adjoining private bathrooms and loos, left the sitting-room part of the wardroom, with its bench seats and tables to the 'military officers' who played innumerable games of Scrabble and Diplomacy (which was very topical) and read books from the small library that we shared with the rest of the ship.

Our accommodation, the 'Embarked Force officers' cabins, was at the stern behind the wardroom proper and included one 2-berth cabin, which was the privilege of Major Gerry Akhurst (the Officer Commanding Troops, for whom this glorious isolation was intended). All the cabins were full and the huge amount of kit we had each was piled up, blocking the passage and cabins. By mutual agreement, the one officers' bathroom (for those officers who cannot bear the thought of taking a shower) was turned into stowage space and was filled to the ceiling with sea bags, bergens, webbing and battered suitcases.

The ship was officered by the Royal Fleet Auxiliary merchant seamen bound by an extra clause in their contract that enforced their participation in such exploits as this. We saw very little of some of them, which was not surprising as they worked the same watches all of the time, so some were nocturnal and others preferred to socialise in their cabin sitting-rooms rather than the crowded wardroom.

The crew of *Sir Percivale* were Chinese from Hong Kong. They lived in the same sort of accommodation two decks below us. In the wardroom they cooked the food, served it up and cleaned the place. Every morning a steward would come in with three cups of revoltingly strong tea with sugar and biscuits and do a balancing act over the bergens, sea kit bags, flying helmets, nav. bags and suitcases that were piled up. This tea was not actually drinkable but its arrival meant that breakfast would be served in half an hour's time. We got up in relays to shave in the single wash basin in our cabin before putting on lightweight camouflage trousers, shirt and desert boots and going to breakfast. (Desert boots are essential on ships because the normal black leather, rubber-soled boots leave black streaks on decks that sailors have spent hours polishing.)

*Sir Percivale* carried a variety of different military units. There were guns and gunners from two commando batteries, 7(Sphinx) and my former gun battery 8(Alma) – otherwise known as "Black Eight". There were a number of people from 45 Commando and its helicopter flight with three Gazelles, pilots, ground crew, fitters, marshallers, and spare parts. The flight commander was Lieutenant Nick Pounds, with whom I shared my cabin.

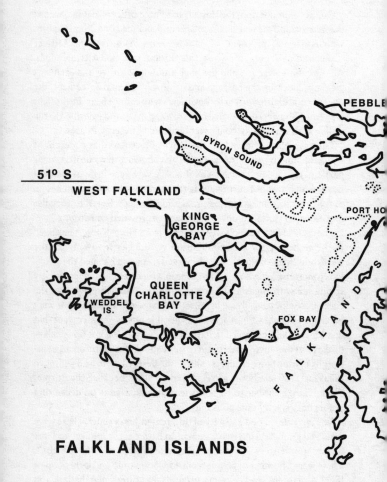

51º S

WEST FALKLAND

KING GEORGE BAY

BYRON SOUND

PEBBLE

PORT HO

QUEEN CHARLOTTE BAY

WEDDEL IS.

FOX BAY

FALKLAND ISLANDS

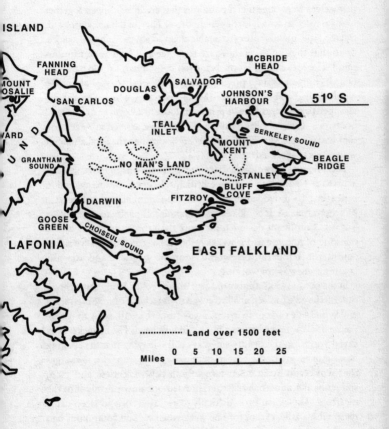

Land over 1500 feet

As part of the ship's company there was the Mexe Float Troop, members of the Royal Corps of Transport (RCT), based in Marchwood and regulars on the *Sir Percivale* who thus had the best cabins, etc. I don't know where the word 'Mexe' comes from,[*] (pronounced like Mexican but without the 'can') but the mexe floats themselves were huge metal pontoons that could be clipped together to form rafts on which lorries could drive. They had huge, outboard, tractor-type, diesel motors to enable them to shuttle vehicles ashore, or so that they could manoeuvre together and form a continuous ramp. The Mexe Float Troop, being self-consciously the old hands on board, enjoying certain privileges, were studiously casual about the whole thing. Later on, the metal 'Mexe' Pontoons, which were carried strapped to the sides of the ship, became loose in a storm and on several occasions were very nearly ditched. When we arrived at Ascension they had to work very hard shifting cargoes around the fleet, and their casualness evaporated.

The ship was very crowded. Its intended role was to move soldiers across the Channel to reinforce British soldiers in Germany, and in peacetime to move supplies across the Channel and soldiers to Northern Ireland. It could cope at maximum capacity for a few days but was simply not designed for more than that, and it was now a question of housing us for weeks rather than days. Also as we sailed south, the temperatures would soon be tropical and the air-conditioning was not working.

In the ocean swell, stumpy old *Sir Percival* rolled badly. At night, in order to be able to sleep at all, you had to put a large orange life-jacket under one side of your mattress, away from the wall, so as to wedge yourself in a V shape between bunk and bulkhead. The lifejacket ploy saved you from the deadly sideways roll – leaving just the rocking horse movement of the bow to stern axis. There were also the surges that woke you up in an instant of panicky weightless and then, suddenly in a nauseous reaction, pressed one down firmly into the mattress. This wasn't too difficult to get used to, and sleep came reasonably easily, except for one week when we had continuous bad weather, seven days of grim insomnia for most of us.

During the bad weather people tended to stay horizontal as much as possible, as this kept the headachy nausea at bay. Meals were taken by all but the most chronically affected, and most found their sea legs eventually. There are some professional sailors who always suffer from seasickness. One wonders why on earth they persist with their career. I watched with some admiration during howling storms, ashen-faced officers-of-the-watch crouching over the chart table to check their position, scanning the heaving horizon with binoculars, turning to peer into radar screens, then ducking suddenly aside to be violently sick into conveniently placed buckets. Their fellow bridgemen, the ratings and petty officers (PO's) had long since ceased being amused by this. I cannot imagine anything worse than the continual curse of *mal de mer*.

The variety of units on board *Sir Percivale* meant that the ship was a tribal community, and this was reflected in the wardroom. To start with, the military 'families' stayed together. 7 (Sphinx) Commando Battery were the most complete unit on board, with all their guns, vehicles, ammunition and men. Gun batteries work, fight and play together and present a united front to the world. Their BC (Battery Commander) was Major Gerry Akhurst, a very capable, affable, easy-going and amusing man. He assumed the mantle of OC Troops with a friendly magnanimity that eased us through much potential friction and strife. The other gun battery (that I had once been a member of) had about 2/3rds of its number on board. It was nicknamed 'Black Eight' because at the Battle of Alma the guns had gone ahead of the infantry (who were pushing forward to storm the heights) and fired so much ammunition that the horses and the faces and skin of the gunners had become burned black with gunpowder and soot.

The units formed groups for training; PT in the mornings, gunnery, weapon drills, lectures and kit preparation. The training had to be centrally co-ordinated so that the very limited space could be utilised fairly and without hindering the smooth running of the ship.

The ship's captain was tremendously helpful in every way and became a great favourite. He and Gerry got us all integrated with the ship's officers by thwarting an attempt by the Chinese head steward to have us all eat at different times. This would have given the wily steward the opportunity to provide different menus and thus lessen the workload and who knows what else besides. Thus we all sat down to eat together, and the ice was broken.

The sergeants had a very lively mess to which from time to time invitations were issued (better described as summons) for the officers to call. One night there was the horse-racing. We stumbled out afterwards very late and were generally rather ill the next day. It transpired that we had taken them to the cleaners in the horse-racing, winning with horses bought very cheaply and avoiding the ones where bidding had got out of hand. (I should say that this was the traditional ship-board game where you 'buy' a cardboard horse in an auction – with real money – and then it races for its owners who get the total proceeds of the auction if the horse wins. The race is run on large squares and the moves are determined by throwing the dice. There are side bets too and normally the officers are comprehensively laundered, especially as the sergeants very 'kindly' agree to allow their officers to sign bar-chits to place their bets rather than using cash).

The soldiers on board were of all shapes and sizes, from the bear-like Sergeant 'Taxi' Kaslyuski (who won the beard-growing competition in spite of forgetting about it and shaving it off half-way through) to the diminutive Bombardier Tulip (known as 'Petal') whose deadpan sense of humour had caught me out more times than I would care to admit. They were animated by events to a certain extent, tempered by innumerable other periods in the past spent 'languishing' on naval ships.

Their accommodation was nothing short of appalling, a nightmare for Lt Bill McRae, the assistant of the Quartermaster of 45 Commando, who was in charge of the administration of the hundreds of tightly packed troops. The mess decks on warships are very cramped, but these ones were designed only for a few night's transit on a trip across to Belfast or to BAOR (British Army of the Rhine). The bunks were suspended in threes, one above the other, and the next three along, nose to toe. The bedding, our own sleeping bags, were simply too hot to use, and were zipped up in a waterproof cover which

58

became the cushion for the divan seat that was formed during the day by turning down the middle bunk and hooking up the top one. Their problem was stowage space for personal kit and there was only minimal locker space.

In these desperately overcrowded conditions, hygiene was our major worry. An officer and a senior non-commissioned officer (a sergeant or above) made a formal inspection every night, called 'Rounds', looking at everything and carefully inspecting each lavatory, sink, shower and drain. The senior hand on each mess deck was present and reported each defect in his bit. We were then able to apply pressure on the already harassed ship's engineers, because delays in the repairs could lead to disaster.

The air-conditioning had never been needed on the European runs and now did not work. Once we got to the tropics the most ghastly conditions developed. We were restricted to only 30 minutes' fresh water every day because the ship's seawater converter couldn't cope. The rules were to turn on the shower and wet oneself, turn off and soap up, and then turn on briefly and quickly rinse it all off. Even so we were running short by the time we reached Ascension. The only way to get a drink was to keep your water bottles and other containers filled at all times, because the water was off for the rest of the day.

The seething mass of humanity was marshalled by an omni-present tannoy system, operated from the guardroom. The duty NCO made the 'pipes' (as these messages are called) and when his accent was very strong or when he didn't quite understand the message, the whole thing was very loud, intrusive and incomprehensible. The awful voice cut through everything and infuriated us because it cut out the World Service news reports – on whose every word we hung – with some trivial announcement about extra parades or something. I now have a strong dislike of any loudspeaker system that is used in this way. They are an unfortunate part of life in warships. (Once battle was joined and people and people were working watches and sleeping around the clock, there was an end to the piping of trivia keeping everybody awake.)

The thought of the long journey ahead and the poor conditions and boredom that would eventually strike everyone led to a plethora of activities. Daily exercise soon started once the storms and seasickness abated. Weapon training and map preparation, first aid and lectures on all imaginable things were programmed and got going.

The padre of 45 Commando decided that he would undertake the production, single handed, of a ship's newspaper, taking the view that this was one of the padre's 'duties in action'. He called it the *Oily Rag*, which was a reference to the many similarities between *Sir Percivale* and the old tramp steamers, whose grimy engineers had coaxed them around the world. Our ship's engineer wasn't too pleased, but it seemed to us to be very appropriate.

The padre's editorial style was distinct. He published everything that people were kind enough to submit to him without any alteration or amendment. He even retained the spelling of the original because it undoubtedly added to the flavour. The only changes were inadvertent, the result of typing errors or poorly written manuscripts.

He would start with the news fresh from the daily teleprinted compilation that we received, which contained summaries of the main UK newspapers. The rest was an open forum for anything at all, and most of the better digs at individuals were anonymous.

I was a regular contributor with a column called 'Don't Get Pissed off...But'. This took the shipboard events and exaggerated them. My penname 'Mack' didn't last more than a couple of days once the level of the humour had been assessed! I have kept a number of these and they give an idea of the background of world events to our strange goings-on and show what we were worried about and how we tried to keep these worries at bay.

The official opening section of the *Oily Rag* consisted of the international news of the day. We were all avid for news and not everyone got a chance to listen to the radio at the right time, and those who had listened had not always taken it in. Naturally, the latest moves in Anglo-Argentinian diplomatic relations, and the Parliamentary debates at home about the Falklands concerned us most of all. We saw ourselves, in our small way, as part of the great international scene, which involved the Super Powers, our EEC allies and the whole complex South American imbroglio. Something had to be done, and we were part of the manoeuvrings; and some of us might die for it. There was another category of international news; this was psychologically good for us, and I'm sure the padre knew it; the tanks were grinding over the desert as the Iraqi and Iranian forces slaughtered each other for God-knows-what end; there were troubles for Israel on the West Bank; there were fatalities from natural accidents all over the world, and so on. We weren't the only ones who were living on the edge of danger; for some people it was the only life they knew.

After the news, the *Rag* would give a few snippets of edifying information, perhaps about one of the ships of our convoy, or about the anniversary of some heroic naval action.

Thus, for the serious reader, the *Oily Rag* on 10 April 1982 described how Mr Nott said that the Royal Navy was prepared to sink Argentine naval ships in the exclusion zone from the deadline on Monday; when told President Galtieri had threatened to respond with war, he had said, 'Let them come out'. Meanwhile, the US Secretary of State, Mr Haig, was in Buenos Aires, greeted by a mass rally in support of the *Malvinas* invasion. (On 12 April the *Rag* was to report Mr Haig as having shuttled to London.) There were reports of the Argentines laying mines round the Falklands and installing sophisticated surveillance systems there; fifteen civil servants in the islands had asked for the evacuation of the civilians before the Task Force arrived, and the deposed Governor had countered by saying that 90% of the islanders would not leave. You can imagine how hard he tried to make all this add up to something hopeful. But it looked as though there'd be no settlement but long delays, during which conditions on the ship would sap our capacity to fight, the southern hemisphere winter would set in, and the Argentines would have the time to perfect their defences.

Lesser items of news recorded the tribulations of people other than ourselves – 500 in Mexico in danger from a volcano and eight actually killed in a volcanic eruption in Indonesia; three guerrillas to be executed in South Africa. And there was a feat of endurance to inspire us; the Trans-World Expedition was nearing the North Pole. Patriotic information was represented by three naval victories taking place on previous 10ths of April – a French ship captured in 1795, the Second Destroyer Flotilla winning the first battle of Narvik in 1940 (Captain Warburton being awarded the VC), and a German U-Boat sunk in 1945. The useful information of the day was the 'vital statistics' of HMS *Fearless* – laid down in 1962 (which seemed a long time ago), its displacement, and the numbers of landing craft, trucks and tanks it carried. Usually there would be one or two notices as well, which were not always what they seemed. The naive volunteers of 10 April who reported to the "Mombassa Rest and Recreation Centre" run by Staff Sergeant Smith were destined to be put on to painting vehicle trailers.

The rest of the *Oily Rag* was given over to free-enterprise journalism, and seeing no censorship was exercised, the licentious wits and would-be entertainers fairly let their biro's flow. Lest the sensibilities of chaste readers be offended, only a few extracts from the numbers of the *Rag* that I have preserved are quoted here. Four-letter words, two in particular, are common coin of discourse in bars and barrack rooms, though normally only during more public eloquence, and not so much in ordinary private conversations. They serve the public purpose of helping to demonstrate that the speaker is browned off, but unbroken. Mostly, they are meaningless, although sometimes, through some paradoxical context application, they can be very funny. War films generally fall down on this aspect of the script; if the four-letter words are omitted, the atmosphere is unreal and manifestly sanitised; if they are put in, they jar impossibly as they resound incongruously in home or cinema. You have to be under the stress or discipline and, indeed, approaching the horizon of danger for the language soldiers actually use to sound at once realistic and inoffensive.

Anyhow, to be a regular columnist in the *Rag*, it was vital to write in the vernacular. There was a very certain sense of pride on board, that the *Sir Percivale* had risen into the international class so far as coarse humour was concerned. As a solemn announcement in the *Rag* stated:

# AT SEA

*The editors of Playboy and Knave wish to announce that next month's issue will consist of cartoons and photographs only. This is because the dirty bastards that write all the letters and articles are on board this ship.*

Our reverend editor knew what he was doing when he provided an open forum for vulgar humour. Loyalty to family and friends and doing one's duty are what padres are concerned with, not 'keeping the party clean' (as if it mattered) as you move towards a battlefield.

My 'Don't Get pissed Off…But' column, derived its whimsicalities from two sources of inspiration. One was to offer my readers what purported to be an account of life on various other ships throughout the Fleet – whether detailing luxuries unknown on ours, or inventing peculiar naval customs and ceremonies that we simple soldiers ought to learn about. The other source was the invention of a comic-opera hierarchy of Argentine military characters and chronicling their rise and fall as fearful news of the approaching Task Force reached them. What can you say about the enemy? It was psychologically better for us – and more civilised – to ridicule them than to portray them as odious. There was not a great deal of hatred abroad in the Task Force.

My column on 10 April described life on the *Canberra*, with 'Phyllis and Desmond' giving ballroom dancing lessons every morning, and growing rivalries among the embarked personnel because Pans People had been left on board by accident when they sailed (and how I offered to put them up on *Sir Percivale* to remove the occasion of their quarrels). In the next number I was able to give more details – how there had been a collapse in morale on the luxury liner because of compulsory cocktail parades and how an escape committee was building a glider in the main ladies lavatory using seat planking from the lifeboats, with all members of 3 Para donating their left trouser legs for the fabric to cover the frame. 'So far no-one suspects a thing, but with them pacing the upper decks using their remaining trouser leg to get rid of dirt from the tunnel, the Paras are being kept pretty busy.' Meanwhile the Royal Yacht, as my confidential information went, was being fitted out for the South Atlantic, and the troops to travel in her were being trained at Windsor by the Brigade of Guards to cock the little finger when drinking tea and not to say 'shit' when things go wrong.

The 10 April number of the *Oily Rag* also introduced the hero of my Buenos Aires saga, Speedy Gonzales, who while attempting a gunboat attack on the *Sir Percivale*, panicked when he saw Captain Nick Pound's bright red helicopter flotation bags inflated by accident when he was in full flight (a true incident). Gonzales was due for high promotion nonetheless, with correspondingly heavier responsibilities, heavier even than his medals which occasionally overbalanced him.

God's representative on *Sir Percivale,* the padre of 45 Commando, was a real gem. A slim, dark Welshman Wyn Jones had endured the rigours of the commando course, which for most padres was a test of character, and a test of their faith. Commando padres are a very special breed.

The commando course is designed to produce soldiers who carry on doing their job despite the worst physical conditions that can be arranged, and regardless of how tired the instructors have managed to make them. A padre on the course is an added bonus for the instructors who devise 'special-to-arm' tests for him, such as stopping the rain on Dartmoor when on exercise or demonstrating his ability to walk on water. He is berated when he fails:

'Come on padre, you can't expect these soldiers to carry on with a padre who can't even walk across this small pond. Even my small son could manage a quick stroll across there. Come on padre, have another go. We'll keep the first attempt a secret from the men. Come on, sir, you're not even trying. If you think that you are going to be allowed into the Commando Brigade and get away with a performance like that you've got another thing coming. All the other padres on the course manage to keep themselves dry much quicker than you. We'll just have to have a go every day until you get it right. And the whole course will have to do it too as a punishment for letting the padre be so idle and useless.'

Of course everyone is loaded with insults that become like background noise and a perverse form of entertainment. Black men are referred to as 'Chalky' and Irishmen run the whole gamut of 'paddyisms'. Officers receive special treatment, being requested to do press-ups in muddy pools, throw themselves into rivers, and so on. The idea is that in spite of constant indignity, you remain the man in charge. The process develops a 'no-nonsense' sort of leader whose judgement is unaffected by bad conditions and stress. The soldiers are similarly undisturbed by their circumstances or by being buggered about, and everyone develops an incredibly strong team spirit. It also produces a very special sort of clergyman.

On Easter Sunday, Wyn gave a service on the forrad hold hatch-cover, with the guns lashed down beside us. There were a lot of people standing by enjoying the sunshine. One of the sergeants major bellowed across to them, 'Come and get your fucking souls cleansed' which got us off to a good start.

Wyn, in his full cassock and surplice, stood out front. 'Without further ado, gents, lets start off with a song. I've got a couple of good 'uns so lets give it rock-all'.

We got stuck into 'There is a green hill far away' knowing that, like us, Wyn knew the disrespectful additional rendition of 'For he's a jolly good fellow' that usually follows military renditions. Thankfully this did not happen. He also gave us a little talk about what we were off to do and Christianity being a man's religion. These few moments of singing and thought were a complete break from the military reality, worry and discomfort, and everyone enjoyed it. We finished with the Naval Prayer:

> *O Eternal Lord God who alone spreads out the heavens and rulest the raging of the sea;*
> *Who has compassed the waters with bounds until day and night come to an end.*
> *Be pleased to receive unto thy almighty and most gracious protection the persons of us thy servants and the fleet in which we serve. Preserve us from the dangers of the sea and of the air*

*and from the violence of the enemy that we may be a
safeguard unto our most Sovereign Lady Queen Elizabeth
and her Dominions, And a security for such as pass on the
seas upon their lawful occasions.
That the inhabitants of or Island and Commonwealth may
in peace and quietness serve thee our God;
And that we may return in safety to enjoy the blessings of
the land with fruits of labours and with a thankful
remembrance of thy mercies,
To praise and glorify thy Holy Name:
Through Jesus Christ Our Lord. Amen.*

This prayer seemed to sum it all up and gave me a sense of the 'timelessness' of our venture. We were, as our predecessors for hundreds of years had done, ensuring the safety of those engaged in their 'lawful occasions'. The beauty of the language, with its succinct brevity and complete relevance, was reassurance and comfort.

I was to hear of Wyn from several people throughout the Falklands campaign for he was constantly up with the soldiers doing his best to take minds off the harsh realities and trying to awaken more happy memories of home. Whatever he really thought, he always appeared cheerful, yet he could read moods and join them, talking about the military side then enquiring about your family to bring you out of yourself a bit. He was particularly incensed when he briefly went to one ship to hear the words of one of his non-commando brethren (who was based on the ship). This padre had been allowed to fly up to the mountains in a Sea King helicopter. There he had seen the preparations being made for the final push to Stanley, and talked to some of the soldiers. He was holding forth with great prophetic gloom about how appalling the conditions were, and how casualties would be severe. As he knew nothing about soldiering he must have found it very alarming and completely unbelievable, but his superstitious pessimism was very damaging to morale. Wyn soon shut him up.

Another story about Wyn came to me from some Marines from 40 Commando, who were the neighbouring unit to 45 Commando. They had seen a strange, muffled figure roaming around in the darkness calling out and waving. (It must have been like that ghastly apparition in 'The Signalman'.) The sentries, who had their weapons cocked and ready to shoot, waited as the strange figure drew closer.

'Zooloo, Zooloo, Zooloo' it cried.

They alerted the whole troop, which stood to in their trenches with their weapons, and the troop commander moved forward to investigate. As the figure drew closer the words that the bitterly cold wind where whipping away, became clearer.

'Zooloo, Zooloo Company. Where are you?'

So the sentry challenged the figure.

'*Halt*, who goes there?'

'Oh thank goodness I've found somebody. Its only the padre and I've forgotten the fucking password'

With a padre like that how could we help but succeed?

Each morning after breakfast we would perch on bar stools under cool air ducts in the ceiling, and listen to the World Service of the BBC. It seemed as if the whole planet was degenerating into violence and tension – which was depressing. Any small development in Falklands negotiations was discussed with strong personal interest. The sooner the politicians and diplomats sorted it out, the sooner we would all be off *Sir Percivale* and back home.

On 11 April, the news was not that inspiring. Mr Nott, having decreed that a 'No-Go' area around the Falklands would be enforced in the next 24 hours, was receiving the US shuttle-diplomat Alexander Haig who was said to have 'specific ideas for discussion'. All sides were girding up their loins; the islanders transmitted an Easter message to the Task Force, addressed to Admiral Woodward and reading 'Onward Christian Soldiers', before the Argentinean invaders confiscated their radio sets. General Galtieri told a rally in Buenos Aires that Argentina wanted peace but would fight if necessary and the EEC announced a complete ban on Argentinian imports.

The only bit of good news was that Lieutenant Keith Mills and his Royal Marine detachment (with thirteen civilians from South

Georgia) were to be repatriated. A sniper in Jerusalem took pot-shots at pilgrims entering the Domed Mosque, injuring eight and killing two, and Israel was building up its forces on the Syrian border as tension in the Middle East mounted. Sir Ranulph Fiennes and the Trans-World Expedition were four days ahead of schedule, having reached the North Pole.

On *Sir Percivale* we struggled from one domestic crisis to another. We were urged to cut down our consumption on water during even the daily half-hour period. Some people were letting their shower continue to run whilst they were soaping themselves rather than turning it off. The main galley was only just coping with the overload of hungry soldiers, and the food was less than wonderful. It wasn't easy to get a drink when the water was off, which in the tropical heat was leading to problems. Everyone had to keep their water bottles filled. Tempers were not helped by one particularly officious Sergeant Major decreeing that the nightly beer issue, two cans per man, was to be made with the cans being opened as they were handed over to prevent anyone storing the cans for a few nights, then getting drunk. This stupidity was rescinded pretty sharply!

By now we were 120 miles north of Tangiers. It was warm and there were few signs of anything like land, fish or birds. The other ships in the Task Force were visible, running along parallel to us but widely spaced. The Royal Navy escorts, the warships, moved about like sheepdogs protecting the flock, using their superior speed, and we ploughed along as best we could. Some mornings we woke to find the horizon empty and ourselves completely alone on the ocean as if we had been left behind - which was a little alarming.

We knew absolutely nothing about what we might have to do. It was realised that we would not now sail straight to the Falklands but would stage at Ascension. The speed of our loading in the UK had left everything hopelessly spread out across the fleet. No one knew what was on-board, what had been forgotten and where everything was. Our hold was piled high and would take days to rearrange. I was expecting several bits of kit on the next wave of ships, but how I was to collect it and when was another matter.

## AT SEA

It took ten days to get to Ascension Island – longer than expected. We had failed to appreciate the distances involved and had thought in terms of a week to Ascension and another week to the Total Exclusion Zone (TEZ).

Our main preoccupation remained the news. Every morning after breakfast we gathered in the wardroom, glued to the World Service. The Task Force was the number one item for months and we followed each new development in the diplomatic round avidly.

As important to us as world news was the news from home. We managed to get mail away at Gibraltar by helicopter as we passed but had received none. At Ascension we knew the mail was piling up and we were desperate for it. As we drew closer, Bill McRae was overwhelmed by the demand for stamps, and he issued two per head with the instruction that several letters be included in each envelope for reposting in the UK. Everyone knows from the last war just how important the mail is for morale, but you really have to be in a situation like ours to appreciate it. Letters from home become the only truly private thing you have, and the only proof of your existence as an individual outside the military machine. Soldiers who didn't receive any mail would often be given letters by their mates to read – usually with the 'sports page' omitted !

*I do now. AAF Modey of Ferndown wrote to tell me that Mexe stands for Military Engineering Experimental Establishment, at Christchurch, where they first built the Bailey Bridge.

# Chapter 4
# Planners and Hoaxers

Once the rough weather abated, seasickness eased and we began to feel better; then the seemingly endless task of planning began. The Brigade Staff on HMS *Fearless* churned out scenario after scenario, appreciations and plans and then counter-plans. A helicopter shuttle service round the fleet was started, one circuit in the morning and back again in late afternoon. Known as the 'SDS run' (Sea King Delivery Service), it was mostly done by Sea Kings from Fearless, which were too big to land on the other ships. So men, supplies and mail had to be winched up and down from the hover while the ships steamed onwards. This process was time (and fuel) consuming and very tiring for the pilots.

As a passenger it meant at least one day wasted; waiting for a SDS to arrive, going with it round the fleet, finding out from the crewmen that they had already been to your destination, landing somewhere else, having lunch and waiting until they came on the afternoon run to deliver you back to where you started. At this stage the crewman usually took pity on you and flew you direct.

The confusion increased as we steamed south. The ships painted out their recognition numbers and letters so that, even to the trained eye, ships of the same type could not be differentiated. People were regularly stranded on the wrong ship and got stuck there if the weather changed for the worse and the SDS could not fly.

I ventured into this chaos in order to go to the fount of all wisdom,

HMS *Fearless*, to see what was going on. There the scene was most unlike *Sir Percivale* (with her lack of water and the beard-growing competition). On *Fearless* they were spruce and brisk, wearing their lifejackets and respirators on belts round their waists and carrying briefcases. The wardroom was very much larger than our cosy room on Sir Percivale and it was crowded with staff officers standing in groups, pointing at files and arguing their point. All the corridors were lined with cartons of breakfast cereal and floored with boxes of tinned tomatoes and baked beans so there was only a narrow passage through and you had to crouch as you walked.

Lieutenant-Colonel Mike Holroyd Smith, a tall, fair-haired man (known by the soldiers as 'Michael Caine' because of the resemblance and by the officers simply as 'HS') was the brigadier's adviser on all aspects of fire support, from naval gunfire, artillery and fighter-ground attack (the Harriers) to the Rapier and Blowpipe air defence missiles. He had been my battery commander in my first posting as a second lieutenant in 1974 and we knew each other pretty well. He smoked a stubby pipe and when he felt his point was not being registered he would remove it from his mouth and poke the stem at whoever was being slow to follow the argument. There was much 'peacetime' sophistry concerning gunnery that had to be dispelled so that realistic plans could be made. Colonel Mike would lecture groups of offending staff officers, jabbing the air with his pipe; and would turn to me with a glint and a smile and say, out of the corner of his mouth, 'These bloody staff officers. They don't have the first idea about artillery.'

He certainly knew what he was talking about and thankfully, by dint of his strong personality, the Brigade Staff listened to him. He had spent his early career in Oman fighting communist infiltrators from the Yemen and his views on artillery were simple, direct, uncompromising and, more importantly, had already been tested in action. He was good to work for because he let you get on with it, didn't mind mistakes (but woe betide if you made the same one twice) and made quite clear what he required. The resident Falklands expert was my friend from RM Poole, Major Ewen Southby-Tailyour. He had commanded the Falklands Naval Party 8901 and, being a very keen yachtsman, had produced a diligently researched book on inshore navigation around the islands - which he had published to very little response. (This book was to be printed and Ewen was to become Yachtsman of the Year.) He was very lively company but, as the expedition progressed, became more and more worried. His judgement and information was to be one of the main factors that would determine where the landings would be made, and he agonized over whether he was providing the right sort of stuff for such fundamental decisions.

Lieutenant-Colonel Mike Rose, the Commanding Officer of 22 SAS, was on board, beavering away in a green-painted Portacabin lashed down on the port Sea Cat deck. Tall, athletic-looking, with a very clear, direct gaze, he was a prime example of that most elite of breeds – the intelligent Guards officer. An historian from my Oxford college St Edmund Hall, Mike Rose was the advocate of the hard-hitting raid and reckoned that the whole thing could be sorted out quickly by a few full-blooded efforts. As he had already commanded Operation Nimrod, the SAS' assault on the Iranian Embassy in London two years earlier, this was to be expected. Various ferocious plans were generated, for instance an 'Israeli-type' raid on Port Stanley airfield with Hercules troop-transporters disgorging a squadron of SAS to created mayhem.

Brigadier Julian Thompson presided over the 'ants nest' of furious staff work with a calm but firm influence. He was universally known and liked and, what is more, he knew most of the officers in 3 Commando Brigade by name and took time to talk to everyone. He was under great pressure - from above, in London; sideways, from the Navy; and then he had to do his own job as well. In the planning stage everyone had to forward their ideas, of which some would be examined in more detail. It was essential that everyone act true to their own role, for example that artillerymen stress the advantage and devastation of naval and field artillery and the SAS the psychological impact (on already tremulous conscript soldiers) of the sickening violence of their methods. From all these ideas the brigadier could put together realistic plans to fit the political options - which at this early stage could mean virtually anything. Some hare-brained schemes resulted and so were eliminated as the staff worked towards a set of workable military options to match political and diplomatic developments.

We continued to be depressed by the gloominess of world news, the routine of shipboard life and our military preparations. Every day that passed made the first-aid lectures, the weapon-training drills and talks about the geography, flora and fauna of the Falklands seem more relevant. Our future was very uncertain - tomorrow there might be a political settlement, or we would continue sailing south toward possible destruction. It was important to stay positive, and divert everyone's mind from the grim options. My small contribution was to keep writing for the *Oily Rag*. First of all there was the report of my visit to HMS *Fearless* and the rumours we had heard (and hoped were true) that they were suffering food shortages. The text of 'Don't Get Pissed Off...But' read:

> "As promised, your faithful correspondent has braved the hungry waves and made the perilous journey by winch and Sea King to HMS Fearless in order to be able to report the true situation there. Firstly the rumours you have heard about food shortages are not true. Every fourth man is not having his left arm amputated above the elbow for the pot, but I do understand that the officers in the wardroom get swan sandwiches for tea only every other day. The passages are paved with 10-man compo boxes and tinned tomatoes and you feel like Alice in Wonderland having taken the pill (the one to make her grow taller, but not one that stops her having babies when the Mad Hatter's Tea Party turns out to be a gang-bang).
>
> There are an awful lot of people rushing round on Fearless looking Terribly Important and Very Busy. They all have briefcases and go to Conferences. I have, however, made a discovery, which may explain everything. At night Fearless is

74

completely empty - like the Marie Celeste, not a soul on board. You see what happens is that they all go home at night. It was partly because they discovered that there were no sheets on board, only nasty scratchy sleeping bags. But mostly because somebody discovered a hatchway that wasn't on the blueprints and didn't seem to go anywhere. I tried it and found myself getting 'filled-in' after the Man United game, so I came straight back. Anyway, at 6 p.m. they all get their little briefcases and when they think no one is looking they slink off home. I thought you'd all like to know."

Another inspiration for frivolity was the developing character in the Buenos Aires comic opera that I had invented, Capitano Speedy Gonzales. By now, he had been promoted and was interviewed by Señor Costa Mendez and Admiral Enrico Frigorifico with a view to taking command of a naval squadron – an heroic role which he could not perform because, under dubious circumstances, he fell into a broom cupboard. I was running out of inspiration now, but luckily discovered that the Argentines had bought the *Veinticinco de Mayo*, their aircraft carrier, from us, after the Second World War, when it had been called HMS Venerable, Hence, a new arrival in my 'Don't Get Pissed Off' column, a very ancient able seaman called Ramsbottom:

"Meanwhile back in Buenos Aires, Admiralissimo Enrico Frigorifico has scored a major psychological victory in his campaign to destroy, little by little, the entire Royal Navy. He has captured a British Matelot! Last night the prisoner of war was paraded before the world's press and here is a transcript of the interview:

'Okay you know. We of the Argentine Navy - the most powerful deadly and magnificent navy in the whole of south-east South America have captured, after a fierce but glorious struggle, this bottom-wiper of a son of a jelly fish whose mother cannot even cook runner beans for tea on Sundays. He is so stupid, this stupid little person, he cannot speak any language at all. I clear my rear passage very loudly so that you will know what I mean.'

"My name is Stanthorpe from the *Daily Torygraph*. What is your British prisoner's name and how old is he?

'We do not concern ourselves with such rabbit-ring questions. You can ask him if you want to know.'

'Can you hear me, sir? What is your name?'

'Eee, boot it's right grand to hear another British voice after all these years. Ah'm called Ramsbottom, Arthur Ramsbottom, Able Seaman, and Ah'm aged about sixty-five.'

'Mr Ramsbottom, can you explain how you happen to be here?'

'Ay, lad ah can. I were a young'un on HMS Venerable in 1945 and I 'appened on the key to the wardroom booze and nutty locker. Woon day I got accidentally locked in there and spent - eee bloody years on the piss, reet grand it were. Then woon day eyes singin to meesen - a bit too loud like - and they kicks the bloody door down. Turns out to be these silly baskets. When they bought tut ship from Royal Navy they bought me too!'

'Can you tell us how the ship has changed since 1945?'

'Aye. They call it some bloody stupid name now. Summat like Vinchento der Maya and put his powder-blue bloody flag at tut mast. In my day tut Captain was called Pumphery-Bandersnatch. Thought that were bloody stupid name until I heard Argentinean Captain's name.'

'What's that?'

'Sounds like cartoon character - has leg in plaster and goes round on crutches, medals all down 'is chest. He's called bloody Speedy Gonzales.'

At this point Able Seaman Ramsbottom is hustled away by thirty-seven members of th special forces counter-terrorist squad armed with GPMGs and LAWs (general purpose machine-guns and light anti-tank weapons)."

## PLANNERS AND HOAXERS

On long voyages with little to do apart from fitness training, weapon drills and nightly mess-desk inspections, with an odd film thrown in, soldiers get rather bored. The difference between life in a barracks ashore and the extraordinarily odd life on board a warship is great, and those who have never been to sea have a lot to learn. The experienced people show the new hands the ropes, and there are a few laughs to be had along the way. One of the usual tricks to be played upon the inexperienced is to run a 'Splash-Target Coxswains course'.

The keen young lads in the on-board commando force are persuaded to volunteer for this fictitious course, and are trained up for as long as their credulity allows, to coxswain or 'pilot' a torpedo-like 'splash-target'. (A 'splash-target' is towed behind the ship on a long cable to allow aircraft to practise bombing and strafing runs, or for the troops on board to fire their small arms.) To want to pilot this target may seem like the most astonishing thing to be volunteering to do, but the young, newly fledged commando soldier is ready for anything, and he accepts that if there is a requirement and a training course then he'll have a go. For everybody, it certainly relieves the boredom of the long voyage.

The perpetrators of the spoof go about planning the course with rather more than the usual thoroughness; to allay suspicions, the students have got to be kept interested. Furthermore, the course has to be difficult, but not so hard that they fail to enjoy it. Although something as ridiculous as a "Splash Target Coxwain's course" could only be credible to its hapless victims, a more 'sophisticated' hoax would create uncertainty in the minds of everybody on board, and would be far more diverting. The circle of those in the know must be kept as small as possible, the whole enterprise kept alive by a debate between the people who have suspicions, and those on the course who must remain convinced that the hoax is genuine.

On previous hoax courses, I'd seen 'graduates' swearing they'd realised it was a spoof all along, and others who'd remained convinced even at the end that it had all been genuine. To preserve this uncertainty, we planned the ending of the course as carefully as we did the beginning. On one previous 'Splash-Target Coxswain's course' they'd 'failed' 'students' when they reached the critical point when incredulity set in, saying that they had failed some test, or been found in some way to be wanting. This had proved to be very entertaining, but a little cruel, as the organisers had ended up with one chap who was absolutely determined to get through. The tests became more and more extreme and ludicrous; he presented himself on the flight deck dressed in flying-helmets and tin-hats, hung grimly on to ropes hanging down from the upper decks for hours on end and clutched water-skiing bars whilst lying on the flight deck being hosed down with powerful fire hoses 'to simulate what it would be like when he had to do it for real'.

So determined was he that the perpetrators of the spoof began to get quite worried about how they were going to break the news to him. When his pals finally told him that it was a put-up job he refused to believe them and was very disappointed and still not too sure, even when his troop officer assured him it was a joke.

We decided to have a similar project but it had to be very carefully thought up and presented, as by now everyone had heard of 'Splash-Target Coxswains', and were on their guard for something similar being attempted. Captain Nick Pounds (the flight commander with whom I shared a cabin) saw an article in a US Army magazine that gave us the idea. It was about a special forces' technique called 'Helocasting' that involved jumping from a helicopter into water whilst the aircraft was at 50 feet and doing 25 mph. There could be military advantages to such a technique, i.e. a radar tracking the helicopter doesn't detect it stopping to drop troops, the speed with which they can be dropped off and so on; spurious advantages that in the real world are more than outweighed by all the problems of waterproofing equipment, dropping safely and then getting ashore. However, we thought the idea sufficiently credible to achieve what we called a few 'bites' – with the potential for a new version of the old hoax.

The ship was ploughing along in the tropical heat off West Africa with no air-conditioning or fresh water. There was a need to divert people's minds away from reality and we reckoned this would be fun for the organisers, giving them plenty to do in the way of instruction and planning; and various levels of diversion for the students and their friends. No one could be sure whether it was a spoof or not, and the debate would be lively.

We started off trying to convert the Wardroom, leaving the magazine article lying around for a few days. With the collusion of the ship's signals officer we then produced a 'fake' Secret signal telegram instructing all the troop-carrying RFA ships to produce one helocast team in preparation for operations in the South Atlantic. We showed the signal to the other officers and the OC troops (Gerry Akhurst, who was in the know), and appointed Nick as the organiser and me as the training officer. We then spent the day talking to people, sounding them out and ostensibly asking advice as how best to go about our task. We were in fact looking for a 'mug' to be the officer in charge of the team.

As it turned out this key part of the spoof proved very easy to achieve; as one Royal Marines Lieutenant Gerry, asked us if we would consider him for the job. Gerry was earnestly keen, solving many of the credibility problems for us. For instance, Gerry reckoned the real purpose of our being asked to train up a helocasting team was so that when the time came to land in the South Atlantic, the RFAs could beach themselves (ramming their bows into the shoreline so they were stranded like whales – which was an option in dire emergency), to get the vehicles and men off quickly using lowered ramps. The role of the ship's helocast team, guessed Gerry, was to be flown off the ship several days before this, to be dropped off into the sea and swim in to recce the beach to ensure it was clear of enemy. He argued that he was the only man for the job because he would be staying on board *Sir Percivale* whereas the rest of us will be transferring at Ascension.

We considered his application carefully, and then appointed him, confidentially and subject to his passing all of the selection tests… We then put a notice into the ship's Daily Routine Orders calling for volunteers and giving a time for the 'selection tests 'to start. We briefed Gerry to keep a sharp eye on the applicants to se how they were doing. At the end of the day he was going to be in charge of them and thus should be the final arbiter.

The debate started immediately Daily Orders came out. As my FO team were in the know and involved in the training, they were closely questioned. They just said that like me, they'd seen the signal so it must be genuine.

About sixty men arrived on the rear flight deck for the selection, all very sceptical and rather self-conscious. There were also a lot of sightseers who didn't have the sense of humour to actually join in. I started off by very abruptly telling these onlookers to push off if they didn't intend joining in. First we had a PT session to whittle down the numbers a bit. We wanted about six for the spoof to be effective – i.e. enough to get into the rear of a Gazelle for whatever the final scene was to be. Thirty melted away in the next twenty minutes or so as they ran around the flight deck and did press-ups until they could do no more. I also sent a couple away that I didn't like the look of; sharp, suspicious characters who I thought would undermine our credibility between sessions. This also started to give our students a feeling that they were to be an elite, a feeling that we were to foster by, for instance, urging them not to talk about the course to their pals. I kept my FO team monitoring who was growing suspicious and what was being said and adjusted our programme accordingly.

The next day we got them wearing fighting order (webbing equipment) and had them hanging from the crane at the front of the ship to 'test' their ability to hang from the skids of a helicopter. Between sessions we conferred in the wardroom with Gerry who was bursting with ideas; and in secret in our cabin. We decided Gerry had twigged that it was a spoof and was playing us at our own game – which we thought could be even better.

Helocasting evolved rapidly; the team would have to be able to get out of the helicopter in pairs so as not to unbalance the aircraft, then hang from the skids until the drop point was reached, when the pilot would signal for them all to let go at the same time so they would all be close together in the sea. They would have to be capable of hanging on for several minutes wearing their fighting order and weapons (whilst the other pairs climbed out) and also to be able to pull themselves back up should the pilot decide not to drop them. As they could not wear headphones, they had to have hand signals arranged for every eventuality. Gerry and the pilots (the pilots were in the know) got the drills worked out and instructed the students. We split the course programme into two sessions per day - one PT and the second aircraft drills.

The debate and scepticism grew, to the point where some of the students went up to the radio room and asked to see the signals log. Our friend the signals officer had put copies of the fake signal in all the right places so our story was very much reinforced. Gerry came to us with a few points; that some of the students thought it was a spoof, that they were wondering what it was really for, and would they actually get the chance to do it. He also thought that there was a case for the helocasters to get special-duty pay like parachutists

And so another 'secret' signal was cobbled up saying that all helocast teams were to carry out practice drops when we arrived at Ascension and that consideration was being given to special-duty pay. The signal also asked for the names of all 'helocasters'.

One young student came to me to say that he had been thinking very carefully and felt that he was not really cut out for helocasting. I thanked him for his coming to see me and said that it was far better that he should come to that conclusion now rather than later. We got a few more recruits to our course, who had seen both the signals and the flight-deck crew stripping out the seats from one Gazelle (in preparation for live, aircraft drills and the 'drops' in a few days time when we reached Ascension). By now those who had decided it was a spoof were playing along and encouraging the students in anticipation for whatever the final act was to be. We even acquired a sergeant on the course, a sure sign that our story was being believed.

We did make one serious mistake however, when we taught them about body armour and then put the heavy chest plates and back plates on them and made them hang from the crane. That was too much and very nearly upset everything.

They were taught a lot of very useful things like first aid, and weapon drills on Armalites and pistols that they had never handled before. We got our diving suits out and had them sweating away, climbing in and out of hot rubber in the tropical heat.

Two days before Ascension, we decided to bring things to some sort of conclusion. The aircraft drills were very slick now, the boys being able to get in and out of the cramped cabin with weapons and equipment, and down on to the skids to balance prior to hanging down and dropping.

We had three too many and we were concerned that a couple of them were not completely convinced and might get through to the others before the climax of the spoof. Nick gave them a very hard time on their aircraft drills saying he was just not going to risk any problems when we did it for real in three days' time. He told our 'doubting Thomases' that they were not really up to it and regretfully now they would not be allowed to go on with it. He then told the remainder that they were 'The Team' and that tomorrow they would practice on the deck then take off and run through the getting in and out actually over the sea.

This last bit would be the finale of the spoof. We could not actually take off with them in the back because the number of flight regulations that would have had to be broken by so doing would have led to us being court-martialled! Instead we'd would have them squatting in the aircraft with all their kit, start up the engine and have them do the getting in and out a few times in the down-wash of the rotors turning. Whilst the noise of the engines cut everything else out, the ships captain would read an announcement over the tannoy system to the rest of the ship to the effect that he was going to present our brave helocasters with their 'wings' and everyone was to make their way to the flight deck to see the ceremony.

Tim Bedford had prepared some authentic-looking certificates (suitably emblazoned and coloured) and there was a can of ice-cold beer for each man. Once the Gazelle engine was going and the scream of its turbine drowned everything on the flight deck, the captain made his pipe. The whole company came streaming up from the rest the ship and gathered quietly around the flight deck, waiting until the engines were shut down. Nick got the team to do one last climb out onto the skids for the amusement of the crowd. In the aircraft Gerry was most concerned about the people on the flight-deck, shouting into Nick's ear that they wouldn't be able to take off until the deck was cleared. (We anticipated that the arrival of the crowd might be a little obvious but we had told the helocasters that there was a PT session scheduled next, so they already knew this was likely to happen.) I set up a presentation table complete with green baize cloth for the rolled-up certificates and the cans of beer.

The Gazelle engine was shut down and the captain called our students forward from the back of the helicopter one by one to shake their hands and award the prizes. He also gave a nice little speech over a loud-hailer to the effect that our students were actually prepared to plunge into the sea from the helicopter and that he personally wouldn't even dream of doing such a thing and so credit should be given to them. Everyone cheered each student, especially Gerry, and we finished off with three cheers for the Captain.

Our students were completely taken by surprise, and to their great credit were amused rather than upset. The nice thing that they all said was that they had enjoyed doing the course, and had found the whole thing most interesting. It certainly enlivened that last week of our voyage to Ascension.

In the outside world the situation seemed to be getting more complicated and worrying. The possibility of Soviet involvement and orchestrated Cuban stirrings made uneasy listening.

Mr Haig had left the UK to return to the US saying that his efforts had been 'inconclusive but both sides were pondering over some new ideas'. In London a government spokesman had said that there were some 'new and serious developments' and that 'optimism would be out of place'. Morale, our swingometer of cheerfulness, took another dip.

Argentina announced that if Britain withdrew the Task Force then she would withdraw her troops from the Falklands but never return again to the same relationship between the islands and Britain. The London response was that nothing short of an unconditional withdrawal by Argentina would be satisfactory. We were, a little later, much heartened when in response to calls in the UN for Britain to back-pedal and prevent bloodshed, Margaret Thatcher said firmly that Argentina must not profit from the use of force. This statement simplified the tangled web of moral issues that could only serve to confuse and keep us over-long at sea, sapping our ability to fight. The offer made by the certain pro-Argentinian South American countries (in the Organisation of American States) to mediate between Britain and Argentina seemed to be another time-waster.

In the tropical heat and without showers or running water, it was getting increasingly warm and uncomfortable. The wardroom bar, directly below the flight deck and the funnel, both of which were baked by the sun during the day, got particularly hot. The Captain, a man with a good sense of humour who loved being one of the boys rather than the isolated man at the top, 'discovered' that hot air rises and that the coolest place in the wardroom was sitting on the floor. So every night the officers lay on the wardroom floor, raising their heads every now and then to sip their beer. The Scrabble ceased, because the pieces got too slippery to pick up and the floor was too crowded with reclining bodies to lay the board out. It was not easy to sleep at night, more especially as the flight deck of *Sir Percivale*, just above the cabin where I lived, was active as the helicopter flight practised night flying from the completely darkened ship.

Every morning we would rise and go out to the stern deck, leaning on huge capstans that wound in the greasy chains that lifted and lowered the rear ramp and cargo-loading entrance. In the fresh, salt air the white wake churned endlessly, dead straight when an experienced helmsman was on watch or dog-legged when the boy was being taught. The sky was china blue and featureless. The fleet were well spread out with the merchant ships surrounded by a 'wagon wheel' of warships which moved individually in a predetermined pattern around the wheel to the eternal confusion of airborne helicopter pilots who were trying to land people on specific ships. Some mornings no ships at all were visible and by the time we were a few days sailing from Ascension they had all pushed on ahead, leaving slow *Sir Percivale* plodding along with HMS *Antelope*, our ever-faithful escort.

*Antelope* was a Type 21 frigate equipped with a 4.5inch Mark 8 gun. There were two sorts of naval gun that we were to control on Operation Corporate: the very modern computerised and fully automated Mark 8 and the older, slower, slightly shorter range but in many ways more reliable Mark 6.

The job of my five-man team (and the four other teams from 148 Battery on the operation) was to go ashore and observe Argentine targets – whether from a mountain hideout, a hole in a bog, walking forward with attacking infantry, in a boat offshore or from a flying helicopter – and direct the naval gunfire to the exact spot where it would do most damage. Each man in the team carried a small but ultra-high-powered radio and we would talk to the ship (which could fire up to 24,000 metres) adjusting the fire in the light of our observation of the falling shells. We sent the co-ordinates of the targets that we discovered to the ship with precise orders as to the type of ammunition she was to fire and how much. We controlled where the shells landed, moved them round and switched to other targets. The way in which we controlled the shells and how the ship (which would be rolling around in the swell, in pitch darkness) fired shells accurately, needed much practice.

Naturally, both we and the crew of *Antelope* wanted to get together to run through procedures and, if the opportunity came, to fire the gun at Ascension. We were now joining up with the means by which we were to fight the enemy – a meaningful and positive moment. The expedition that we made to *Antelope* was also very enjoyable – we were received with great hospitality, enjoying their showers and the change of scene. The captain and crew were keen to find out what they were to be doing. In particular, they wanted ground maps of the Falklands (in addition to their nautical charts), which they would need when firing inland for us. We spent a morning putting them through their firing drills and talking about the type of land targets which we might attack – the latter mostly conjecture.

Their air-conditioning worked very well indeed, the food and company was excellent and the sick-bay provided a comfortable berth; the ships' surgeon John Ramage was a friend who had been the

Medical Officer at Royal Marines Poole, and put me there as it was the only spare bed they had on board.

We spent the night on *Antelope* and their Lynx helicopter delivered us back to *Sir Percivale* next morning. Nick Allin and the boys were carrying large, brown-paper sacks which they kept clutched carefully to their chests. The pilot put me out on the winch and playfully lowered me so that my feet were in the sea. He flew along towards the stern of *Sir Percivale* then reeled me back up and plonked me on to the deck. He had similar fun with the other four. The brown-paper sacks were full of chilled beer cans and dubious magazines, donated by the matelots who had heard that we were short. We put the beer in Sir Percivale's meat store to stay cold for a celebration when we reached Ascension.

On April 16<sup>th</sup> the *Oily Rag* told us that the Argentine navy, with the *Veinticinco de Mayo,* put to sea 'as a defensive measure'. This was seen as a morale booster for the Argentinians and was not thought likely to lead to armed conflict. Mr Haig had been back in Buenos Aires and Mr Reagan had spoken to Galtieri – with no result. The Russians, after reports that they were supplying the Argentineans with information about the Task Force, had accused the US of 'acting in collusion with a colonial power and supplying intelligence material'.

The Common Market ban on Argentinean goods was applied, initially for one month. This would affect about 25% of her exports.

In the rest of the world, tension and violence continued in Beirut, China was unhappy with the US over the supply of goods to Taiwan, recent arms finds in Zimbabwe led to some desertions from the army there, HM The Queen was formally to proclaim a new Canadian constitution in Ottawa and Bjorn Borg would not play at either Wimbledon or Paris this year.

In that same number of the *Oily Rag* I reported my visit to HMS *Antelope*. We had heard of lots of ships having to throw unessential furniture overboard so I thought we'd invent an orgy of destruction on *Antelope*:

> Yesterday I went across to HMS *Antelope*, the Type 21 frigate
> that is looking after us. These boys have got one or two

problems, which I will try to explain. There seems to be something wrong with the victualling system, which has resulted in there being no water and stacks of beer. This means everyone is on the piss and no one is washing.

Whilst I was on board I overheard the First Lieutenant discussing their programme. Apparently when RN ships enter hostile areas they go into what they call 'Defence Watches'. This involves no one being allowed any sleep, everyone eating ham sandwiches and drinking mugs of cocoa, carrying a penknife with them at all times, and *throwing all the fittings over the side!* Well, can this be true? I investigated and it was.

They start traditionally, with the wardroom carpet and pictures, then the antelope's head followed by the wall plaques. The chief petty officers' mess beer-cooler is last of all.

'Sorry Captain, sir, if you could just stand up a second. Right, Leading Radio Operator, chuck that chair over the rail. You didn't want these photo's of the wife and kids did you sir?'

When eventually this orgy of destruction is over (it includes shaving off beards – and hair if worn) the ship's officers put on their best uniforms and go to Divisions (this is a parade of the whole company). On Divisions everyone helps each other to rip the pockets and buttons off their best uniforms and jump up and down on their hats. Finally the captain, head completely shaven, has a handful of shit rubbed on his bald pate by the Master of Arms and snaps his telescope in two over his knee.

By this stage they are pretty pissed off and go round their ruined ship dressed in rags and tatters and getting more and more angry.

'Right' they say, 'We're getting really pissed off now. You Bastard Argentinians. We're really going to sort you out now. Look at the fucking state of my head! You Bastards, we're really going to make you pay for this, you bastards.'

So when this happens, before we reach Ascension, don't be alarmed if you see wardroom furniture come bobbing past us, or the main galley tables, or the darts board, or the film library.

Its only Jack getting himself into the right frame of mind.

My invention of barbaric, anarchical ceremonies onboard *Antelope* contained a grain of truth. It was being said that *Invincible* had chucked her wardroom carpets and piano into the sea and had gone on Defence Watches (meaning that the usual night time routine of just a skeleton crew plus team of cleaners ends, and half the crew stays on duty all night, the ship remaining on full alert around the clock).

As danger intensifies, life in a naval ship becomes more and more uncomfortable – and the psychological effect is enormous. On *Antelope*, they were about to follow *Invincible's* example so far as Defence Watches went; as for throwing things overboard, they had almost reconciled themselves to the possibility that the sacred antelope's head would have to be jettisoned. Another element of naval preparation which took place came to the fleet by courtesy of the French armed forces, since most of the Type 21 frigates on their way south were able to practice their anti-aircraft drills against Super Etendard jets flown at them as they sailed along the West African coast. It was to prove invaluable practice.

By now we were nearing Ascension Island, so I now wound up my Buenos Aires saga by having the Argentine fleet sail (not very far) under the command of Speedy Gonzales. Alas! Admiral Enrico Frigorifico was not available to take command in person; he was in hospital having popped cartilages in both knees and slipped a disc because of the weight of his medals.

Now we had come to the point when the Task Force might well come under Argentine attack – and the time for frivolous inventions was over.

# Chapter 5
# Ascension Island

*Sir Percivale* arrived at Ascension early in the morning, one day behind the other faster ships who had steamed on ahead. There were dozens of ships at anchor when we sailed in – merchant tankers, car ferries, sleek Type 21 frigates, the larger and more sinister-looking DLGs (Destroyer Light Guided), RFA's like ourselves as well as the POL (petrol, oil and lubricants) tanker versions, and deep-sea salvage tugs. There were also a few American ships, no doubt bemused at this ultra-quiet backwater becoming suddenly so busy.

The island itself is remarkable, made of volcanic lava which forms black pinnacles that look absolutely solid. The shore is indented and has sandy beaches, but there are only a few places where the surf permits landing. The foreshore is covered with every kind of radio mast, from dish antennae to the long runs of pylon and cable for long-distance HF communications. To the south there was a lot of helicopter activity, all going into the single-strip airfield that served the tiny island. Originally, and presumably ironically, it had been called 'Wideawake Airfield' but this name was very appropriate now. There was every sort of aircraft, Phantom jet fighters, old Vulcan jet bombers, Nimrods, Hercules and Victor Tankers.

In the centre of Ascension Island, the black volcanic pinnacles went gently upwards to form foothills to the sudden grandeur of Green Mountain – which dominates the whole island. In a dramatic contrast to the barren oven-baked moonscape of the rest of Ascension, Green

Mountain was a misty, ethereal feature with its own localized cloud. The sudden upward movement of moist air, condensing into cloud near the top of one of the few bits of high ground between Africa and America causes a miniature rain shadow on the upper slopes of the mountain where vivid green vegetation caps it like the topping of an ice-cream.

Sometimes the mist completely enshrouded that implausibly green paradise – which, from the crowded heat of the ships at anchor, and surrounded by the conical piles of arid black pumice stone, appeared like a Hollywood visualisation of Shangri-la.

When eventually we got ashore and climbed Green Mountain it did not disappoint us. The long, hot walk up the sweltering tarmac road into the cool greenery, with the tiny pub near the summit and the nineteenth-century barracks (once used by the garrison troops), was well worth the effort. The sudden profusion of tropical fruits was truly remarkable and delightfully unexpected.

We awoke that morning to the unaccustomed sound of the anchor being dropped. It was a very bright, warm day and the calm water around the ship was very clear, blue and alive with fish. After breakfast we gathered by the rail to look at dry land for the first time for a fortnight. The well regulated bowels of military men and the very basic plumbing of the ship (the same as BR trains) soon disturbed our idyll. It was just after breakfast, that most popular time, when pirana-like black fish appeared in large numbers voraciously seizing every morsel that appeared and lurking hopefully near the outlets. They were immediately christened 'shit-fish'.

The Chinese stewards got out fishing lines and horrified us all by being very successful. They fish apparently at every possible opportunity and although the word had been put out very firmly that nothing was safe to eat, only the top Chinaman (the Bo'sun) spoke and understood English, so we were never totally sure about fish on the menu from that moment onwards.

We got our Gemini inflated, ostensibly to test it and our engines, but really to be ready to get across to *Canberra*, which when she arrived would berth close by. We were curious. There were rumours of the normal cruising staff still being on board, which meant 'ladies'. Having completely fabricated so much about her in the *Oily Rag* I wanted to see for myself, and also after the rigours of *Sir Percivale* any ship would be a treat.

In the meantime we were keen to get on solid land and take some proper exercise. There was a stone jetty with steps, petrol bowser, and cranes at the end of the rocky pinnacle nearest to the main group of buildings in Georgetown, the main settlement. We tied up the Gemini at the Fort Thornton pier and went ashore wearing webbing, with plenty of water, shorts and boots. Des, being very pale, was wearing a jungle hat, but the rest of us were acclimatized enough not to have to worry. As we walked up the road in the direction of Lady Hill, which we had decided to climb, we passed a long, two-storied building with a verandah round the top storey from which a lot of chat and conviviality could be heard. Voices assailed us, friendly voices that we knew and had heard oft-times before in equally unexpected, remote and unlikely places. Members of 148 Battery Sergeant John Rycroft and RS (Radio Supervisor) George Booth were leaning over the rail with cold pints of beer in their hands. We managed to resist the strong temptation not to bother with the march and join them, and bravely tramped off into the heat haze.

The black pinnacles turned out to be loosely granulated and very like a fine coke, in lightness and colour. The wind blew the dust from these piles for quite some distance and all the ships in the bay at anchor were soon covered with granules. We flogged up to the top of the hill, running most of the way, until the heat became almost unbearable. The summit had an unmanned US radar station, and there we paused for the view, looking across to the centre of the island where Green Mountain disappeared upward into the mist.

John Rycroft and George Booth had come ashore from *Fearless* the day before and had set themselves up on the first-floor verandah of the 'Exiles Club', in which they had been 'refreshing' themselves for most of the morning. The place was packed with the green-denim uniforms of marines, some of whom had flown out from the UK and had been on the island for a while; and there were also newcomers like us – many who turned out to be friends I had not seen for years. It seemed particularly strange to be meeting up with old pals in what must be the most remote and unlikely spot possible; like a comedy film about dying, to find yourself in the celestial waiting-room prior to the completion of entry formalities for the After-life.

It was also far too much fun to last. Something was bound to go wrong, the military 'System' would object, or some clown would misbehave and spoil it for the rest. However, I was completely wrong. Everyone behaved and it was only when it was realized that in a few days the island's entire supply of beer for the year would have been drunk, that Brigadier Julian Thompson reluctantly banned us from the 'Exiles Club' – to the club manager's great disappointment. This was the first example of how when military operations are for real, nobody gets uptight about trivia.

That night we decided to drink the beer that the boys on *Antelope* had so generously donated. Some of our huge pile of cans, carried like swag in a blanket, was brought up from the meat store and wrapped in several other blankets to keep cool. The strategic place to hold what was going to be a most civilized piss-up was the deck immediately outside the wardroom, facing Ascension and the dying sun, conveniently close to the nearest heads.

The best knees-ups start very slowly, almost by accident, and evolve with gently sipping and the reflective broaching of crisp, fresh cans with that most satisfactory sound as the ring is pulled. We leaned over the rail and watched the sun go down, chatting quietly. People passed by, were offered a can, then stayed, adding to the conversation and going into the wardroom to fetch out a round of cold cans in return.

Leaning over the rail in the dark, staring down into the phosphorescent water, we reflected on what the future might have in store. We had no idea, but that night I decided to resist any attempt to rearrange the composition of my Forward Observation team (as our Battery Commander had mentioned he might yet do before we left the UK). Nick Allin and I were pleased with the way our training and preparation was going and we, as a team, were all happy with each other – which was the most important bit of preparation of the lot.

When we finally managed to get on board SS *Canberra,* we found that it was in reality more like my fictional portrayal in the *Oily Rag* than I could have imagined. And she had most of her normal crew still on board, including the ladies.

The 'Crow's Nest Bar', the first-class cocktail lounge below the bridge, had been operating as normal until the more exotic drinks ran out. A few of the ne'er-do-wells had been testing the skills of the barmen with their cocktail shakers and crushed-ice machine. The novelty had worn off after about two weeks and now the ship had a far more military air about it than poor old *Sir Percivale.* The facilities on board were ideal for keeping fighting troops fit and their skills up to standard. The quarter-mile-long promenade deck was constantly crowded with crocodiles of runners, often wearing full combat kit and festooned with equipment. The wood planking was buckling in many places and the metal plates bowed from the constant heavy pounding – so different from the more gentle use envisaged by the designer. The length of the ballroom deck had been stripped completely and was waiting to be converted into a large surgical hospital – rather along the lines of *MASH*. The carpets had been taken out in Southampton and the piles of oxygen cylinders, cardboard boxes of dressings, sutures, tubes, blades, syringes and all the medical impedimenta lay heaped around the dance floors, against the pianos and where the tombola machine stood under a dust cover.

The 'Crow's Nest' resembled the pit propped gallery of a mine, with a spider's web of scaffolding supporting the steel plates of the helicopter flight deck above, built over the forrad swimming pool. Metal ramps ran down from the flight deck to the ballroom, to move the wounded in stretcher trolleys from the CASEVAC (Casualty Evacuation) helicopters when they landed above. This conversion work had been accomplished in the few days before sailing – with much cheerful use of cutting torch and large hammer. The steel flight deck had been very rapidly prefabricated and the last bits assembled after the ship had sailed, with the shipwrights being flown off as *Canberra* sailed past Gibraltar (no doubt to their great relief), abandoning all their oxy-acetylene gear on deck where they had finished, and where it still lay.

At Ascension there was further 'robust' marine construction work going on, the most notable being the skipper of *Atlantic Conveyer* cutting off the entire bow superstructure at the front end of his ship to make a flat flight deck so that Harrier jump jets could land and take off. A vast amount of steel plate was thrown into the sea so he could become the captain of an aircraft carrier. This transition was achieved with astonishing rapidity. The first time a Harrier did land on board, it looked alarmingly as though it was going down into the water.

The normal luxury cruise shops on *Canberra* were still open, so the assembled soldiery could select from the full range of Pierre Cardin scarves, luxury perfumes, and souvenirs. However, the hair-stylist had completely changed his outlook on life, and now produced the most stylish 'short back and sides' ever experienced by the British Army.

There had been a few 'incidents' between male crew members and the embarked military; the odd black eye had resulted and all was well. Rumour had it that a few crew members had quit the ship for various reasons at Ascension, but it is very much to the credit of Canberra's crew and also P&O's recruitment system, that there were no actual problems in these extraordinarily stressful circumstances.

The contrast between conditions on *Canberra* and those of *Sir Percivale* could not have been greater. I can only imagine that for those on *Canberra* it must have been very difficult to keep the overall aim of the expedition in the forefront of the mind and prepare seriously for what it looked as if we were going to have to do. Somehow living under the more realistic conditions of the RFAs and the warships, in what for us were familiar circumstances, kept things properly in perspective. At least we on *Sir Percivale* could only be moved to a better ship – it could hardly be worse! Certainly members of 148 Battery on *Canberra* were actually relieved to be getting off her and onto the RFA that took them southwards in the wake of Rear-Admiral Woodward and the small force that re-captured South Georgia. It was much better to be getting on with it than hanging about waiting – even in such comfort and splendour.

The conditions under which battles are planned and fought can be summed up in a single cliché – 'the fog of war'. This is the one factor that you cannot include in training exercises. Armchair strategists listening to the wireless news, and historians with their critical hindsight rarely understand it. The fog of war obscures some things and not others, suddenly lifts and just as suddenly falls again, makes you think you are going faster and then slower, or puts you into a blissful state of false security. The only way to deal with it is to be infinitely flexible, which involves constant changes of plan. In turn this demands resignation and a sense of humour from both the troops being buggered about and from the 'loggies' (logisticians), who in a nightmare of eternal chaos were trying to plan for every eventuality.

During this the final preparation for the campaign, we talked endlessly about strategy – we were all planners, logisticians, brigade commanders – but of course what was really being planned was above our heads and beyond our ken. I do not think that a record of what we debated in this tense period of waiting is worth reproducing. Nor, when talking of the planning of Operation Corporate, will I indulge in the wisdom of hindsight. Best, I think, to limit what is said to the worm's eye view that is all any individual, short of the higher commander, has of any war.

When attacking an enemy position you need at least a superiority of three to one. The arithmetic gets worse if your enemy has a very well prepared defence, particularly if you have to assault from the sea. This is known as an 'opposed landing', and because of the probability of suffering high casualties while leaving the ships and getting established on the shore, requires very much more than three to one. But if you don't have the requisite numbers of troops, you have to use deception and brilliant planning to increase the effect of the troops you do have, so as theoretically to increase their numbers, and thus satisfy the ratio.

In our case, for getting ashore in the Falklands, the Task Force had only sufficient helicopters and landing craft to assault with one battalion – flying in one company by helicopter and the remainder by sea using landing craft. Of course we could bring in further reinforcements after this first wave, but strictly by the application of military mathematics, we could only do an opposed landing against one enemy company at the most. Thus by basic deduction, it seemed that we were not going to do a direct, full-frontal assault on Port Stanley – thank goodness.

We practised assault landings interminably (or so it seemed) at Ascension, which was to be invaluable for the partially opposed landing that we were eventually to do at San Carlos. I discovered afterwards that the option of a full-frontal assault by sea and by a *coup de main* helicopter force was still being actively considered by the planners – but was moving down the list in terms of its probability.

HMS *Antelope*, the Type 21 gunship who's company had already been so hospitable, asked us to fire their gun and so FO1 flew across to them for the day. The fire would be at smoke flares dropped by helicopter into the sea to the north of Ascension. I would adjust the shells on to the smoke flares from the rear of the aircraft, while Nick and the rest of the team worked with the ship's navigator and PEWO (principal executive weapons officer), so that the ships operations room staff would understand what to do when we called upon them to fire for real.

The first part of the morning was spent running through the computer and operation-rooms drills and talking to the pilot and observer of the Lynx about the best way to do the job. I wanted to give them as much of the firing as possible, thinking ahead to when it might be in my interests to have a helicopter crew who were confident and able to adjust the gun on my behalf.

I came back into the wardroom having completed the arrangements for the afternoon's firing, to be introduced to the ITN television reporter Jeremy Hands, who had come on board to film the firing practice - as it was certainly the most visual of the preparations currently being made at Ascension. He asked me what my part would be and what I thought I would have to do when we sailed down south. I had no brief for this and said that I did not think that I could help him. Jeremy Hands made the point that he could not produce the right sort of report if he had no idea of the background, and could I talk to him on such a basis? I could see that a well-founded report was better than nothing and that realistic reporting of our preparations and capability might actually lend weight to diplomatic negotiations.

Therefore, I explained in general terms how my team operated and what we did on land to get the naval guns firing into their targets. (As far as I am aware my confidence was respected and I hope that this talk provided useful background. It did seem that most of the reports from media men actually with the Task Force were similarly well researched and that the line between informative reporting and breaches of security was respected.)

TV reporters have vaguely familiar faces. If you have absolutely no recollection of having seen them on the screen, this vague familiarity is puzzling. I suppose this sort of *déja vu* is because the TV set occupies such an intimate position in most people's homes. Jeremy Hands was interesting to watch working. He had a two-man crew: a cameraman and sound recordist who seemed to delight in chasing him and pulling his leg. As the front man, he had to look spruce for the camera and plant himself firmly with some suitable background, to deliver his lines. On ships this would very often be a precarious position at the edge of the heaving deck with spray breaking over, from which he would retreat rapidly when the shot was complete. His crew frequently pretended they thought him to be rehearsing, kidding that they hadn't been filming, so he had to risk another soaking by doing it again.

Jeremy Hands made one report from the flight deck of *Antelope* with a Lynx in the background preparing to take off. When the rotors started turning, the down wash rearranged his hair, made the firmly planted stance hard to maintain, and presumably he had to shout. Afterwards I asked if he had been a reporter before he went into television. He replied, 'That's like me asking you if you were a soldier before you were an officer'. Point taken.

In the hazy, tropical sun-glare, the featureless ocean became like a greasy mirror and was painful on the eyes. The firing practice went well, although the first few smoke flare targets dropped into the sea and failed to burn, and when they did ignite, were hard to see. The Lynx helicopter landed back on board and we stayed for dinner, being delivered back to *Fearless* by Gemini assault boat later that evening.

The huge restowing programme had got underway as soon as we arrived at Ascension and the air was constantly black with helicopters and the choppy swell of the mid Atlantic alive with 'Mexe' floats and landing-craft. The logisticians were working round the clock as they tried to get everything put into the ships in something like the reverse order in which they would have to emerge when eventually we landed. There was as yet no firm operational plan, so the loggies were as usual doing the impossible; giving the 'ops' planners as wide a set of options as possible by loading to allow as 'flexible' an offload as possible.

In war nothing can be achieved without good logistics. 3 Commando Brigade was very fortunate to have the excellent Commando Logistic Regiment and its unique experience. The 'load' had to be got as near correct as possible at Ascension Island. Once we sailed south, the seas would not be calm enough to allow any but a very limited reshuffle of troops, and hardly any reallocation of the mountains of stores. We did not know that South Georgia would fall without a struggle so even the likely theatre of operations was uncertain – from the snow, ice and mountains of South Georgia, to the wet moor land of the Falklands – totally different places in which to fight, requiring different stores and equipment.

To further complicate the restowage programme, all the commando and parachute battalions needed to practise fly-offs and landing-craft assaults, taking up most of the helicopter lift capacity and clogging up the loading routes through the ships. These rehearsals entailed running through the complete routine of battle preparation; the assembly drills, the complex assault routes through the labyrinth of ships' passages, hatchways and ladders to the landing-craft bays and flight decks, the calling forward of the platoons and companies in the correct order for the assault plan, then getting them to the right boat or helicopter at the right time. The practices started in slow time by day without heavy equipment, working up to doing it at night carrying huge bergens, through bolted down hatches (to minimise flooding if the ship is hit). The troops needed to be totally familiar with all this, and the ship companies needed to practise their part as well. Pilots and landing craft coxswains had to go through the routines until everybody could do it slickly, in the dark, in bad weather and heavy seas, and possibly against enemy opposition. (On 21 May, the actual landings at San Carlos ran late because of many unforeseen difficulties; for example, a soldier falling into one of the landing craft and breaking his pelvis. Without the practising at Ascension the delays would have extended long into the next day, with the certainty that troop carrying ships would have been hit by the Argentine air force.)

For the proposed landings, my job was to be in a helicopter, ahead of the assaulting wave of helicopters, directing the naval shells and Harrier strike aircraft on to enemy positions. We practised the sort of flying that would give the helicopter a chance of surviving yet allow me to set the targets. This involved sickening turns and dives, while flying very low indeed.

FO1 got out and about as best we could, off *Sir Percivale* and on to the island to go on long marches in the blistering heat, to fire our weapons on a makeshift range and to scrounge the odd dinner on board *Canberra*. We were told to move across to *Fearless* – which couldn't be done immediately as our equipment was still buried in the hold of *Sir Percivale;* and in the restowage programme could not be 'excavated' from the pile for several days. There were several panics when we were told that *Fearless* was sailing south, including one when our source of misinformation thought that her normal water replenishment trip to sea (to get clean sea water for her desalinizer) was her actually sailing for the South Atlantic. FO1 were literally set adrift in our Gemini and very nearly left stranded one mile off Ascension at night with no fuel.

But eventually we were able to get all our gear out of the vehicle deck on *Sir Percivale* and had it flown across to *Fearless*. We followed in our Gemini, leaving the RFA that had brought us to Ascension and all the friends we had made.

On *Fearless*, the large number of officers in 3 Commando Brigade HQ had filled all the dedicated officers' accommodation, and so the overspill lived in one of the other ranks mess-decks - 'Four Mike One' (4M1). Naturally whenever there had to be a fire practice in a mess-deck it was 4M1 into which the smoke-cannisters were thrown, or the fire-hoses 'accidentally' let off. Officers are rightly considered fair game.

Despite being regularly awash with water and very crowded, 4M1 was more physically comfortable than friendly old *Sir Percivale*. I slept at the top of a bank of three bunks, directly above an unfamiliar padre who couldn't stand the close living. (He was found other more congenial accommodation.) The bottom bunk belonged to Brigadier Julian Thompson's ADC (Aide-de-Camp), who was much very smarter than the rest of us (not difficult), and far more serious (also not terribly difficult), with what struck me as the splendid name 'Montefiori'. (I was reading a comic but very disreputable book by a writer called "Kyril Bonfiglioli", who I also liked.) With his head by my feet, was a cheerful REME Captain Trevor Wilkins, a computer buff who I knew well from my days as an officer cadet at Sandhurst. Trevor's wife sent him computer magazines that he kindly left in the wardroom for others to read when he had finished. However, Trevor hadn't seen that she had filled in some of the advertising coupons with sweet little personal messages – until we showed him of course. Trevors' bunk was festooned with his smalls – like bunting.

There was also Flight Lieutenant Denis Marshall-Hadsell, an RAF Phantom Navigator, a forward air controller, who with me, formed the core of a small and very select deck-quoits-playing club, which met before tea every afternoon on the upper Sea Cat deck.

There were eighteen others in mess-deck Four Mike One, crammed in rows three high. It was never particularly cluttered or claustrophobic because we were all used to it, and because everything had to be stowed away for action stations every morning. When a ship gets hit, anything loose goes thrashing round the deck space and catches fire. The stowage of kit was practised and inspected *ad nauseam* until it was automatic.

The ever-present tannoy blasted forth from a loudspeaker in one corner of 4M1 and had two positions, on and off. I think there should have been a volume control but ours, being in the officers' mess-deck, must have been sabotaged. Because the tannoy is a key part of the ship's organization, it could not simply be turned off when we were trying to sleep. I used to tape a towel across it, which at least muted its stridency. "Pipes" are broadcast from the bridge, and are made by ringing the Bo'sun's mate, who with the permission of the officer of the watch, picks up a hand microphone and speaks to the whole ship; and like the guard on an old British Rail commuter train, the volume is usually too loud and the accent indistinct. There were certain particularly disliked pipes that would be made many times each day:

> "D'yer hear there. For Exercise, for Exercise, for Exercise. Fire, Fire, Fire. There is a fire in 4M1 mess-deck space. Secure all watertight doors aft of 2 Kilo. Fire party to assemble at the base of the 2 Kilo hatch. Damage-control party stand by.
>
> D'you hear there. This is the Commander speaking. There have been many useful comments about the pipes being made. I know many of you are unhappy about unnecessary pipes, and the use of irritating clichés. I've hoisted in the point about this. I'm going to cut out all the clichés and get straight to the nitty-gritty. But more of that later.
>
> D'you hear there. This is the officer of the watch speaking. There have been far too many unnecessary pipes being made which disturbs everybody as well as cluttering up the smooth running of the bridge. I ask you to co-operate to reduce pipes to only those that are strictly necessary. That is all.
>
> And a particular favourite: "Hands to flying-stations, hands to flying-stations. No more gash to be ditched. No smoking or naked lights."

There was one particular Bo'sun's mate who always seemed to be on duty, who had a high-pitched 'George Formby' accent that really grated on everyone's nerves. His classic pipe, repeated many times every day, was 'The AOO is requested to go to the AOR. The AOO.' Translated into English this reads – the Amphibious Operations Officer is requested to go to the Amphibious Operations Room. He is 'requested' and not ordered, as the AOO is senior to the person who authorised the pipe.

After a delay, and no AOO appearing in the AOR, the mate would then decide to add a sense of urgency to the pipe: 'The AOO is to go to the AOR. The AOO.' Someone on the bridge would then tell him that he couldn't order the AOO, so we'd get a third version:

'D'yer hear there. Disregard that last pipe. The AOO is *requested* to go to the AOR. The AOO. That is all.'

By this stage in this oft-repeated round of pipes we would be singing, in George Formby voices: 'The AOO's in the AOR and I'm still cleaning winders.'

Lieutenant Montefiori, the Brigadier's ADC, was also a key man, like the AOO. But the ADC had succeeded where we had failed. From the constant piping that went on for him, he must have discovered a room without a loudspeaker. We heard this pipe, with the Bo'sun having no qualms about his tone, many times every day:

'Lieutenant Montefiori is to report to the Brigadier's day cabin. Lieutenant Montefiori.'

These were the sounds of HMS *Fearless* at war.

The easiest way to forget these cramped and uncomfortable circumstances was to slip into a routine. The day would begin with the pipe 'Call thee Hands' – "Call thee 'Ans, call thee 'Ans, call the 'Ans."

We would get up in waves to use the washbasins, and pack up bedding and loose clutter. Breakfast entailed quite a long journey, up two ladders, along the main side passage and up another ladder. This took you past the chief petty officer's mess and the gunroom (a mess-room traditionally for the junior officers which now housed the intelligence cell).

After breakfast and the 8 a.m. World Service news, the morning would be taken up with whatever work there was to be done. Lunch and more BBC news, then in the afternoon a very comprehensive PT session on the flight-deck, or the Sea Cat deck aft, or the steep metal ramp down to the tank deck and dock. FO1 would normally do that together, although for variety John Rycroft often came and took the session to give the boys a break from me.

We were getting quite good mail with very little delay from the UK, so I did much letter-writing. The mail came at 1830 and was the high point of the day. The 'postie' always had plenty of helpers to sort the contents of the bulging blue sacks that blocked the narrow gangway past his office.

In the evenings the wardroom was absolutely jammed and we ate in two sittings. The more junior of us had to eat between seven and half-past, and the senior ones after that. The beer was terrible and sometimes the ice machine broke, so decisions about what to drink were far from easy. Once the Pimms ran out we were really pushed! It was very hot even with air-conditioners going flat out. For historical reasons, the restrictions on drinking that applied to the other ranks, did not apply in the officers or Petty Officers' Wardrooms. The end result was much the same; drink so much that you appeared to be impaired, and you were in serious trouble.

After dinner our group would drink the same thing – it was Irish Mist for a while until it ran out (thankfully). When the senior officers finished eating, the chairs would be arranged in rows, 'cumfiest' at the front, for the film. The commander and the senior officers sat at the front, and I slipped into the pecking order in about the fourth or fifth row – on hard-backed dining-room chairs. We would watch the film with the pauses between reels to recharge glasses. At the end the bar would close and we would totter back off to the 4M1, being very careful with the ladders.

# Chapter 6
# Our War Begins

On Saturday, 26 April we heard the news that South Georgia had been retaken. This caused jubilation. It also gave rise to a hope that the Falkland Argies might be ready to surrender by the time we got to them – although no one counted on this. The poor performance of an isolated garrison being set upon by what must have seemed to be an overwhelming force was not an example on which to base future operations.

An assumption of Argentine lack of resolve did however flavour the early actions of the battle for East Falkland, the SBS operation for Fanning Head that we were to be part of, and the Paras' battle for Darwin and Goose Green. In the Paras' battle for Darwin, Goose Green, the amount of artillery support provided was limited. The helicopters were desperately unloading the ships at that time, so could not be spared to fly off more guns and ammunition. It was also hoped (rather than thought) that the Argentine garrison would surrender fairly readily. The easy-surrender concept was certainly behind the planning of our Fanning Head operation. Nevertheless, with the taking of South Georgia it seemed that the war had started and that everything we were doing had entered a new dimension.

On Monday night, after reports of unidentified and possibly Argentine merchant vessels in the area, the Navy started to become twitchy about the possibility of an attack on our anchorage at Ascension. The intelligence people advised that Argentina had bought at least two mini-submarines and some chariot-type submersibles that could be used to get into the bay at night to place limpet mines on ships' hulls. The Argentine Navy had one Guppy-class sub remaining in good working order, which had not been located, so when strange sonar reflections were detected we suffered an inevitable series of submarine scares.

The first of these submarine scares took place just after the news of the South Georgia surrender. A successful attack on the Task Force at this stage would have been a very good Argentine counter-move. Just after 4 a.m. the duty sonar operator heard a foreign sonar emission and sounded the alert. The klaxons went off for the first time without the caveat that it was 'For Exercise'. In what was to become the established pattern, the HQ staff grabbed their respirators, lifejackets and something warm to wear, and rushed up the ladders and through the hatches that were already being closed and screwed down, on their way to the Amphibious Operations Room. Only a faint red glow of light came from the emergency lighting system (to allow the retention of partial night vision). Sailors went to their fire-hose positions, stretcher-party mustering points and first-aid posts. Everyone was wearing their 'anti-flash' – the white asbestos hood and gloves that were soon to prevent so many serious burns when ships were hit.

We remained, like the others on the ship without specific jobs to do, languishing in our mess-deck. We were almost exactly amidships and well below the water line – the ideal torpedo impact area, but safe from Exocet missiles, which are programmed to hit amidships, nine feet below the top of the ship's radar silhouette. All the hatches were screwed down tight, and to get out into fresh air required the opening of four hatches and the negotiation of several tortuous corridors and ladders. The claustrophobia of an iron grave. Four young sailors were unfortunate to have the bilges underneath us as their action station. They would arrive breathless in 4M1 pulling on sweaters and anti-flash hoods, armed with torches and a hammer, to scramble down the ladder into the dank bilges below. We screwed down the hatch, their pale faces looking up at us in the red gloom. From their position standing on the hull of the ship, if they heard the sounds of frogmen trying to place mines they were to give the alarm by using their hammer to bash on the hatch which we had screwed down tight after them.

The tannoy burst into life again: 'D'you hear there, this is the Captain speaking. We have picked up what seems to be an unidentifiable sonar operating from the west. You all know that there is a submarine and swimmer threat, and so we are going to initiate full preventative measures, which will include dropping of scare charges every three-quarters of an hour or so. Those of you below the water line may find these quite loud at first. We will remain at action stations until first light and then revert to "Damage control state Two, condition Yankee modified". That is all.' These damage control states were a mystery to most of us, but eventually we learned what they meant in terms of hatches bolted tight, and companionways sealed.

The first of the swimmer scare charges, lumps of high explosive thrown into the sea, was shockingly loud and we waited, sweating in the darkness, for the next one. The air-conditioners and anything else that makes a noise were turned off lest it be picked up by the enemy sonar operator. (I presume the explosions, because of their severity are a hindrance and not a help.)

After a couple of minutes of this terrible tension, there we heard a hesitant, metallic 'tap tap' on the hatch leading down to the bilges. I got off my bunk to see what the problem was. I unscrewed the hatch bolts and lifted the heavy, steel plate. A pale and worried little face, two eyes staring out of an anti-flash hood looked up at me. The other three young sailors were hanging on to the top of the ladder that went down thirty feet to the wet bilge bottom.

'What's the matter?' I asked.

'There's been an explosion – we heard it just now, outside the hull. Is everything all right?'

They hadn't heard the captain's broadcast and had thought we were under attack. But they had been debating whether they should bother anybody or risk alerting an enemy sonar operator by banging on the hatch to find out what was happening!

We were annoyed by the news from home. It seemed as though some of our politicians were trying to make political capital out of the situation. We reckoned that any sign of weakness in Britain would give hope to Galtieri, that he would gain strength from the merest hint of any British lack of resolve. On the other hand I felt there was also a danger in forcing him into a corner from which – like a wounded bear – he would have no alternative but to fight.

At Royal Marines Poole the previous year, where the Falkland Island Garrison Naval Party 8901 were trained, we had listened to the Parliamentary debate on whether to scrap the Royal Navy's ice-breaker *Endurance* with growing anxiety. The immediate reaction of more senior officers, who were already concerned that NP8901 was too small to be more than just a token force, was that the Falklands would be invaded. It was well known that the Argentine military academy regularly practised the invasion of the "Malvinas". Getting rid of the relatively small expense of HMS *Endurance* was certain to be taken as an indicator of Britain's lack of interest and resolve in the South Atlantic. And now, with this prediction come true, the same politicians whose penny-pinching had so thoughtlessly contributed to this crisis, were urging us ever closer to bloodshed.

We knew that Galtieri had seriously miscalculated every aspect of his 'Malvinas' project, which put us in a classic bind; if we appeared feeble, he would certainly stay there. But if we were tough, far from forcing him to admit his mistake and withdraw, would pride oblige him to fight? The whole adventure seemed so large scale, unreal and unlikely, that we were still thinking in terms of this crisis being resoved without us having to land in the Falklands.

So far the Task Force had struck several blows in the battle. Port Stanley airfield had been bombed twice by the RAF – a psychological operation that heartened us, rather than disheartened the Argies (as it did little damage and did not affect the operation of the runway). South Georgia had fallen easily and we had captured a submarine at Grytviken. Several aircraft had been shot down (Mirages, Pucaras and a Canberra bomber) and several FPB's (fast patrol boats) and a second submarine had been damaged. The bombing of Port Stanley was followed up by daytime naval shelling of the racecourse and airfield.

On Tuesday, 4 May, we heard news of the sinking of Argentine cruiser *General Belgrano*. I went from the Wardroom to the operations rooms to read about it in the Signals Log. There was said to be large loss of life – we supposed that the other Argie ships in the area had fled in case they were the next targets, leaving the crew of the cruiser to their fate. The cold seas would quickly kill anyone in the water.

When *Belgrano* went down there was universal sadness and disgust on *Fearless* that the whole thing had got to this stage. In the next few days we were to see newspaper headlines that were gleeful and victorious. I wrote this in my diary[*] for that day (Tuesday 4 May):

My feelings are not of the glee reported by the idiot press on board *Canberra*, but more akin to the Royal Marine Colonel who when told of the sinking by a press man, used a four-letter expletive and returned to his office to carry on with his work. Of course there are clowns who are pleased. They seem to be the ones lest likely to be personally involved in future fighting.

The lines of battle were drawn over the next few days. Events became an odd mixture of momentous news and trivial activities. The five of us went ashore with our rifles and pistols and our webbing. We marched across the island and zeroed our weapons at a makeshift range, marching back and having a swim on the beach. That night Denis Marshall-Hadsell introduced us to Harvey Wallbangers before dinner, as the draught lemonade for Pimms had run out. I was up in the AOR looking rather blearily through the signals log (bleary on account of the Harvey Wallbangers) when we got the news about *Sheffield* having been Exoceted. Very rapidly the news of the number of deaths came in which was a great blow to us all. I suddenly understood how it is that morale can fluctuate so much according to the news. My diary noted:

*Thursday, 6 May*: The sinking of HMS *Sheffield* was a very low point that shook us all. It looks now as though 30 men have died. What a terrible waste.

My morale is not very high at present as I feel that we are being premature is rushing off to invade. We cannot do this whilst there is still a risk from Argie air. To remove this means bombing mainland Argentine airfields which I hope is politically unacceptable. Therefore why all the talk of landing? [I was thinking in terms of a naval blockade and possibly a battle at sea.]

After lunch Denis and I decided to cut each other's hair so as to avoid being scalped by the Chinaman who, to add insult to undoubted injury, charges too much. We thought of taking a trip across to *Canberra* for an appointment with André but apparently he is booked up for at least three days and we may well have sailed south by then. Denis in fact did mine quite well but chickened out when I set about doing his. He is very wise.

Yesterday I sat on the upper deck – the roof – got red in the sun and did my exercises. An officer quite new to the Commando Brigade rushed up to me saying, 'Come quickly and look at this'. He was going to do a parachute jump later in the day out of a helicopter into the sea (for fun) and said that he had just seen something that worried him. He pulled me over to the guard rail talking about being eaten by shark, gesticulating downwards. It was an incredible sight – at least 40 porpoises in twos and threes converging on the bow of the ship, bobbing rhythmically right our of the water and blowing air from the breathing holes in the tops of their heads. They were a really beautiful sight, like quiet, curious children from another world – and he thought they were sharks!

The practice fly-offs took up most of my time and I wrote in my diary:

Up at 0400 to bolt down the hatches and go to action stations again. The matelots put on their anti-flash and let off smoke grenades to exercise the fire and damage-control teams.

We go up to the wardroom for the mandatory pre-flight breakfast to find that the stroppy petty officer steward was using action stations as an excuse not to produce early breakfasts. We 'explain' to him that it is only a practice and that certainly on the day of the race the cookers would be turned off because of the fire hazard, but that in practice exercises you do not risk air accidents at night by having hypoglycaemic air crew (who have not had their breakfasts as they are by regulations required to have done). As we also complained to the Chief Petty Officer – who is a pillar of strength amid much distracting confusion, this did not happen again - *and* we got breakfast.

We eased along to Flyco [Flight Command] to get into Major Peter Cameron's Scout, but there were no lifejackets. The deckies were very difficult (it being early morning) and wouldn't give us any, and the storeman's action station was miles away. Nick Allin sorted it out and acquired three lifejackets, we strapped into the seats and eventually took off. Things went from bad to very near disaster. Denis had, accidentally in the rush, firmly strapped his safety harness around the cyclic control (it was a dual-control aircraft so he had all the controls duplicated in front of him). Peter had to land again very hurriedly as he discovered he couldn't move the controls.

As the delay had lasted several minutes, the ship had turned on to a different heading but Flyco sent us off in the original direction – directly into a mountain covered with radio aerials. We only just saw this in time – as it was beginning to get light. Then only one radio worked and Denis had forgotten his torch so we couldn't see the maps! This was developing into a comedy of errors.

Peter Cameron had to repeat everything that I said on his pilots' radio (because of an electrical fault) as well as fly. Things went as well as you could have expected under these circumstances. Denis, on his radio set, was for some strange reason called 'Hairy Mary' and his base station on the ship was 'Thunderbox'. At one stage the ship went very faint so Peter Cameron, (a very experienced but unflappable Royal Marines officer) told him to get his head out of the box. Peter then got into a fit of hysterical laughter, and in a scene of general chaos the helicopter went into a dive until he recovered. The radio operator on the ship, having retuned his set to get better communications, came back to us using a very high-pitched voice, saying he was sorry he couldn't do any better because his head was stuck too. More hysterics, diving and spinning.

There is a Russian AGI (a very sophisticated trawler bristling with radio antennae) spying on us and monitoring our frequencies. I wonder what Ivan made of all that?

The last of the commanders that I must introduce into my narrative had come aboard and was sharing the Portacabin with Colonel Rose - Major Jonathan Thomson, the Officer Commanding the Special Boat Squadron. Jonathan had joined *Fearless* at Ascension where, whilst waiting for the ship to arrive, he had acquired a tan and become rather bored. In his comfortable, and rather fashionable, cut down lightweight camouflage shorts and sandals he was rather envied by the rest of us who suffered the heat in long trousers and desert 'wellies'. He is quiet and grave and listens very carefully. A stranger might accuse him of a lack of sense of humour – probably because he had, without realising it, become the object of the gentle sarcasm with which Jonathan prods people. He was a member of the British National Orienteering team and although now out of proper training, was very capable of taking quite good runners to the cleaners in the rough woodland used in orienteering competitions. I was soon to be under his command.

On 7 May, FO1 and Denis Marshall-Hadsell with his Tactical Forward Air Control party, transferred from *Fearless* to her sister ship HMS *Intrepid*, for whom (like *Hermes*) the spectre of the scrap yard had been on the horizon. It seemed ironic that Britain should have sent a fleet of ships that had either been sold to someone else or promised to the breakers, in order to sort out a group of renegade scrap metal merchants in another hemisphere.

*Intrepid* was altogether better than *Fearless,* being much less crowded. Denis and I shared a cabin just along from the wardroom and were able to enjoy food and drink unheard of (or run out of ) on *Fearless*. Ewen Southby-Tailyour was still incarcerated on *Fearless*, whose many discomforts included the fact that the port had run out. We were able to send a food parcel to him by HDS (helicopter delivery service) containing two bottles of port and one of the excellent currant loaves baked by Intrepid's chef.

*Intrepid* was old, and out of service for a radical refurbishment. But she had been brought out of the shipyard and refitted in just ten days – a process that normally takes a year or more. The layout was ostensibly the same as *Fearless* with a few very confusing differences. There were bare wires hanging down from the light fittings that had not been connected up in the rush to put to sea. All her crew had been drafted to other ships or to shore-based jobs and so to get the ship seaworthy in such record time they had simply asked them to come back. The wardroom CPO had left the navy after completing his 22 years, but he had come back and was marvellous at keeping the place 'homely' in spite of everything that was to happen.

On the third night we were on board, a message was received saying that *Intrepid* was to be made ready for use as an emergency operating theatre. We sat and watched a film in the wardroom (*The Omega Man* – a strange film about the one surviving man after an atomic war who is not tainted with a terrible mutating disease), while the ship's engineers started the conversion in the gunroom next door. When the Navy is at war, things happen very quickly.

First they got oxy-acetylene cutters to slice eight feet of steel out of the bulkhead to make a doorway wide enough for stretchers. We could hardly see the screen for smoke and fumes. Next they set about removing the sink from under the bar counter and replumbed it in next door. By the time the film was over, the room was ready for the installation of specialised bits of medical kit to complete the transformation. The oxygen cylinders and cases of instruments had been stored in the bowels of the ship as part of its basic equipment, waiting for this very day. The plans the engineers had followed came with this kit.

But the next morning, some very senior medical officers resplendent in gold braid, arrived to survey the wreckage of our wardroom. It was too small they observed loudly in fruity tone, the access was too restricted, and clearly, they said, it would be absolutely *impossible* to use the *Intrepid* for this purpose.

We finally sailed from Ascension Island to join up with the rest of the Task Force outside the Total Exclusion Zone (TEZ). Even now we still thought in terms of spending time bobbing about waiting in the South Atlantic. I was concerned with the thought of the Argentine Air Force and the effect of bombs hitting one of the liners; or how a landing would fare if the enemy jets were able to bomb the troops on the ground. But at least we had left Ascension and were on our way south.

The geo-political aspect of the situation when seen from our worm's eye level was disturbing. There was the possibility of escalation to involve other Organisation of American States (OAS) countries and Cuba, and possibly the use against us of Cuban troops operating as a Soviet proxy force. I saw the bombing of mainland Argentine airfields as a sensible military pre-condition to our landing but I did not think that we could actually do it, for political reasons. And so it seemed we were on our own.

The next nine days were full of uncertainty as we ploughed south through seas that got steadily colder and rougher. The various drills were practised daily and carefully revised and refined to cut down the times taken still further. There were no problems over the realism of these exercises. My diary continued:

*Sunday 9 May*: The usual 0700 shake followed by a shower and breakfast. The Beeb is being sporadically jammed by

Spanish voices and music so I've not heard the complete news today. An Observer reporter was commenting on the situation and said confidently that we were destined to fight. Cheers, pal.

We had a church service and hymn singing in the senior rates (Senior NCO's) dining room in the memory of the 20 officers and men killed aboard the HMS *Sheffield* and the three Harrier pilots that have died. I had to go for a quiet walk on the flight-deck afterwards. Several others did too. We carry with us everywhere we go our respirators, anti-flash gloves and hood, lifejackets and bright orange 'once only suits' (immersion suits).

*Tuesday 11 May:* another day much as yesterday. The excitement started after lunch with two Russian BEAR high-level; reconnaissance aircraft flying low and slow over the fleet giving it a very thorough going over. As they took our photos we took theirs and eventually they flew off.

Then as I was waiting for a helicopter to take me to *Fearless* for a conference the alarms went off and we all ran to our action stations pulling on our anti-flash. A Periscope had been seen off our port bow and so we went through the routine of securing for action; tying up the wardroom furniture and lashing it to walls and supporting pillars, put the freshly laid afternoon tea back in the galley and waited. I fell asleep on the wardroom carpet. The fleet turned away from the position of the sighting, the ASD (anti-submarine duties) helicopters were launched and the frigates *Ardent* and *Argonaut* were sent to investigate. There seemed to be two submarines, both of them Russian, and a school of whales behind which the boats were sheltering. This was the High Seas, so all three parties had a perfect right to be there, but it did seem an affront to the whales.

We've just had the Harriers from *Atlantic Conveyer* scrambled to intercept and shoot down the Argie Boeing surveillance plane (as Maggie threatened if it comes snooping). This radar contact turned out

to be one of the Victor tanker aircraft that we kept over the fleet to refuel
the SHAR (Sea Harrier) when doing CAP (Combat Air Patrol). These
pilots must be doing many, many hours – all the way from Ascension.

> *Wednesday, 12 May:* have been across to *Fearless* to see the
> Battery Commander (BC) and get briefed. We are to land (in the
> Falklands) sometime soonish – after 18th May – and I'm to start
> off with 45 Cdo, in a LCU (Landing Craft Utility) with the CO
> in the assault landing, and after that in a forward OP
> (Observation Post) to the south of the landing area (San Carlos)
> overlooking Darwin.

Had a letter from New York today. Some of [my friend] Alice's
friends are Argentinian and are embarrassed by all this. They blame
Galtieri for the whole thing.

We received, by signal, orders to join 45 Commando for the landing.

> *Saturday, 15 May:* I've got to go across to RFA *Stromness* (the
> ship bringing the bulk of the 45 Commando) for orders with
> CO 45 Cdo. There has also been a problem with the wrong
> secret codes being issued, so I've got to sort that out.

We completed a course of medical refresher training and issued the
morphine – two ampoules of Omnopon each, packed in urine sample
tubes to prevent them getting damaged. We also finished making up a
comprehensive medical pack for the patrol to carry in addition to our
normal individual first aid kits. These were complemented with as
many vacuum packed field dressings as we could fit into our fighting
order and pockets.

The morphine and our compasses, the two most important bits of kit
we had, went round our necks. The rest of our kit was carried in the
following way. Personal weapons were always in our hands with two
full magazines taped together loaded on the weapon. (If you do this to
reduce the time it takes to reload, you have to be very careful not to
allow any dirt or grit to get near the weapon). In our pockets we carried

24-hours worth of food (chocolate and biscuits mainly), several more loaded magazines and first aid gear, penknife, water purifying tablets and a set of maps – all completely unmarked, the positions having been memorised. Our fighting order, pouches suspended on a belt with shoulder straps, contained more loaded magazines, food, medical gear, a small cooker, chopping knife, emergency flares, a radio beacon, at least two quart water bottles, a tin mug for cooking, and grenades. The Bergen rucksack contained a resupply of food and ammunition and also a camouflage net and waterproof poncho shelter, a radio, spare batteries and a hand generator, a quilted 'Chairman Mao' suit, spare socks and foot powder, a telescope, binoculars and a night-vision device, a camera, and spare film and other items that I have now forgotten about. We always used to take tins of curry powder on exercise to brighten up the compo rations, but now no-one seemed to bother with this small extra weight, preferring to carry more ammunition.

This list is by no means exhaustive but it does give some idea of how our bergens and fighting order came to weigh an average of 120 pounds and often much more. The clothes we wore, with the pockets filled with food, ammunition and medical kit, weighed about 20 or 30 pounds, plus the pistol on a belt around the waist or in an inner pocket, and binoculars tucked down the front of the windproof smock. Naturally, as you ate the food it got a bit lighter, and it was very noticeable that mortar teams were very keen to start firing, to lighten their bergens.

Because of the weight, you could only really carry ten days supply of very meagre rations with you. This would mean one tin and a couple of packets of biscuits a day, and a lot of very sweet "wets" of tea and coffee. I had taken up smoking small cigars, which were light (most important!) and good at staving off the hunger. It meant that towards the end of longer operations, even with extra rations brought in and buried in caches, we would end up stripping out our bergens, our pockets and fighting order, to find the last bit of chocolate or packet of squashed, frozen then melted Rolo chocolate toffees, to keep the wolf from the door.

Our physical training on the way down had continued relentlessly despite the changes of ship and the conflicting demands on space. Running round a small flight-deck on one of the RFA's during heavy weather was quite exciting, the secret being to time your run so that as you got near the side of the ship was on an up-roll and the first half of your run back was downhill, changing into uphill as you reached the rail again. If you got this wrong you could easily end up in the sea.

I made much use of my skipping-rope and became quite adept at crossovers and double-jumps. FO1's daily regime was a warm-up in the morning, wearing boots to keep our feet from going soft, and then a hard session in the late afternoon light, in rubber-soled training shoes. This consisted of a series of warm up exercises followed by a complete sequence of strength and mobility exercises to cover every muscle group, especially our backs which were going to have to carry the heavy loads. These were accompanied by and followed by heart-lung exercises.

As Britain is now so 'keep-fit' conscious (a trend of which I approve greatly) here is an example of a typical training session, specially tailored for the very confined space of a warship. (It might save some readers from spending money on Jane Fonda videos – one could certainly do it all in a high-rise flat! Do consult your physician first.) A typical session was as follows:

*Warm-up:*

- 30 bends to toes
- 30 trunk twists
- 30 double trunk twists
- 30 trunk side stretches
- 15 neck arches (neck straight)
- 30 rowing sit-ups
- 15 neck arches (legs drawn up)
- 15 leg lifts and roll over
- 15 humping and hollowing
- 15 'pluto waves'

*Circuit:*

Run up ramp 2 times and then 20 press-ups – on the LPD's (Landing Pad Dock – generic term for HMS *Fearless* and *Intrepid*) there is a ramp joining the lower decks and the dock to the flight-deck. It is 30 metres long and very steep.

> Run twice up ramp
> 20 dorsal rises
> Run twice up ramp
> 20 sit-ups with twistsRun twice up ramp &
> repeat all 5 times
> 20 squats
> Run twice up ramp
> 20 toe and heel raises
> Run twice up rampRepeat 5 times.

The session finishes with a warm-down run around the flight deck with silly games like leap-frog and building up elaborate series of hand signals as you run round to do different things, i.e. one hand up means jump up in the air and run around in the opposite direction, two hands means run around in the same direction but backwards, an even number shouted means touch both hands on the deck, etc. etc. this seemingly ridiculous activity has the benefit of keeping people thinking when tired, and became so chaotic, especially in rough weather, that we would eventually have to stop because we were laughing too much to continue.

After these exertions we would go down to the flat where the vending machines were located and have a cup of tea, or if the ship's ice-cream machine was working, a cornet from the kiosk! I would then go off to the wardroom and have tea and stickies to stave of the hunger of the wait before Wardroom dinner, which was two hours later than in the main galley.

Events seemed to move faster and faster as we prepared for the landing at San Carlos Water. D-Day was firmly established as 21 May, which became an open secret throughout the ship. I began to spend much of my time in the Amphibious Operations Room reading the bulging signal logs and trying to make sense out of the various agencies that were sending me conflicting orders. Everyone was going flat out on their little section of the jigsaw puzzle and you had to work out everything for yourself.

A multitude of last-minute preparations kept us busy; we had stripped down our rifles and pistols, checked and oiled the working parts and dismantled all the magazines to ensure that they were completely free of dirt and that the springs that pushed the rounds up to the chambers were not weakened. Our maps were glued together and cut so they could be folded into a trouser pocket. We applied waterproof plastic film to the surface to seal out water.

In the quiet of the ship's chapel, the only space not already booked up from some activity or other, I went carefully through the various Geneva Conventions and Rules of War with the boys. It sounds strange to have 'rules of war' – indeed almost a contradiction of terms. War is such a terrible thing but without the moral constraint of the Geneva Conventions it could very easily become very much worse. I was particularly concerned with the rights of prisoners of war. It is essential, if captured, to know exactly your rights within the Geneva Conventions – if only to identify whether or not your captors are keeping to the rules. You are only obliged to give name, rank, number and date of birth – referred to as the 'Big Four'.

It was also important to be quite sure of the rules that determine who on the battlefield is a combatant, and to whom the status of prisoner of war is given under the Conventions. Anyone who openly carries arms, regardless of whether uniform is worn, counted legally as a combatant and therefore could NOT be shot as a spy. The threat of summary execution would make it very hard to resist interrogation if you were not absolutely sure of the law – a small comfort under the circumstances, but preferable to ignorance. This clause was particularly important to special forces people, as we wore what suited us best, rather than what was officially provided.

My study of the thick, classified signals log started to pay off. It was invaluable to know the background to the decisions that were eventually being made, and when eventually a series of signals came in giving me my instructions, I knew more or less (as much as anyone) what was going on.

The orders to go ashore with 45 Commando had been a red herring – as I had suspected. We were now told that FO1 was to work exclusively with the Special Boat Squadron, in keeping with all the training that Nick Allin and I had been doing with them for the previous four years running the Battery's amphibious operations teams. Des Nixon, Steve Hoyland and Tim Bedford, our new boys, did not know the SBS so well, and were understandably uncertain whether this was a good development or not. Nick and I had no such reservations, and were delighted to be back to working with our friends again.

The Special Boat Squadron has been described as the Royal Marine equivalent of the SAS. This is an unfair (although understandable) comparison, because the two organisations are very different. The SAS are recruited from the Army and have the same structure as an infantry regiment, with training wings and other oddments tacked on. They have the whole British Army from which to select the people they want. As each Army unit is very different from another (e.g. the Grenadier Guards from the Royal Signals) the SAS have a very wide range of experience, background and type of person from which to draw. The SBS recruit only from the Royal Marines, a much smaller number from which to select, and all from the same, already highly trained background. This is hardly a disadvantage – indeed it is one of the strengths of the SBS that they are all Royal Marines that have undergone an extremely taxing period of training and selection.

The SBS are only one squadron strong (the SAS are considerably larger) and their role demands that they operate in four-man teams and rarely in larger groups. The SAS operate in anything from four-man teams up to squadron strength.

The SBS are concerned only with the sea and its immediate hinterland, and are the experts in covert and clandestine amphibious operations – having pioneered this field since the days of the

'Cockleshell Heroes' of the last war. Their motto, 'Strength through Guile' describes their unique approach, which is based upon what a four-man team can do with explosives, automatic weapons and brainpower. We would add our thoughts, expertise and the 4.5-inch guns of the Royal Navy and the 105-mm Light Guns of the Royal Artillery to their arsenal.

My Orders said to prepare for special operations lasting three days, taking all our radios and 'light scales' (i.e. no sleeping-bags or shelters but as much ammunition as we could carry without becoming too ponderous to fight). This meant that we would not be doing our normal covert-surveillance job, but probably becoming part of a raid.

But first 148 Battery needed to have a last get-together on *Fearless* to talk over procedures and decide exactly how we would operate for the rest of the campaign – as it was most unlikely that we would be together again until the end.

Since we had all been together in Poole six weeks earlier, our world had changed radically. For some, the six weeks had been a period of boredom at sea; for others an odd period of preparation and waiting in Poole (punctuated, so they told me, with many hilarious 'last' nights in pubs and wine bars), with a short VC10 flight to Ascension, then on to various ships.

Two 148 battery teams, led by Captains Willie McCracken and Chris Brown, had played a key part in the recapture of South Georgia, directing the naval gunfire with great accuracy to frighten but not kill the Argentine garrison, causing them to surrender.

After South Georgia these teams had been joined by two more (FO1 being the fifth team and the last to arrive in the area of operations) and started a programme of naval bombardment of Port Stanley (part of Operations Paraquet, the operations of Admiral Woodward's naval force before the main fleet arrived) organized by Lieutenant-Colonel Keith Eve, the Royal Artillery Liaison Officer Naval Gunfire Support (RALONGS). Keith Eve had been constantly moving about the fleet from gunship to gunship and on the *Hermes*. The bombardments were still taking place in daylight and the ships were going in close to Port Stanley, so he had experienced a few hairy moments. The NGFOs

(Naval Gunfire Forward Observers), adjusting the gunfire from helicopters flying into the east of Stanley, had quite a harrowing time too.

And so Nick Allin and I were summoned to *Fearless* on 18 May for orders and a detailed communications brief. All the FO team were to be there so I decided to take Des, Tim and Steve as well in the helicopter so they could catch up on the adventures of their mates.

We were delighted to see the others again and news was eagerly exchanged. Colonel Keith Eve told of his lucky escape when the ship he was on was attacked by Mirage jets and two bombs went through the side – the first of several incorrectly fused bombs that were to do the same thing. He had even managed to take photos of all this happening which required a lot of nerve. (Keith is one of the oldest paratroopers in the British Army and keeps himself fit by his ferocious, and sometimes violent, hockey playing. His enthusiasm and constant movement about the fleet made him very well known.)

Captain Bob Harmes also appeared, larger than life and very noisy. He had started an additional and uncanvassed career as a naval fire-fighter in the first of several ships that he was to be on when they were hit. He was another of our invaluable liaison officers – who moved on to gunships when we were ashore firing them. (He had yet to have the first of several shipwrecks that led to his becoming the 'Jonah of the Fleet' - feared by captains and ship's companies alike.)

The NGFO's, Captains Kevin Arnold, Chris Brown, Nigel Bedford and Willie McCracken, were also travelling from ship to ship to keep the bombardment of Port Stanley going. The RAF's morale-boosting feat of logistics and airmanship sadly had only put two iron bombs on the runway, but the NGS (Naval Gunfire Support) was doing damage and was the next stage in the escalatory process.

Initially bombarding by day (until the threat of land-based Exocets), the gunships were leaving the main *Hermes* group and steaming south to a gunline that was only a few miles east of the airfield. The ship's helicopters would be launched with an NGFO strapped into the co-pilot's seat. He would order the targets and adjust them, bobbing up from the cover of hills or the sea when the shells were due to land, then watching for the smoke. The first time they did this, in daylight, Chris Brown was the NGFO in the Lynx helicopter from HMS *Alacrity* (a Type 21 gunship). He had persuaded the pilots, Bob Burrows and Rob Sleeman, to remove their anti-ship missiles and mount two GPMGs (General Purpose Machine Guns) in the rear, one pointing out of each side door. Chris manned one and the 'Schoolie' (the Royal Naval educator), who had been for a time in 41 Commando, manned the other – a terrifying duo.

They took off from Alacrity south of Port Stanley and flew in a wide loop north, around and well clear of Cape Pembroke and the airfield. Once in Berkeley Sound they came in over Kidney Island in order to land on high ground east of Mount Low, where Chris would shell Stanley using *Alacrity*'s gun. The spotted a fishing boat with soldiers on board flying a blue-and-white flag so swooped down on it with both machine-guns blazing away. After one pass they circled round behind Kidney Island and made another run. As they did so a fast patrol boat came out into the bay with cannons firing. Some eight bullets hit the helicopter but no one was hurt and nothing apparently damaged. In fact the pilots were unaware that they had been hit at all, and did not see the shattered hole on the windscreen a few inches to the right of the first pilot's head. In the back Chris shouted to his partner that on no account should this bad news be shared.

They landed on the spur to the east of Mount Low and Chris leapt out – incidentally to become the first member of the Task Force to set foot on the Falklands – and discovered that one of the enemy bullets had gone through their helicopters' petrol tank and fuel was streaming out. They very rapidly took off and radioed that they had been hit. Captain Willie McCracken, on standby in the second helicopter, was ordered to take off and intercept them in case they ditched in the sea. They flew direct, and over the FPB (Fast Patrol Boat) which fired some more rounds to no effect, landing back on *Alacrity* with a bone-dry fuel tank. Only then were the bullet holes pointed out to the pilots, who were not impressed!

Willie McCracken had been strapped into the second helicopter listening to the radio transmissions and making notes for his sorties.

He told me that as the drama unfolded the pilot's face – and he presumed his own – went white and whiter.

It was also Chris Brown who had been widely reported in the newspaper account of the Pebble Island raid as the 'cool, calm voice' directing naval gunfire on to the airfield a few hundred metres from his position during the SAS attack. His team gleefully reported to us that on this occasion his voice had been everything but 'cool and calm'.

The Orders Group and the 'Comms' brief were held in the chapel of *Fearless*. Because of the great pressure on space the proper chapel had become the COMMAW (Commodore Amphibious Warfare – Commodore Michael Clapp) staff office and the chapel was now a Portacabin lashed down onto the upper Sea Cat deck, and was the only spare bit of space for this sort of thing. The code sheets and communications details (frequencies, schedules, etc.) were handed round like hymnbooks, but the grim note taking during the sermon rather ended any similarity to the Portacabins' proper use.

We were one team short, that of Captain Willie McCracken. With Bombardier Jackson and crew, Willie had already been inserted (a week ahead of the main landing) into the area of Sussex Mountains, to the south of San Carlos Water. Their task was to send back information if it was important enough (i.e. if the area was suddenly reinforced); and then when the landings actually took place, to be prepared to fire the gunships at enemy targets. Once the troops were ashore they were to link up with the Paras (who were to take up a defensive position to the south of the beach-head). They had been dropped off by rubber boat, from a mother ship that had steamed right into Falkland Sound. Having landed, they buried a cache of spare food and ammunition. They were now making their way very carefully and slowly to their OP position to await the rest of us.

Afterwards Willie told us of a very nasty shock that he and his team had experienced after they had been dropped off south-west of San Carlos. They had carried the cache well away from the landing point, dug a hole and buried it – with careful camouflage. This activity would have been the most worrying part of their insertion phase, as they did not know if their landing had been observed. The cache was too heavy to be moved any great distance, but once concealed the team moved away as fast as possible.

Once clear of the landing-place, they slowed down and started the very careful business of surveying the ground ahead with night-scopes, checking behind that they were not being followed, and then moving deliberately forward. Jacko, Willie's Bombardier, was 'tail-end Charlie' and in checking behind, got an uneasy feeling that they were being followed. They stopped and went into 'all-round defence', lying on the ground in a circle facing outwards, weapons at the ready.

To their horror, a figure appeared moving up over the ridge behind, coming towards them. Then several others appeared carefully spaced apart, in single file. The were moving cautiously, stopping and peering forward, then moving on with balanced steps. This was the nightmare that the team had hoped would never happen. They had been detected. They made their 66-mm anti-tank rockets ready, laid out their grenades to hand and prayed that this patrol would not find them.

More figures came up over the dark ridge and as they drew closer they seemed to be talking, and it certainly wasn't English. This patrol grew from being a section to a platoon (thirty or so) and then larger as more of the figures shuffled carefully up out of the gully. The talking became louder and the peculiarity of the gait more pronounced as they got closer, until Willie realised that they were penguins!

The relief and release of tension gave way to amusement, but this was short-lived. There was now a very large number of these birds and they had sensed the presence of the team and were investigating. When they got close enough to decide that they were men, there was a sudden and very alarming panic, and they all rushed off screaming with outrage. The patrol carried on, fervently hoping that there were no Argentineans in the area to notice the disturbance and investigate.

Already I was thinking not only about the first operation to come but what we would do after that and how to minimise the confusion. I decided to take Nick, Steve and Tim across to *Antrim* for the three-day op' for which we had been warned – leaving Des on *Intrepid*.

Experience told me that a sensible person who knows exactly what you are doing is invaluable for looking after the kit you have left behind, getting anything to you that might have been forgotten and getting things ready for when you return. Des was not at all impressed with my choice of who was to stay behind – but he did understand and did a good job. I promised him that he would be in 'pole position' on the next operation. (It is extraordinary how dreadful it is to be left behind – especially when the others are off on something dangerous. The strong desire to be there with the team is opposed by the sense of self-preservation which tells you that you are much better off in the warm, safe ship. Unfortunately the balance achieved in this way is upset by a strong feeling of guilt at being safe when the others are not.)

Once the orders were given, our questions answered and our farewells to each other made, we dispersed to our home ships. FO1 went back to *Intrepid* to get the gear ready to move across to HMS *Antrim* and join the SBS. After all the confusion and uncertainty it was a relief to know what we were doing.

My worries and misgivings, for instance over the effect of Argentine air strikes, were put aside and I concentrated on the things that I could actually do something about. I had no time for anything outside my own little bubble of activity. (I was glad that it was someone else's responsibility to worry about the Argentine Air Force.)

The next day, 19 May, was spent in a very typical way – waiting for a helicopter. We flew to *Antrim* with our equipment via several other ships in a nautical version of musical chairs. Lunchtime saw us temporarily stranded on an intermediate ship, so we had a meal and arrived eventually on *Antrim* as night was falling.

We learned that one of the Sea King helicopters had crashed into the sea whilst shifting men and equipment ready for the assault. A search for survivors was being made. As we left *Fearless*, the SAS had been coming in from the RFA. They were to be making a diversionary raid on Darwin and Goose Green at the time of the main landings at San Carlos. It seemed that is had been one of these Sea Kings that had gone in. I later found out that this was true – the aircraft had members of D Squadron (SAS), one of whom I knew. The pilot turned out to be a friend as well (he escaped, thankfully, with only cuts and shock). All these details however only emerged later.

One of the SAS troopers who survived said that as the helicopter was under water and going down he had managed to get out, except for his ankle, which was caught in criss-cross webbing in the back of the seat. He said that he felt a hand grab his ankle and then felt a sawing movement. The hand tapped his ankle firmly twice – like a judo wrestler when he submits to an arm lock. His ankle had been cut free and he swam to the surface and was rescued. His benefactor was one of the eighteen who were drowned.

I felt it had only been a question of when such a disaster would strike. There had been so much flying that statistically something was bound to happen. It was psychologically a very great blow to me, worse than the sinking of *Sheffield*. I was always nervous when in helicopters from this point onwards.

*Antrim* is a destroyer equipped with a Mark VI gun system, and several sorts of missile. Her corridors are spacious and her cabins and mess-decks comfortable. The crew clearly enjoyed having Special Forces on board and were very confident after their success at Grytviken helping to capture the submarine *Santa Fe,* and co-ordinating the recapture of South Georgia. The food was also good!

All the SB Squadron were based on board *Antrim*, having finished the first stage of their war (which had been the thorough recce of all the Argie positions). They still had teams out, including one to the north of Willie McCracken's location in the south of San Carlos. They had had a few narrow escapes, including one of the team that had got separated, losing one man for over a week. (They had withdrawn the remainder of the patrol, then having got more rations and ammo, went back, searched for and found the lost member who had followed procedures and was waiting at one of the pre-designated rendezvous points – an emergency RV).

Constant living in soaking-wet holes in the moss, wading rivers and the lack of anything but snack food on these long recce patrols was already sapping their strength, and most people were suffering the first symptoms of trench foot. As special forces units are able to order the equipment they need – as opposed to having to make do with what they might be given, SB Squadron had ordered a set of seemingly magical, waterproof, Swedish ski-march boots to replace the virtually useless Army issue boots - but they had not yet arrived. Although our friends were visibly tired, they were quietly positive, looking forward, well ahead beyond the complications and dangers of the landings that everybody else was absorbed with. We were all part of what military planers call "Advanced Force Operations" – the shadowy world of concealed work that precedes more overt operations. Their work for the main landings done, the SBS had moved on to planning what they were going to do next, predicting what the main force might have to do once on land, and the reconnaissance missions they would have to do to prepare the way for those operations.

## Chapter 7
# Fanning Head

FO1 had been warned by signal from HMS *Fearless* to pack for a three-day operation, with all our radios and with light equipment scales. Once on *Antrim* we were told exactly what we were to be doing. A fighting patrol, to be landed well before the first troops ashore, was being mounted with naval gunfire (from *Antrim*) as the key element in the plan. The purpose of this patrol was to ensure that the strait, between which the ships would have to pass in order to enter San Carlos Water, was safe.

The feature that commands the narrow entrance to San Carlos Water is called Fanning Head and is surmounted with a steep hill that offers a splendid view all round. Our patrols had reported that there was considerable enemy helicopter activity in the area and troop movement. Our SIGINT, the top secret signals interception people, reported that a 'heavy weapons company' had been moved into the area, although they could not say whether it was located at Fanning Head or somewhere else around San Carlos Water. This lack of detail was because of initial uncertainty about the way the Argies transmitted map references, and was resolved once we captured a few Argie maps.

Our mission was to 'neutralize the Argentine heavy weapons company' and we were to do this by bluffing them into surrendering to a numerically inferior force equipped only with small arms and with a gunship in support. We were to pretend to be a infantry battalion (of around 650 men) by carrying a vast and disproportionate amount of firepower. This rather strange mission came as is usual with Special Forces operations, from the highest level, where war planners needed to assess the resolve of our enemy. They had already seen the Argentine garrison at Grytviken surrender without a fight after being shelled, and wanted to see if the Falkland Island troops would do the same.

This was a psychological operation, complicated by having two aims (the assessment, plus ensuring the safe passage of the fleet by the "neutralisation" of the enemy unit). It was also left to me to decide how the "neutralisation" was to be achieved – and indeed if it actually had been achieved. This was a far cry from standard military planning, where each mission had to have one clear aim with a few simple caveats, but nothing like the almost open-ended instructions we'd been given. But in a special forces operation, every person knows what is required, and if nothing else worked, individuals could be relied upon to achieve the overall aim - on their own if needs be.

There was also a strong humanitarian aspect to the mission we'd been given. I was urged to keep the naval gunfire falling beyond the enemy gun position, and move it slowly forwards to "herd" them away from their guns. Once they were no longer able to fire at the fleet at sea, we were to try to take them prisoner. We took a Spanish linguist and a portable loudspeaker system with the idea of getting within loudspeaker range (having dropped a few salvoes from the gunship behind), and calling on them to give up. I was then to creep the shells up to them and if in the end they still refused to surrender, I was actually to hit them.

The linguist was an RM officer, Captain Rod Bell, who had been brought up in South America and his Spanish was good enough to pass as a Cuban or an Argentinean. He was not however in the Task Force as an interpreter, but as Adjutant of the Logistic Regiment – itself a very responsible and important job. It had taken Rod quite some time to encourage the system to 'discover' his abilities as a linguist, and he had only been relieved of his many adjutantal duties quite recently.

With his extensive South American experience, Rod believed the Argentineans were alarmed by what they saw as a huge British

# FANNING HEAD

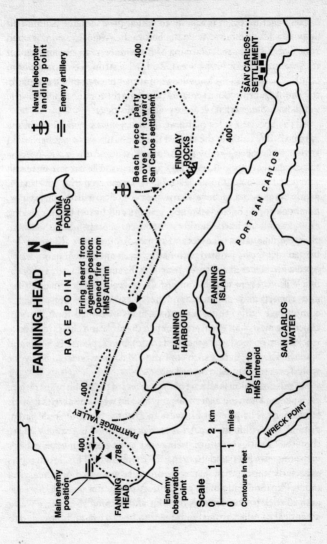

over-reaction to an invasion, to which they thought Britain had acquiesced by default. (At Poole, before the Argie invasion, we had regarded the proposed scrapping of *Endurance* as an encouragement to Argentine claims in the area). Rod, with strong emotional ties to South America and his knowledge of its people, felt much sympathy for the Argentine position and particularly for the plight of the individual soldiers that we were going to dislodge.

All the Special Forces planning on *Antrim* was being done in the Admiral's day cabin in the bow of the ship. This was a once splendid sitting room occupied by the Admiral (when *Antrim* was used as flagship) for receptions, meetings and parties. The carpets were still down and the magnificent oak table was protected by a covering of army blankets, and bore maps, half-filled armalite magazines, notebooks and pencils, sellotape, scissors and bits of black masking tape (known as 'harry maskers') and map sheets embellished with chinagraph squares, triangles and arrows. Around the walls were piled bergen rucksacks, painted with black, green and brown paint, many open with their contents spread out over the surrounding area of deep-pile Wilton. There were 9-mm pistols, several sorts of armalite rifle, and rocket and grenade launchers; camouflage nets, shaggy camouflage 'gilly' suits, tent-poles, bags of tinned food, bars of chocolate many half eaten and lying on the table and chairs (everyone stocking up on food while they still could), boots, plimsolls, socks and waterproof suits; in fact such confusion that one wondered if anyone would ever sort out who owned what.

But this confusion is all part of the process of thorough preparation; each person knowing exactly what is his and where he carries it in his equipment. The piles of kit were in groups, the four-man patrol groups, and within those patrols each person knowing exactly where the other kept everything, being just as at home in each other's webbing, pockets and bergens as their own. This intimacy is especially important when someone gets wounded or when vital things like food and ammo get short. Also it is not possible for each man to stick to humping his own kit and nothing else. There was a great deal of other bits of equipment to be carried, and these had to be shared out amongst the patrol to even out the weight of the loads.

All the ships in the fleet were at action stations permanently during the daylight hours. This meant wearing anti-flash hoods, white gloves and belts with respirators and 'once-only suits'. Food was 'action snacks' (hamburgers, cheese rolls, cold sausage rolls) and urns of tea. The corridors were crowded with recumbent figures sleeping or reading to while away the hours. Some would be dressed in stiflingly hot asbestos fire-fighting suits and others had stretchers and first aid boxes close to hand. The blue belts of their lifejackets were looped through the handles of plastic mugs hanging down ready to hold the sweet tea from flasks that did the rounds every hour or so.

The SBS patrol commander, a small, fair-haired Royal Marine lieutenant called Roger F., was busy writing his orders, which he would give at noon the next day. He was not so much planning as coordinating the various arrangements. There was much advice on offer from the very experienced senior NCOs in the section, almost too much in fact.

The SBS patrols were not used to operating grouped together, as they normally worked on their own. Their strength was their individuality and this was hard to suppress in the compromise that was a necessity to mount this large and unusual combined patrol.

The operation was quite complicated, especially the insertion phase by helicopter. A Sea King would have to be used in conjunction with a borrowed Wessex from *Fearless*. As *Antrim*'s flight-deck could only manage one helicopter at a time, the spare would have to take off and hover, then land back on again once the other aircraft had taken off. These complications would take place at night, and in what looked certain to be rough weather.

Our biggest complication was the lack of information about the enemy. We had a choice of three fairly widely separated locations that our intelligence said they might be occupying. They might also be at many other places and not necessarily all be in one place or in the numbers expected. Several secure-speech telephone calls to the OC of the SBS failed to get any clarification and so we were left with a most imprecise aim for the operation. My view was that Fanning Head was the most important geographical feature and that failing everything else we should aim to neutralise it in order to ensure the ships safe passage to enter San Carlos Water. Any other enemy that materialised would have to be dealt with on an *ad hoc* basis.

We were not going to have enough time to carry out a full recce of the area. The dictates of security meant that we would have to go ashore on the night before the morning of the landings, locate the enemy and 'neutralise' them. If the planners had assessed enemy morale correctly our Spanish speaker should be able to persaude them to surrender. The fleet would enter the anchorage, the brigade would then land and we would recover by landing-craft to *Intrepid*. Thus went the plan!

The spare helo, the Wessex, had a very new bit of equipment lashed in, to enable us to locate the heavy-weapons company – a thermal image camera, video recorder and TV screen. An RAF Flight Sergeant, our parachute instructor Doug Fletcher, had been instructed in its use from the manufacturer's handbook, and it was suspended in the doorway of the Wessex using parachute strops, away from the heat of the exhaust. The thermal imager (TI) produced a heat picture in which living things were said to show up very clearly, which could be recorded and played back on the tv screen.

We were to fly slowly over the whole area, 'vacuuming' it with the 'TI' and recording the picture, then land back on the *Antrim*, play back the tape and determine the enemy location. I fervently hoped that they would prove to be in Fanning Head area and that there would only be one group of them. The patrol would already have been briefed in every way except for the details of the location, so it would take but a few minutes to decide on the helo landing-sites, RV's (rendezvous sites) and the objective, tell everybody before the first lift (helicopter load) clambered aboard the Sea King and flew off to secure and prepare the LS (Landing Site) for the rest of us.

Facing the nemesis of a possibility of being wounded, I decided to have a tetanus booster injection - just in case, like a good luck charm that I hoped was not in fact a temptation of providence, before the sickbay stopped seeing ordinary patients. Once the whole ship closed up to action stations prior to leaving the rest of the fleet and sailing for

East Falkland, this would be impossible. The wardroom then becomes the traditional place for the medical centre for an RN ship in action, as it is a deck space otherwise unused. It rapidly became littered with stretchers, medical equipment boxes and oxygen cylinders.

Throughout the day of 20th May tension mounted. We moved our kit from the admiral's day cabin to the main galley, which was more accessible to the flight-deck. The day was spent eating and packing kit, as well as continual planning conferences in the admiral's cabin. The formal Orders Group that afternoon was a tense affair, with wrinkles in the plan being ironed out as we went. Everyone had a sleep in the afternoon and woke for a huge supper and a last meeting. The captain of *Antrim* came to this as he was (in theory) in charge of the operation and wanted to give the plan his approval. We were not best pleased to have to present the plan to him at this late stage.

We then went down to the main galley to load our ammunition. Small-arms magazines are always stored empty to stop the springs weakening. Mortar bombs and 66-mm rockets were kept safe in the ship's magazine and had to be unpacked. Our personal weapons had to be prepared for firing (cleaned, pulled through to remove any dirt, or oil from the barrel that would make smoke when the weapon was fired, and then lightly oiled). Hand-grenades needed to be cleaned and primed (the addition of the detonators that would set them off), then carefully stored in pouches. Everyone settled down to some sleep if they could manage it, and rest if they could not. Special Forces operations are characterised by many hours of tense waiting.

Outside it had grown dark and *Antrim* was steaming very fast away from the Task Force to the point at which she would launch the Wessex for our recce flight. This point would be quite some distance from East Falkland (about 100 miles), and so not only would our insertion take some time, but any disasters would take place a very long way from any help. It was a totally dark night, with no moon and sparse cloud cover. It took some time for the eyes to become adjusted, in spite of the dim lighting below decks. Standing shivering (in spite of thermal underwear) on the sharply moving and vibrating deck was a very lonely experience.

Roger and I were called forward to the flight-deck for the thermal-imager recce flight. The sea was very rough and the wind very strong indeed. The occasional faint light on the deck indicated that the crew were doing their pre-flight checks, staggering to keep up with the steep rolling of the ship. The Wessex was 'burning and turning' and we were escorted to the door, handing our weapons to the crewman before climbing aboard. The TI camera was blocking most of the door and so we had to climb around it. Flight Sergeant Doug Fletcher, the self-taught cameraman, the crewman and the two pilots were all wearing immersion suits and lifejackets. Roger and I felt very vulnerable in our heavy fighting order, without the protection of an immersion suit.

Take-off under these conditions is always fraught. The pilot has to get the helo "flying" into the safety lashings, so that when they are released, the rolling of the deck doesn't pitch the aircraft into the sea. There are only the briefest of flashes of light to indicate that the straps are about to be removed and that they have gone; and then the pilot lifts off into the howling wind as best he can. Once away from the ship the wind doesn't matter, but the need to fly as low as possible to avoid the enemy radar and the total blackness of the night were alarming to say the least.

The open door sent very cold air roaring in and very soon I was shaking with cold. The fate of the SAS Sea King was very much in my mind during that flight. Through the headphones I could hear the pilot and the co-pilot making gallows-humour comments to each other – black comments about helicopters crashing to ease the tension.

It took about 45 minutes to reach the northwest of East Falkland just north of Fanning Head. We climbed to 300 feet and began a Thermal Imaging sweep of Race Point and Middle Bay to the immediate north. In spite of reports from our patrols in the area earlier, reporting enemy activity, the television screen images of the Middle Bay area revealed nothing. We hoped the system was working. We then came south to sweep the area to the north of the Head itself.

The image on the screen showed the coastline and the ridgeline very sharply, with darker and lighter patches that were boggy places, showing a distinct difference between rock and peat. This second sweep showed nothing until we came round to higher ground to where Port San Carlos settlement lay. To our astonishment, it was ablaze with lights; street lights and a warm glow from the windows of the weather-board bungalows. Our sweep took us right over the top of the settlement which (thankfully) dreamed on and remained apparently undisturbed by our interest.

The sweep back along the ridgeline to Fanning Head showed clusters of small but bright glowworm objects on the screen, in pairs and in groups of about fifteen. There were several of these groups to the north of the Head, and a group actually at the top of the feature. The TI system worked extraordinarily well. We had found our heavy-weapons company.

The sweep continued along the coast, and over Port San Carlos Settlement again, to the area just beyond, and then south from Death Valley Hill and Lookout Hill. We turned back west across the Water, before over-flying San Carlos Settlement; vacuumed Ajax Bay and Wreck Point before (with relief) heading back out to the sea and a long flight back to the warmth and security of *Antrim*. The landing was tricky in the heavy seas. Once the deck crew had lashed the helicopter down so the pitching of the deck would not throw it over the side, we played the tape through again to confirm the enemy locations. Roger and I then went down to brief the patrol.

Blinking in the strong light of the admiral's day cabin we quickly went through the details of landing-site and enemy locations. We had all smeared black 'cam' cream on our faces to remove the tell-tale shine of normal skin. Individual identities were thus also masked. The landing-site securing team began humping their heavy bergens up from the galley to the flight deck hangar, leaving them in rows so they could be quickly identified in the dark.

From the very start, our carefully worked-out fly-off plan hit snags. With the huge load of ammunition that everyone was carrying, the Sea King was well over its maximum lift capacity and simply would not take off. The stick orbat (the names of everybody on the operation – "orbat" order of battle – as allocated to helicopter flights or "sticks") had to be rapidly changed, creating a strange atmosphere of hushed chaos, in the darkness and freezing turmoil of the flight-deck.

Nick Allin and I took off in the third lift. The pilot had to try several times to lift off the deck because the aircraft was so overloaded. The door was completely blocked contrary to regulations, by piles of very heavy bergens, and with the weight of our fully bombed-up fighting orders, Navy issue inflatable lifejackets would have been useless had we gone in. So by mutual consent we broke some more regulations and took them off once we were on our way. The SAS' tragic Sea King accident was very much on our minds.

This flight took about 25 minutes as by now the ship had steamed closer to the islands. We approached over Middle Point and came in low and steady until the brief coded flash of a shielded torch indicated the landing site. As the pilot went into his final hover, a 'T' shape of muted torches came on below to show him the exact spot and the wind direction. We landed quickly, jumped down then unloaded our kit, and lay in a wide circle facing outwards until the roar of the downwash faded and the helicopter had vanished into the darkness.

We lay quietly in the heather facing outward into the night waiting for the next lift to arrive. After the exertions of the landing I was quite warm and actually glad to be lying out under the stars in the lee of the hills, very like those of Cape Wrath in Scotland. This sweet-smelling hillside was free of the hum of ships and the ever-present smell of Avgas and diesel. There was no movement and the air was fresh; in short, in spite of the circumstances I was pleased to be on land again.

Faint engine noise alerted us to the returning helo and the landing-site team lined up once agin with their torches, first flashing on one torch the recognition code letter and then, when the pilot briefly flashed on a light in his cockpit, illuminating the 'T' shape. (The 'T' tells the pilot it is a helicopter landing-site, and the letter's orientation tells him that the wind is blowing from the top of the 'T', so he must approach from its base.)

During the waiting, cold had started to permeate through my layers of clothing. So once the last lift had arrived, I was ready to move. We shouldered the bergens and started off up the ridge towards Fanning Head. We had with us a smaller version of the TI observation device, which went at the front of our long and heavily laden 'commando snake'. There were frequent halts to scan ahead and the odd pause while our suspicious 'tail-end Charlie' (the last man of the 'snake') investigated noises to the rear. We were not sure if we would encounter enemy before we got to the positions we had scanned, so we were cautious.

The going was very rough with large tussocks of grass and strange out-crops of what in the darkness looked like waist-high seaweed and huge lettuce plants. We were soon perspiring and opening our smocks to ventilate. (Perspiration makes you terribly cold once you stop and cool down). We plodded upwards onto the top of the ridge and sent scouts ahead with the TI to vacuum the ground, which appeared to be clear. On the top of the ridge it was rocky and although I was relieved because this meant that it was unlikely to be mined, we slipped on wet rocks, stumbling and occasionally falling under the heavy bergns, which is very tiring.

We could see Fanning Head looming in the darkness, and again vacuumed ahead. Whenever we stopped, the scout group would move on ahead a little, and the 'snake' would move up to form an outward-facing circle with ankles touching. We became a little nervous of the Head, which although beyond effective small-arms range, was beginning to overlook us and it was possible that our slow progress was being observed.

Then we heard firing coming from the dead ground to the north-west of the Head. The whoosh and roar was certainly anti-tank guns firing, and the bangs were possibly artillery and certainly mortars as well. From the muffled sound, I decided that the weapons were being fired out to sea where our ships were gathering prior to coming in through the strait to San Carlos Water. We were now running late, and as *Antrim* was on station and ready to fire I decided to use her to silence the enemy gun positions.

It takes some time to get a ship ready to fire and she hit a snag with one of her twin-turreted 4.5-inch guns. The rest of the patrol had never had anything to do with ships' guns (or any other big guns) and became impatient. We had a small mortar with us and the SAS mortar-man (a rotund, but very tough sergeant who had instructed me on a jungle warfare training course in Belize, Central America) was very keen to use it (by firing the bombs he was carrying in his own bergen, thereby as one consequence lightning his own load). We had a muted disagreement, and unfortunately impatience got the better of prudence and about twenty mortar bombs were loosed off in rapid succession to absolutely no effect whatever. As I knew would be the case, their impact, wherever that might have been, could not even be heard let alone observed. On the other hand anyone in our vicinity would certainly have seen the muzzle flash, which advertised our presence rather nicely.

As well as waiting anxiously for the ship to be ready, Nick was having trouble with communications, but by walking around on the hillock, we were able to get through. After the argument about firing the mortars, our troubles with the radio and the delay, there was muttering in the ranks... muted complaining, and worried doubting about the wisdom of waiting so long in the freezing cold. Nick and I were standing about 15 metres away from the rest of the patrol when the ship's radio operator finally reported that they were ready, I ordered her to fire twin salvoes (one shell from each barrel), and they were bang on target. Apparently at the other end, on the gunship, they had our radio broadcasting over the tannoy and after the anxiety of our helicopter insertion, their passage to the gunline, and the final unleashing of these first shells of the landings, when our message came back, 'On target, 20 salvoes fire for effect', they all cheered.

I had ordered our patrol to lie down when the ship reported to me that the rounds had been fired and were on their way. The first salvo can, by the nature of the system go anywhere. We could see the faint flash of *Antrim*'s guns far out in the Sound as the remainder of the twenty salvoes were fired – a total of 40 shells. Then followed a silence, an eerie whistling noise and a brief silence. I had ordered airburst (which explodes 50 feet above the ground) and as it arrived, night turned into day. The hollow crash of the explosions came seconds later. The gaps in between were filled with gasps and expletives from the patrol, who had never seen naval guns at work. I felt a bit like Merlin unleashing the forces of darkness.

The bombardment stopped and there was no resumption of the Argentine firing. We decided to press on towards the enemy positions under the cover of a sporadic NGS bombardment to make our enemy concentrate on his own survival and so be less likely to become aware of our presence. Every minute a shell crashed down. We tramped along the ridge to the end, with Roger F. and me in front, from which we could observe the northerly slopes of Fanning Head. I peered through the viewer of the TI and swept the slopes, and was astonished to see two lines of figures moving steadily over the ridgeline down into the valley in front of us. I counted 40, with more coming over, all in our direction. We were outnumbered, so we had to make the most of our position on high ground, and that other vital military factor surprise.

We ordered a line to be formed along the ridge with all the machine guns on the flanks, a small fire team behind us to protect for attack from the rear, and the mortar set up in the gully behind. We had sixteen GPMGs (General Purpose Machine Guns), one carried by every other man, which were loaded with tracer ammunition – which burns red in the darkness, so that the streams of fire would be terrifyingly visible to the enemy. Only a battalion, or at the minimum two companies, would be able to deploy as many as sixteen GMPGs. In my diary I wrote:

> The night was very cold and we rapidly chilled when we stopped. The heavy work of moving caused perspiration which made us colder still when we stopped again. We got to our ridge position, moving very carefully with snipers out in front. Initially there was no sign, but then silhouetted against the spur of north Fanning Head we could see six or so figures of men digging in. (Afterwards we found that the shelling had caused them to dig in, their not having bothered until the shells arrived.) I opened up [with the NGS] well beyond them [800m] and crept the fire backwards towards them. (Not only did I not want to hit them, but I did not want to hit *us*!) The bright-red figures on the imager ran around, lay down or just stood still

when the shells came down. Then a strange thing was seen – a line of two parallel files of men marched over the spur and lined up on our side, appearing to be deciding what to do next.

The figures then started to move towards us, moving away from their gun position and the NGS shells. We decided that this was the time to try and get the loudspeaker into action. It was very windy, blowing from the enemy towards us. A stream of tracer was aimed using an Armalite fitted with a night-scope, and then one GMPG opened up on the same line, placing a burst of tracer over their heads. But predictably I suppose, the loudspeaker, that had been so carefully devised, packed and carried, failed to work. Rod Bell tried shouting something about 'Royal Marine desperadoes', but even if they heard, it must have seemed like the voice of an angry god, after the shelling and machine-gun fire.

The main enemy group now split and men were moving in different directions, towards and away from us. The situation was very rapidly getting out of control. The Squadron Sergeant-Major who was in charge of the rear protection party, stamped angrily around behind Roger and me, swearing with worry and saying, 'This, gentlemen, is *not* the way to do business.' One group of enemy was sitting down as Rod had ordered them to, but there were a number of others trying to sneak off over the spur and back to their gun position. Using tracer rounds from a weapon with a night sight to indicate the target, GPMG bursts were fired at these would-be escapees, initially to cut them off and 'shepherd' them back to the main group, but then directly at them – shooting to kill.

Rod's sympathy showed through at this stage and he became very angry. He shouted out that he was going to try to stop them from all being killed, and that he was going down the hill to talk to them. I urged that a section with a radio be sent down to protect him. So in this highly tricky situation, we let our humanitarian instincts get the better of our military logic and split our force in the darkness. Dawn was approaching and we were in a very vulnerable position, overlooked by Fanning Head, which we knew (from our thermal sweep in the helo) to have enemy on it.

It was not clear what to do; we had neutralized the Fanning Head "mob" as this enemy unit came to be known, and so had achieved our aim. So we should now do something about the enemy we had in front of us. Further down the hill Rod was not able to establish any contact with the enemy because he couldn't find them. He very sensibly didn't go too far and came back directly when asked.

With very great reluctance we decided that as the Argentineans were not surrendering we would have to shoot to kill. We were beginning to feel like butchers, but the knowledge of what was to happen later, and the thought of what might have happened if they got to their mortars, guns and anti-tank guns, tempers my remorse. My diary noted:

> The next problem was the approaching dawn, which would reveal our rather poor position – on a hill being overlooked by Fanning Head. We detected movements on top of the Head and so I shelled it with NGS yet again. We dug shell scrapes (a shallow trench). As it got light we saw enemy trying to get up to the top of the Head and into the bushes at its northern side. We tried to get them to surrender by firing over their heads but in the end we fired at them. They must have thought us terribly bad shots.

> Suddenly, shockingly, from off to the right of this action, a long burst of machine-gun tracer fire hit us from the foot of the hill, blasting my shell scrape and ripping the bergen of the man next to me. I forced myself to look up but the enemy had taken cover. Next to me, Wally P. wrenched his GPMG round to the right and fired long deafening bursts at a clump of bushes further down the spur. I put a dozen rounds of rifle fire into this small area. The firing stopped.

A white flag appeared from a group at the bushes halfway up the hill, and a group of men started to walk down towards us. The four that arrived first were very young, uneducated and poorly equipped. Rod questioned them and said that he was very glad that his Spanish wasn't as bad as theirs. Their boots had holes and they had one blanket each. They said they had been flown in a few days previously and had no food except a sheep they had found and killed. They said that their sergeant and officer had gone off earlier. They also said that their group had several casualties.

A section was sent down the hill to search for enemy wounded – another unsafe thing to do in view of the numbers of enemy that had disappeared in this area – but again our logic was still humanitarian not military. The section found four casualties who were suffering from bad gunshot wounds and were made relatively comfortable with morphine and dressings (and eventually later in the day were flown out to a British hospital ship). The search was a very lengthy process and thankfully, there was no more firing from whoever remained at large from the heavy-weapons company.

By this stage it had got completely light to become a beautifully crisp, clear day – just the sort of day we really didn't want, because it would be ideal for the Argentine Air Force. The main landings had become inexplicably delayed, to the alarm of one of the SBS beach recce teams, who had found themselves right beside an enemy position and didn't know whether to attack it and risk the landing being delayed and themselves overwhelmed, or leave it there and have the beach rendered insecure. I tried to find out what was happening from our people in the Ops Room on *Fearless*, but they didn't know what was happening either.

As it got light we could see there were ships in the Sound and in San Carlos Water. I flicked around other frequencies on the radio, and could tell from the traffic that the landing-craft were at last going in. We tied white bandages round our heads like bandanas, the agreed recognition sign that would give us safe passage through the Parachute Regiment's perimeter, when it was time to return to *Intrepid*.

A British Scout helicopter clattered in to land on our ridge, and SBS commander Jonathan Thompson and a medical officer and medics clambered out, both grim and angry. They had been trying to rescue the two-man crew of a Gazelle helicopter that had been shot down by enemy in the Findlay Rocks area. The helo had gone in the sea and the crew had been swimming ashore when the Argies had machine-gunned them, killing both. They were very hard-faced, and concerned to take our prisoners off our hands as fast as possible. Jonathan said that he now realised why military text books say it is important for prisoners to be taken from their captors and to the rear areas so quickly. The Argentine soldiers were flown away, to one of the ships.

As the news of this atrocious incident went round the patrol, we decided not to pussy-foot about in the future. The Squadron Sergeant Major, with all his operational experience, had been right. We resolved not to take so much trouble over surrenders – although we also agreed that we would not descend to such depths of killing for no purpose. As I was shovelling, deepening my shell scrape, I began thinking that this whole thing was like the usual sort of big NATO exercise, but with a dreadful difference. It was the clearest, most beautiful day and the rising run was warming me through the layers of chilled clothing.

I clearly remember the first Argentine Mirage jet screaming in over our position, using the narrow gap between the Head and our ridge as a screen from the missiles loosed at it by the fleet down in San Carlos Water. He flashed by, about 50 feet away, the aircraft painted in air show colours, a gaudy camouflage in contrast to the oily, drab, green and black of our own Harriers. The underbelly was white with red-and-green stripes and the pilot wore a white helmet and black sun visor. We watched the first pair flash through, too quickly for any action on our part; then positioned the GPMGs and everything else available to put up a hail of lead into the path of the next batch. I could see *Canberra*, huge and white, stationary in the water, the most impossibly easy target.

The two LPDs (Landing Platform Dock: *Fearless* and *Intrepid*) looked very vulnerable, and the destroyers and frigates steamed urgently into their positions as air defending goal-keepers. The desperate twisting and turning of the Argie jets and the roar and explosion of the Sea Cat and Sea Wolf missiles were too far away to be more than just background noises. We saw smoke billowing from the stern of *Ardent* (where our Captain Bob Harmes was fire-fighting) and heard confusing reports on the radio of which ships had been hit. It all seemed unreal watching this in the bright, clear sunlight from the grandstand view of that wind-swept hill.

Once the prisoners had been taken off our hands we shouldered our kit and set off down the ridge to the eastern side of Partridge Valley, which we followed for a time before cutting back up the ridge and down to a sandy beach on the west side of Fanning Harbour, where we were to meet the LCM (Landing Craft Medium) that would take us back to *Intrepid*. We moved down through the brilliant green and brown of virgin heather in a diamond formation with one section forward, each section moving as an arrowhead, all spread out over a very wide area. We were still nervous about Argies who might be left and also about any trigger-happy paratroopers who might have forgotten that we were coming through. (With our long hair and combat waistcoats we did look vaguely Argentinean).

The first wave of the Argie air attack had been dissipated and we gained the shelter of the cove before the next wave swept in. The radars on the 'flat tops' (*Hermes* and *Invincible*) were giving good early warning to the landing-force. The enemy jets were having to fight their way through the CAP (Combat Air Patrol - the Harriers) who were reporting their direction to the landing force ships. We were able to receive this information on our radio net.

We used this information to arrange a phalanx of GPMGs so as to put up a screen of lead through which any aircraft that flew over our heads would have to fly. A lookout was positioned on the hill in the direction of the attack, and the 'curtain of lead' would go up 100 metres further along the beach. As soon as the lookout saw the aircraft he would raise his arm and the curtain of lead would go up. The 100 metres space would give the rounds time to get up to the jets before they passed by overhead.

No sooner had we taken up our positions than another air raid started. A wave of four Argentine jets went through the fleet flying very, very low, and I think that at least two were Mirages. The four jets screamed over our quiet cove running for cover and home, but ran right through our lead curtain. As they flashed away over the scree slope at the end of the beach some bits flicked off the tail of one of the Mirages and brown smoke started to come out of the side. All four vanished from sight, and it is impossible to say for certain whether the explosion we heard was it going into the water, but certainly he wasn't going to make it all the way back to Argentina.

There were a few shouts of congratulations, then a number of expletives as our little cove was enlivened by a sudden hail of explosions from which we all took cover. These were rather mysterious, but then it occurred to me that all the fireworks being let off in San Carlos Water in the direction of these four jets, had to end up somewhere, and as the jets were vanishing northwards over our heads, then inevitably the missile and gun operators were aiming towards us. When the rockets ran out of fuel or the operators lost sight of the target, the missiles would hit our beach and the cliffs at the end.

The cove really was beautiful. There were small dolphins jumping just off shore and a pair of seals bobbing about like little old men in a bath tub. The noise was rather a novelty to them at that stage, but I had the very strong feeling that the peace and tranquillity that I had so suddenly and rudely shattered the night before was possibly never to be restored.

# Chapter 8
# HMS Intrepid in Bomb Alley

We arrived back on *Intrepid* in an LCM (landing craft medium – a flat bottomed assault craft capable of carrying two Landrovers), leaving the bright, fresh sunlight for the cavernous exhaust fumed atmosphere of the now very busy dock.

As FO1's home base was HMS *Intrepid,* this was where we kept our Gemini inflatable assault boat and the outboard motors, the spare radios and batteries, the huge pile of rations and ammunition, and all our spare personal kit. I had a cabin, in the small passage to the left of the wardroom door, in which I dumped myself and my kit whenever we got back. I had a large parachute bag in which I stuffed my belongings, leaving the toiletries handy at the top ready for immediate use. This huge bag was looked after in my absence by Lt Commander Roy Laney, who had the cabin opposite.

The other empty cabins in the passage were also full of kit, belonging to various other nocturnal folk including Chris Brown, John Hamilton (the SAS captain killed later at Port Howard) and several other shadowy people. We would appear, pale, haggard, and filthy, stay for a few nights, then vanish again in our separate directions. An empty cabin, with me sleeping on my own, would suddenly be filled, stealthily, without the lights being turned on, and in the morning there would be snoring, dead-tired bodies on all of the bunks and floor space, and weapons ranging from pistols to rocket launchers hanging on pegs and lying on desk tops. The corridor outside would be blocked with muddy bergens and neatly piled webbing with the peculiarly distinct smell of peat and rifle oil.

Lieutenant-Commander Roy Laney handled half of the workings of Flyco, organizing all the flying to and from the ship for twelve of the twenty-four hours. He virtually lived in the glass-windowed control box that overlooked the flight deck, from which everything from the servicing of aircraft, their landings and takings off, refuelling, reception of wounded and prisoners of war, etc., were handled. I was constantly poking my head into their glass-fronted office, bothering them, wanting to be taken to other ships or asking for estimated times of flights. In spite of the pressure and constant confusion under which they worked, they bent over backwards to help.

Roy also looked after my interests when I was away, collecting my mail and keeping it for me – putting it in the top of my kit bag so I could get at it if he was working in the Flyco when I got back aboard. He never asked about what we had been up to, just provided a beer – even when the wardroom was closed – which was absolutely magic.

The wardroom chief petty officer was also a very helpful man. He had left the Navy when *Intrepid* had gone to the shipyard for its refit. The Naval postings branch had then asked all the previous ship's company if they would come back for Operation Corporate, and so our CPO had stayed in the Navy beyond his retirement date to run his wardroom throughout the war. (I would think there were times in Bomb Alley when he wondered if 'Civvie Street' would not have been a better idea.)

Coming back on board *Intrepid* to a hot shower, food and sleep, was wonderful. Roy would wave from Flyco as we ran out of the helicopter and humped our kit over to the ramp. When the engine noise had died away he would make some crack about us over the flight deck tannoy. We would heave our kit over the slippery flight-deck and down the steep ramp to the lower tank-deck where our mountain of food, kit and ammunition lay. The boys' mess-deck was very close by, just through one of the watertight doors.

I would walk back up the ramp to the flight-deck and along the starboard rail to the hatch that led into the galley area and the senior rates' dining hall. A short climb up another ladder onto the wardroom flat and, passing the gun-room and the wardroom galley, I could enter the sitting-room-cum-dining-room of the wardroom proper.

The ship's officers, working their standard watches under the most unpredictable conditions, worked hard to keep things as normal as possible. There would be tea as usual at 1600, the bar would open at 1800, and if we were at sea there would be big, chunky hot chips and relish on the counter. There were newspapers on the tables (dog-eared and hopelessly out of date), letters lying around unclaimed in the letter-rack, waiting until the addressee returned, and the ever-cheerful and sometimes cheeky mess staff topping up the constant supply of coffee on the hob.

If there had been a lot of air raids, the furniture would be lashed back against the walls and central pillars, and everyone not at action stations would be sitting around in the armchairs or lying on the floor reading *Motor Magazine* or *Illustrated London News* for the third time, and mumbling at each other through the grubby, white cotton of their anti-flash hoods. The padre held regular Holy Communion services in a wide variety of places around the ship as his chapel was occupied by other more worldly activities - Special Forces operational planning – and was divided in half, occupied by the SAS and the other half by the SBS.

The hot shower was the most enjoyable *après*-operation activity – one of the greatest advantages we enjoyed over the troops digging in ashore. It was sometimes however, during air raids, quite difficult to fit in. After the Fanning Head operation, I got myself completely lathered up, and shampooed, eyes shut and fumbling for the soap, when the tannoy blasted out an 'Air Raid Imminent' and ordered everyone to take cover. I debated the pros and cons of climbing into my filthy clothes and donning anti-flash, covered in soap. I decided that I simply could not be bothered and as I was rinsing my hair, the deck above my head reverberated with the pumping bang of the Oerlikons, the clatter of the GPMGs and the whoosh of the Sea Darts as the raid came in. I was completely unaffected and continued my toilette as if inhabiting another warmer, more peaceful, soapy world, but the thought of my completely bare body and a flash fire makes me shiver.

It was on 21 May, the morning that we came back on board after Fanning Head, that San Carlos Water was nicknamed 'Bomb Alley'. The first captured Argie pilot said they named had it 'Death Valley'. Both names were equally appropriate.

It was ideal flying weather for the Argies, almost unnaturally bright and clear. Falklands experts had told us that the clearness of the air made things appear much closer than they really were. The Daggers, Mirages and A4 Skyhawks with their almost parade ground coloured stripes seemed like toy planes when they came screaming in over the low hills surrounding San Carlos Water. The LPDs, RFAs and particularly the 'great white whale' herself (*Canberra*) looked so terribly vulnerable.

It seemed to be the 'goalkeeper ships' that got hit, perhaps because they were positioned in the most likely attack approaches, or because the enemy pilots had been told to go for the escorts. I would think the latter less likely to be true. The enemy pilots had just split seconds to acquire a target and get through their weapon-release drills, while all the time avoiding missiles and flak. I think they went for the first thing they saw. Also, it would not make sense to target the escorts above other ship, as they could have been replaced. But the troops and their troop-ships were irreplaceable – and very vulnerable. The loss of *Canberra,* with the political as well as military implications of the destruction of such a large and well-loved ship, with so many people on board, which was so vital for getting troops safely back home again afterwards, would have put the whole expedition in jeopardy.

We got back from the cove at Fanning Harbour to *Intrepid* in between air raids. The route to the wardroom was virtually impassable because the ship was at Action Stations (with all hatches bolted), so I decided to climb up on to the forrad Sea Cat deck and go in through the hatch below the bridge. This was incredibly foolish as I soon discovered.

No sooner had I got my kit heaved up on to the deck than another air raid came in very suddenly. The Sea Cat juts feet away missiles started to rotate in those peculiarly sinister jerky movements they use when tracking a target. The Oerlikon guns on the bridge started to pound and a sailor dragged me into the Sea Cat missile stowage space and bolted the hatch. We all sat there in the red glow of the emergency light smoking cigarettes, listening to the sitreps over the tannoy from the officer of the watch, and grimacing as the Sea Cats launched with a 'bang, roar and a whoosh' just outside the door. It was an hour before I entered the forrad hatch and made it to the wardroom.

The daylight hours were filled with Red Alerts and tense waiting. We were grateful now for the constant pipes being made from the bridge, which informed us of the number, direction and type of air raids that were on their way into Bomb Alley, the number of casualties and, most important of all, the number of Argies 'splashed'. On the first day of the air battle we shot down 18 and lost one Harrier, with *Ardent* being set on fire and sunk, the *Argonaut* severely damaged and *Antrim* having a bomb through the flight-deck on which we had so recently been standing (and which thankfully had not gone off).

The Argentine effort was redoubled on the Sunday, with wave after wave of jets coming screaming through, running the Royal Navy's air defence gauntlet, frantically dropping bombs then jinking and weaving their way northwards, to face the Harriers, on combat patrol, astride their route home. My diary reads:

*Sunday 23 May '82:* No respecters of the Sabbath, these Argies. It has been another air-raid day - a progression of sudden, very terse pipes:

'Air raid warning Red.'
'Raid imminent'
'Raid now 40 miles red and closing'
'       Two Skyhawks and three Mirages detected'
'CAP [Combat Air Patrol] moving south to close'
'CAP dog-fight 10 miles south'
'Air raid imminent, air raid imminent, 4 Skyhawks from astern.'

At this point we throw ourselves on to the floor, me under the stout oak wardroom table, and cover our heads with our hands.

'This is the PWO [Principle Warfare Officer, pronounced peewoe] speaking, the score is so far two Skyhawks and a Mirage. *Antelope* is reported hit.'

'This is the Captain speaking; *Antelope* looks to be OK, *Brilliant* and *Argonaut* claim hits each..'

Rumour and counter-rumour abound.

'*Antelope* has a hole in her starboard side but seems to be steaming alright.'

'The air raid of the six Mirages is about 80 miles due NW and seems to be holding.'

'The air raid seems to be escorting a C130 transport aircraft possibly with a food resupply. There are several ideas on this one'

'Air raid condition Yellow, relax anti-flash.'

Everyone gets up and pulls off the white asbestos hoods and gloves. The briefings and planning sessions continue.

'Air condition Red, don anti-flash. Raid detected 40 miles and closing.'

'Raid is 6 mirages, CAP moving from *Invincible* to intercept.'

'Raid imminent. From starboard bow. Take cover, take cover.'

Everyone literally hits the deck and the ship reverberates with the clatter of machine guns and the steady popping of the Oerlikons. The 'bang-whoosh' of the Sea Darts as they go off, adds to the racket, which fades as soon as it started.

'CAP has shot down one Skyhawk and two Mirages are believed destroyed.'

When the jets are hit by missiles they completely explode so you'd think that they were never there and that the missile simply went off in mid-air. The missiles operate on an 'expanding rod' principle in that a

156

wriggly steel rod is compressed tightly from about 100 feet long to form a single 6" diameter cone interpacked with explosive. The missile has a sensor that explodes the rod outwards at a certain distance from the aircraft, which is simply chopped up by the scything tumble of now uncompressed metal.

When jets get hit by guns they generally lose bits and then crash. If a vital part is hit they explode leaving a small oily, brownish-black cloud. The Argies are at present losing about 50%, which cannot be good for their morale. They do not seem to veer away when the Sea Darts are launched (this is a steered missile and therefore not nearly so good as a 'fire and forget' missile like the Sea Wolf). Bob Harmes was on *Ardent,* which was sunk yesterday, but we heard that he is OK.

We heard that a patrol from 3 Para had been ambushed by about 50 Argies only a few thousand metres from where we had been dropped by helicopter two nights previously. This was a great blow because it seemed to me that these were remnants of the company who might have slipped away from us on Fanning Head. We had found only a few bodies and taken but a few prisoners. My diary entry read:

> We had eight casualties brought on board – two were left on the wardroom floor for most of the afternoon. They were the worst, bullet wounds in the head and both thought likely to die. One had a fractured skull and was haemorrhaging into his face. His head and face were slowly swelling up. He had a drip up (intravenous drip) and his eyes opened occasionally, but blankly. Only a very good surgeon with the best facilities could have tried to sort him out. The other was worse, with another bullet in the head. His eyes were open and kept darting about, even seeming to follow what was going on, but there was that very disturbing blankness of expression that all serious head wounds seem to have. They were both very pale and still, their heads swathed in blood-soaked first field dressings with bits of mud and heather where their mates had patched them up.

I stayed with them for a time to give the medic a coffee break. I felt physically sick because they were so corpse-like, and mentally sick because they could have been shot by the enemy that escaped from us that first morning. They vanished later this afternoon, probably dead. They were both very young blokes. I reckon that Paras will be undergoing a radical reassessment of the situation and that their future ops will be fairly ruthlessly prosecuted.

That sad and reflective diary entry was very soon overtaken by events. The two head-injury cases were flown ashore and the surgeons were up all night operating on them, saving them both. One awoke from the anaesthetic and quoted his identity number when asked. The ambush itself turned out to have been another 'blue on blue', own troops firing on each other. A Para patrol had returned to the battalion lines through the wrong section and was opened up on at long (thankfully) ranges, so the wounds were not so bad.

Much later on, I was told that a lot of bodies were discovered in the area north of Fanning Head, mostly killed by shell splinters. I felt regret that I had killed them, but I felt relieved that my 'nagging worry' about the 'humanitarian' conduct of the operations was over. I had not left any survivors who had gone on to kill any friends.

I wrote a letter home (to my parents) once I had got back on board *Intrepid*. After it had been posted I began thinking about what I had written, and went with the orderly to retrieve it. It was a dreadful letter, full of matter-of-fact statements that were fine for me but would make the blood run cold back in sleepy Oxford. So I decided to write completely innocuous letters, one of which I reproduce here:

> Well here we are, actually in the Falklands, which are not unlike NW Scotland, except that it is sunny at present although when the wind blows it is very cold. The air is very clear and you can see for miles.
>
> The ships are pretty well battened down all the time and we

spend a good deal of time under the wardroom tables wearing our white hoods and gloves, telling jokes. We eat 'action snacks,' have 'action cups of coffee' and 'action soup', etc. etc. All this action stuff couldn't feed a rabbit so is a bit of a contradiction! We get a big stew in the evenings when the action bit is relaxed, so we all top up.

I'm sharing a cabin with Chris Brown and we have managed to prevent anyone else from encroaching. This is just as well as we have a mountain of kit between us. I have acquired, of all things, a fighter pilot's helmet. The others who arrived here more recently are crammed four to a cabin, so we are sitting pretty.

There are many animals, birds and fish here in startling profusion to contrast the rather sparse scenery and barrenness. The heather is in fact like out-of-control lettuce and is very hard to walk through. The tussock grass is very much higher than its Brit counterpart and is reputed to have fierce penguins that attack you as soon as look at you, living in holes! There are seals and dolphins and even monster walruses that go for Land Rovers without hesitation. What sort of an Easter holiday did this turn out to be?

Life on board the ships was certainly far from normal. Everyone was on Zulu time, i.e. UK time, to make things easier to plan. In this way there could be no confusion over signals sent from the UK, and all we had to do was register that sunrise was at about 11 am and sunset was about 10:30 pm. The ships watches all got up at the normal times and got breakfast eaten before going to action stations at about 10 am. The first air raids were generally coming soon after that and didn't stop until 10 or 11 at night. 'Action snacks' or hot dogs, soup sandwiches and 'nutty' (chocolate and other sweetie bars) carried in respirator bags, kept hunger at bay until a cooked supper was produced at midnight or a little later.

On *Intrepid* the PWO started using a few very old, traditional Royal Navy pipes to announce air raids. I can only remember the one:

'Air raid warning. Don anti-flash. Knock out pipes.'
'Air raid warning. Yellow. Relax anti-flash. One, all round.'

This always made me think of our predecessors on the gun decks of tiny wooden warships, having fired their guns broadside into the enemy ship, turned away from the enemy and reloaded, then all relaxing with their clay pipes until they came downwind again and once more brought their guns to bear.

On several occasions when ships were attacked, the Argentine's thousand-pound iron bombs failed to explode, passing through the superstructure and out the other side, or lodging harmlessly to be dealt with by our bomb-disposal experts. It seemed that the armourers who loaded the jets back at the Argentine bases were giving the safety fuses on the bombs too long to run. These fuses prevent the bomb exploding too close to the aircraft on low-level attacks.

Aerial bomb fuses use a small wind-vane device that measures the distance the bomb has travelled, and arms it after the predetermined interval, to prevent the blast occurring too close to the fragile aircraft and damaging it. When unexploded bombs were examined, these fuses were found to be intact with time to spare, probably because the bombing runs were being made at much lower heights to avoid flak and missiles, than had ever been experienced in training. The bombs were probably fused correctly according to the manufacturers' handbooks, simply because neither these aircraft nor their bombs had ever been used in a real war, against hostile ships.

We were urged not to make any mention of unexploded bombs or fuses in our letters home as it would be simple for the enemy armourers to make good their mistake and have the bombs explode. There was no censorship of our letters as it was felt that we all understood the problem and could be trusted to be sensible. This specific point was emphasized to everyone several times.

But the night after the commander of *Intrepid* had reminded us not to mention the fuses in letters home, the World Service of the BBC announced it for us. The freedom to print the truth is obviously a cornerstone of democracy, but it would seem that editorial common sense practiced by professionals, is concerned with selling copy rather than with any other implications the broadcast story might have. Suffice to say that we were not impressed.

**FALKLANDS COMMANDO**

# Chapter 9
# The Fox Bay Raid

I visited Fox Bay settlement a few weeks later, when the war was over. It's a small, sheep-rearing community situated to either side of the bay itself, where it narrows into an estuary. Several farmhouses are grouped around a jetty, where a rusty cargo vessel lies holed and aground in the mud. The houses are weatherboard with corrugated iron roof, with small gardens enclosed by low wooden fences. It is surrounded by wet, green turf and low hills. There are no trees at all, and when the sun shines, the sea gleams blue, the flocks of gulls are brilliant white and the heather is bright green with tints of brown and purple. When it is not raining Fox Bay is a very beautiful place, and is completely peaceful – at least it was until the Argies and then the Task Force arrived.

On 22 May, Major Jonathan Thomson, the Officer Commanding the Special Boat Squadron, got us all together in the main galley of HMS *Intrepid*, For more than an hour, with the clattering and shouting of the kitchen in the background, he spelled out the tasks that we were to undertake for the next phase of the operation.

Outside, the air over the ships in San Carlos Water was filled with the clatter of helicopters; Sea Kings and the older trusty Wessex, often with large nets suspended underneath, filled with less fragile things like ration boxes, jerry cans or crates of ammunition, shuttling relentlessly from ship to shore unloading the incredible amount of stores that the 'loggies' had crammed into the ships.

In the bowels of *Intrepid* the piles of equipment were melting away to reveal the extent of the foresight of the logisticians. Behind the rows of vehicles, rations, barbed wire and ammunition appeared lengths of piping and enigmatic crates. Nobody knew what this was, until a group of commando engineers arrived asking for their water pumping kit. Their enquiries were greeted with blank faces, until somebody remembered this mysterious equipment. The engineers loaded up an LCM with this gear - a water-pumping pipeline with huge rubber torpedoes that could be filled with water from a ship then towed ashore to link up with the pumping system ashore. The purpose of this equipment, hidden behind the other more immediately important stuff, was now revealed.

Landing craft chugged to and fro, and on the green hillsides the paratroopers and commandos deepened their trenches while sentries scanned the horizon, GPMGs at the ready. It was bitterly cold, wet and windy.

In the noisy warmth of Intrepid's main galley, Jonathan Thomson started his briefing. Whilst the off-load and defensive preparations were continuing at San Carlos, the special forces were to push inland, the SAS in the centre of East Falkland and as close to the Argentine positions around Port Stanley as possible, probing and testing their strengths and weaknesses. The SBS were to investigate the northern coastline of East Falkland, especially the indented shore of San Salvador Water – into which, in due course, 3 Commando Brigade might move. In addition, we needed to keep the Argentine garrison in West Falkland occupied to prevent them attempting to interfere with the San Carlos landings area, until some time in the future, when they could be properly dealt with. This latter task was to be my concern.

The scene in the galley was warm and cheerful, greetings being shouted across the room and much good-natured chaffing. We all wore a peculiar mixture of green and brown assorted mountaineering clothing and normal camouflage military stuff. The long hair and beards fitted in with the general tone of the gathering – which was like a convention of friendly pirates.

'How are the Gunners then?'

'We're all right judging from the state of you. You lot want to worry about yourselves.'

'Dropped any short lately?'

This referred to the uncomplimentary nickname that the Royal Artillery have acquired; 'the Drop Shorts' – i.e. shells that drop short and onto our own troops. This happens, but rarely, and with mortars too, and is generally the result of battlefield confusion, infantry advancing too quickly and of mistaken identity. Nick Allin was very quick to bite back on such occasions - in the nicest possible way of course!

'Yeah, loads. Drop one on you if you like?'

'Don't mess with that lot, for fuck's sake. They're actually quite useful ... at times.'

The Special Boat Squadron seemed quite impressed with naval gunfire and were keen to use more of it. This was to be the key to the bottling up of the West Falkland garrison.

The islands of West Falkland seemed to be occupied by an enemy brigade, with a battalion or larger plus artillery, anti-aircraft batteries, helicopters and a field hospital at Fox Bay, and a similar force at Port Howard, with other smaller garrisons in the remote western islands. Both these places had airstrips, which were probably still in use and could therefore be the mounting areas for a helicopter-borne counter-attack on our anchorage at San Carlos.

The Royal Navy had the Falklands Sound virtually sealed off, with none but the occasional Argentine-crewed fishing boat creeping in or out at night. On one occasion a particular boat known to be making regular trips, was detected in daylight by the Navy, and the SBS were tasked to capture it. This operation was mounted in a very short time with all the rushing around and pandemonium that the reader will be becoming familiar. Unfortunately, in the intervening period, Harriers returning towards *Hermes* after being on combat air patrol (CAP) spotted the boat, recognised it and finding military uniforms being worn, attacked and severely damaged it. The SBS had been looking forward to capturing this boat, as it would have been a perfect floating base for small-boat operations – and extremely useful back in the UK! Their attack turned into a rather bloody first-aid exercise, patching up seriously injured Argentine military personnel, and the fishing boat was lost.

Eventually the Navy stopped all movement and the blockade of West Falkland was made absolute.

The task of keeping the enemy in the west out of mischief was given to a single SBS Troop, consisting of three four-man reconnaissance teams and a headquarters. This was quite a task for such a small number of men – but once all the special forces' tasks had been identified and the resources allocated, only one Troop could be spared to do the job, so we had to work out how to achieve the aim with what little we had.

After much discussion, it was decided to plan a series of night raids to get FO1 in very close to the enemy positions so I could shell them with naval gunfire. Being as close in to the targets as possible meant that the effect of the fire could be assessed and added to if required, as well as to avoid damage to houses, and civilian casualties.

Then once the Argies had put in the effort of repairing their installations, these raids would be repeated. The draining effect this would have on enemy morale in the west we hoped would prevent them from interfering with the main operation in the east.

The rhetoric from Buenos Aires stressed that should Stanley fall the fight would continue in the west, with reinforcements being put in, and Fox Bay and Port Howard being strongly defended. As it was, if we needed to attack and capture either settlement, we should need more than a brigade for each. They were also both very good defensive positions, easy to defend, so our siege had to start as soon as possible.

We wanted to hit both places on subsequent nights to throw the enemy garrisons into the maximum confusion. I decided to split FO1 in two with both groups equipped with the necessary radios, but needing to be accompanied by an SBS recce team as protection. Four is the absolute minimum number with which you can operate, because if one man is injured, then two can carry him while one goes ahead as scout.

For this phase of the operation, I was to have Steve Hoyland, and Nick Allin was to have Des Nixon, with Tim Bedford staying behind – having drawn the short straw – as our anchorman to look after things on the ship.

Nick and Des were to go to Port Howard, and Steve and I to Fox Bay. At first we planned three-day operations – inserting on the first night, recce'ing all day, shelling on the second night and, if the hours of darkness ran out, boating back out to sea to meet a ship on the third night. In the end, a lack of time and the need to simplify things led us to do the whole thing on one night – a somewhat busy evening's work!

There was a reasonable amount of information available to us about Fox Bay – an SAS patrol had been lurking there for several weeks and had just been extracted so we were able to debrief them. Also the radio intercept people had been hard at work. We knew there was at least a battalion of infantry, an artillery battery, a number of anti-aircraft batteries, a fuel dump, an unused airfield and a hospital.

The SBS Troop commander was Lieutenant David C., another friend from RM Poole. He had been stationed in the Falklands as a member of NP8901 and we had first met several years earlier when he had been preparing for the year's tour in the South Atlantic. He had not wasted that year in the remote barracks at Moody Brook for soon after his return to England he married a lovely Falkland girl and started his SBS training.

For Dave, Operation Corporate was a more personal business. His wife was safe in the UK but her parents were still at home (in a remote place to the north of Stanley). It was as if we were ejecting the Argies from part of Ireland (his own home) and his enthusiasm for the job was infectious.

The first raid would be on Fox Bay, the southerly of the two settlements. With Steve Hoyland and me, Dave C. brought five of his section for protection. Sergeant Pete E. was the coxswain of the boat (we would use an RIB –Rigid Inflatable Boat – belonging to the ship that would deliver us and fire the shells). Pete E. is well known in the small-boat world as the often ferocious canoeing and boating expert who makes that phase of the SBS selection course so hard. He is slight with a gaunt face and crew cut, which when fresh makes him a frightening sight for young children and the poor unfortunates just embarking on their basic 6-month Swimmer Canoeist course.

The gunship for the raid was to be HMS *Plymouth* with her twin-barrelled, Mark 6, 4.5 inch gun, firing 55-pound shells up to a range of 18,000 yards. As we were borrowing *Plymouth's* RIB, all we needed to take were the radios, lightweight dry suits, lifejackets, our webbing, fighting order and weapons with a couple of days' emergency rations (chocolate mainly, and biscuits) and stacks of ammunition. A GPMG was put in the bow of the boat with several 66mm anti-tank rocket launchers, which were becoming a favourite weapon because of their very satisfying effect on snipers, and the sheer impact of the tank killer rocket.

Under the dry suits we wore our complete combat kit, pockets stuffed in the usual manner with ammunition, field dressings and food. Over all this we wore as many sweaters as would fit. Thus when later we struggled into the dry suits the wriggling and the pulling on the rubber soon had the sweat pouring off us – but after a few minutes being soaked in the very cold Atlantic Ocean as it swamped over the bow of the RIB, we were soon shivering and getting colder. Several of us had swapped conventional webbing for combat waistcoats in which pistols, rifle magazines, torches and knives could more handily be carried.

We transferred to *Plymouth* on the afternoon of Tuesday 25 May by LCM in San Carlos Water – nipping across between air raids. WO2 'Brum' Richards was the Liaison Officer for the raid and was already on board going through the gunnery procedures upon which we would be depending. The officers and crew of *Plymouth* were clearly very impressed with his efforts – they made a point of saying so – which augured well for our operation. Brum was by a long way the most experienced Liaison Officer we had, having been in the NGS business all his military life. I was delighted that he was to be on the other side of the radio.

I gave Brum a copy of my fire plan and we talked it over before speaking to the PWO (Principle Warfare Officer) and gun-direction crew. Pete E. was at the stern sorting out the RIB, and the launching and recovery routines. The captain of *Plymouth*, David Pentreath, received us in his day cabin and, surrounded by charts and mahogany surfaces, looking over his half-spectacles, listened to the plan in detail.

Work done for the time being, we settled down to an excellent steak and glass of Beaujolais. As last light and the threat of air attack faded, we sailed slowly out of San Carlos and turned left to go south down Falkland Sound toward Fox Bay. Once in the Sound, *Plymouth* wound up her engines and steamed flat out towards the drop-off point, so that we would have the maximum amount of darkness to wreak havoc on the Argentineans.

The drop-off point was five miles south of the West Head and there was another mile and a half for us to run before the point where we would land. We would motor in towards the Head in its lee in case there was an enemy observation or radar-post, or a gun position on the high ground. The Chatelaine (the appropriately named portable thermal imaging device we had used so successfully at Fanning Head) was in its waterproof box in the bottom of the boat. We wanted to vacuum the coast as we crept into Fox Bay but wished to be as sure as possible that it was clear. We would motor quietly (an outboard motor is surprisingly quiet and the sound does not carry very far) as close to the coast as possible so that our image on an enemy radar-screen would be lost in the clutter caused by the coastline.

The weather, calm in San Carlos, was bad and getting worse here, Fox Bay being notorious for sudden changes. It was overcast, there was a very stiff wind and the sea was getting up. The RIB was suspended from the davits and we stood huddled in the darkness braving the elements in order to acquire our 'night sight', clutching our rifles, faces blackened, wearing black balaclavas and dark-coloured woollen climbing hats (in two warm layers) to try to keep our heads warm.

The deck was taut with vibration as *Plymouth* made her best speed through the blackness. All we could see, after our eyes had become adjusted to the darkness, was the white foam of the bow wave. It is a very lonely feeling waiting like that – no more talking with anyone else to be done, nothing really to say and only the job to get on and do. The odd whispered joke and then a tap on the arm to move up to the boat and get in. Everyone checked the safety catches on their rifles and cocked, pulling back the slide and carefully feeding a round into the breech. Anyone who had completely dismantled their weapon recently to clean it fired off a round or two to check that all was well and we clambered into the RIB.

The ship suddenly slowed, wallowing as her engines went into reverse. The RIB was winched down into the darkness and as we touched the now very choppy sea, Peter E. started the engine. He had spent time checking it and warming it up so it started immediately, and we set off heading towards the invisible mass of West Head, five miles north of us. It was 26 May at 0030 hours.

After 30 minutes the weather started to get much worse, the waves were starting to break over the boat and we began to fill with water. The engine was faltering but kept going so we pressed on. The bungs started leaking water and then the engine decided to stop intermittently; we began bailing desperately.

Eventually West Head loomed out of the darkness but as sea conditions were so bad we forgot our good intentions about using the Chatelaine (it stayed dry in its case) and pressed on without doing a thermal sweep.

Once we had entered the relative shelter of the Bay, the sea was not quite so bad – it had got to Force 7 or 8 outside. We found that we could not get close to the shore because of thick belts of floating kelp* that clogged the propeller and was being towed along behind our boat like an oversize bridal train. It was much too wet to use any of the night observation devices – the moisture appeared as red spots, which obliterated everything else.

The landing space was identified but we couldn't get in close because of thick seaweed. There was a prominent island in the middle of the channel, at the mouth of the estuary, called the Knob Island, which looked like the only place where we could land and observe. It also looked like just the place for a standing sentry, were I defending the place. So two of our team swam ashore and searched the island, which

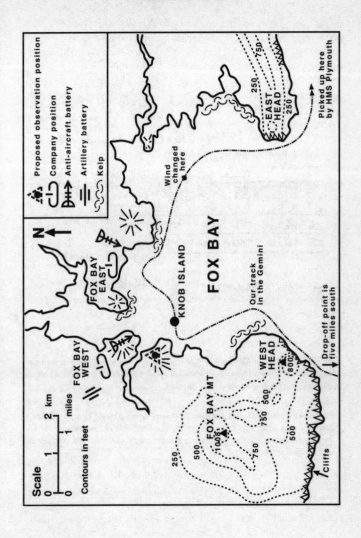

ZJ 1069   Fuel Dump (Stip RH Point) *
           creep N.   VT Low in Effect

ZJ 1066   ARTY  (L & R) LH beyond jetty,

ZJ 1068   AA near (LH)

ZJ 1067   Tents gully (LH) VT (High)        *

~~XXXXXXXXXXXXXXXXXXXXXXXXXXXXXXXX~~

ZJ 1074   B ECH worried?) LH FAR VT         *

ZJ 1071   AA RH Hill) Speeding Fire D500 LF 500

ZJ 1070   Centre Trench RH

                                    ┌─────────────┐
                                    │  FIRE  PLAN │
                                    └─────────────┘

ZJ 1072   Runway Centre (RH)  45 HA / 7257  ³H458

*above* The Fire plan for the Fox Bay Raid. Target numbers, brief description and method of fire required in the order I thought likely. The ship's and all our call signs for that night are on the bottom.

Both this document and the one opposite were placed in a waterproof envelope and, with my unmarked map, were the only documents carried on the Fox Bay Raid. The envelope was handy; ready to be thrown into the sea had capture seemed likely.

SA7C    BC0Z    H45B   KGS0

FOD1    ~~0AP6~~    72S7   QD6R

Y5AR    ~~9188~~    Y927   7PHG

P7LY    ~~MDS4~~    45HA   WJ6U

3888    3535      20·028

530S    3590

7044    5115

       5098

       6806    | 4gHA | !

1065 →

*Four nights' worth of ships' and our call signs and radio frequencies, crudely jumbled up to confuse a captor. We might well have been forced to stay for several nights had our luck failed.*

was only fifty feet high and a hundred feet in diameter, with waist high tussock grass all over. We brought the RIB in close and waded ashore.

Steve and I sat on the top, in between the thick clumps of grass, and I contacted the ship on the radio – which unfortunately in the soaking wet trip had got damp in its headset terminals, in spite of the numerous plastic bags etc., that under more usual sea conditions, keep things dry. We sat there blowing on the terminals, and then cannibalised some connectors from a spare radio to get it working.

The ship reported ready and shells started coming down. I put some 60 rounds on to the enemies' main fuel dump (ZJ 1069) mixing VT (variable time fuses that make the shells explode 25 or 50 feet above the ground, spreading a hail of shrapnel forwards and downwards) with ground-detonating shells to puncture the cans and try to start a fire. Unfortunately the water in the radio made it transmit and receive intermittently and we wasted a lot of time once more blowing on the connections and swapping leads with our spare set. Also the tide was receding and Pete E. decided we should get out into the middle of the bay before the kelp got too thick to allow us to move. The bridal train was slowing us down greatly.

Our shelling had been accurate and several fuel tanks had exploded. There had also been panic firing from various Argie positions, which helped me to confirm the information I already had as to their locations and to get my bearings. In the darkness, the ground only became visible when shells went off or through the nightscope (a small image intensifier). The deep boom of the gun firing far out to sea and the tremendous crash of the 4.5-inch shells exploding quite close echoed across the quiet bay.

As we motored away from Knob Island, the RIB's engine suddenly revved up. Pete E. fished around in the water then announced that we had lost the propeller and we had no spare. He made an ironic announcement:

'You know how I tell you on the basic canoeing course that the only way home is to paddle? Well, we are in literally just that situation and I suggest we get used to the idea of a very long paddle.'

So in twos we started off paddling back out to sea where the ship was waiting, about seven miles out. There was a stiff wind blowing us onto the shore towards the (by now) very wide-awake Argie battalion defensive position. Our paddling kept us more or less in the same place, and was very hard work. As we were being slowly blown ashore, I started working out how if we had to land, we could get back round on foot to East Point and our emergency pick-up point.

The bailing had to continue quite rapidly as we were filling up due to the missing bung (which was in an inaccessible place). It was now about 0300 and as our cut-off time with *Plymouth* was 0600, it was very important to get a radio set going. Both my radio and the VHF set were now wet, but by cannibalising some more parts we were able to get through on VHF. Brum Richards recognised my voice and was invaluable in interpreting what we needed as the reception faded and crackled.

Peter E. had noted a change of wind away from the Argie positions and to WSW. We stopped paddling, made a cruciform out of the paddles and lashed a poncho on as a sail. This blew us sideways, but away from the enemy, and with much adjustment and paddling we actually started to move back out to sea. I was bailing, and as we had communications it seemed a reasonable opportunity to carry on with the bombardment.

My procedures were minimal; 'Ten salvoes on the far right-hand target', but they worked. I bailed furiously, then looked up when the shells came over. When Steve took his turn paddling, he gave one of the others a quick course in NGS signalling:

'Whatever the ship says you repeat it back to them verbatim loud enough so I can hear it, and whatever I say to you, you repeat over the air word for word.'

It was very comforting when it became certain that we were moving away from the shore, because the shelling was making the Argies very excited. The anti-aircraft battery to the east of the settlement had started firing into the air so I shelled him and he went permanently quiet. We were drifting now towards the eastern shore, and as time was running out we were becoming reconciled to landing and walking to our emergency shore RV. (This pre-determined point was about 20 miles up the coast and was where, if we were left behind, someone would call to pick us up in a few days at pre-set times. All our evasion RV's were on the other side of the bay, having assumed in our planning that we would land on that side, so we were not at all happy about our predicament.)

The cut-off time of 0600 was getting closer and we started sending bearings from ourselves to the ship, using the muzzle flashes from her gun, to allow her to search on radars.

The RIB was ankle-deep in water which was coming in as fast as we could bail. The GPMG and the Chatelaine box were somewhere underfoot, the radio having become the most important piece of equipment to us. Steve Hoyland sat beside me on the inflated rubber side of the boat, with radio earphones over one ear (and the other free so he could hear what was going on), hunched over the radio – which was on his knees, shielded from waves breaking in over the bow. I bailed and shouted the fire-control orders into his ear, which he sent to the ship.

In the bow, two men stood precariously holding up Pete E.'s poncho to the wind, which made the RIB, which did not have a keel, move very sluggishly in a sideways direction, but now definitely away from the enemy positions. This kindly change in wind direction was not enough to get us out to sea and so to avoid being blown onto the rocks on the eastern side of the bay, so the cruciform of paddles holding up the sail was dismantled and the paddling began in earnest. I now alternated between bailing and paddling at 10 minute intervals. The waterproof suits that we were wearing, the layers of clothing underneath and the heavy, ammunition-filled combat waistcoats worn over the top made paddling very hard. We were very cold, shivering constantly, and the cutting wind seemed to drain away any body heat we were generating.

HMS *Plymouth* could not come into Fox Bay to pick us up because that would have exposed her to too much risk. In the operations room, they had detected an enemy *Fledermaus* radar being used from the Fox Bay settlement to investigate the location of the ship. As there were intelligence reports of shore-based Exocet missiles having been deployed ashore, this radar was a very great worry.

# Pizza!

Temple Sinai

Toastmasters

7-8:30 am

Holiday Inn
S. Burlington

862-5725

2nd & 4th
Tuesday(?)

*above:*
HMS *Fearless* moored off
Ascension Island.

*left:*
Mess deck 4 Mike One,
where itinerant officers were
housed.

A "Razz" or resupply at sea taking place in typical South Atlantic weather.
Equipment and supplies are pulled across from the supply ship using a line and
pulleys.

Brigadier Julian Thomson being winched down onto a ship with no helipad, as he travelled constantly round the fleet for meetings with his commanders, and to talk with his troops.

Keeping fit at sea. The rope across the bottom of the picture is our improvised deck quoits net, with Dennis Marshall-Hasdell just visible to the left of the Sea Cat missile launcher - which is loaded and ready for firing.

The cross-decking operation in which D and G Squadron SAS men and their equipment were moved from carrier Hermes to LPD *Intrepid*, shortly before the tragic helicopter crash, which was the SAS Regiment's worst single operational loss of life since World War Two.

Lt Paul Humphries, one of the pilots of the Sea King helicopter which crashed into the sea killing 16 members of the SAS. Flying at low level is always dangerous, even over the sea. The sudden catastrophic engine failure was thought to have been caused by a sea bird being sucked into an engine intake. Paul managed to punch his way out of the escape canopy above his head.

SBS and 148 Battery troops zeroing their weapons on a makeshift range near San Carlos before Operation Brewers Arms, including GPMGs, and AR15s or M16s with nightscopes or grenade launchers.

SBS men searching Argentine prisoners taken just after a fire fight on Fanning Head early on the morning of 21st May.

Steve Hoyland and Nick Allin resting on Fanning Head, wearing white head bands as identity to the Paras through whose defences we are about the walk on our way to the shore and an LCM ride back to *Intrepid*.

Dawn on 21st May, as SBS lieutenant Roger "F" and his troop sergeant make the formal perimeter check f our defences - just before another fire fight broke out.

Red Beach at San Carlos, with an LCVP (a landing craft for carying vehicles and troops), and the rickety jetty from which vessels had to be unloaded.

The author digging a shell scrape on Fanning Head (as protection from enemy fire) soon after dawn on 21st May, with passenger liner *Canberra* and other ships in the background.

Captain Rod Bell interrogating prisoners beside Fanning Head on 21st May.

A badly damaged ship in the harbour at Fox Bay.

Lieutenant Roger "F" with two SBS men, as we discuss what to do next on Fanning Head at Dawn on 21st May. *Canberra* and other ships have just entered San Carlos Water.

The peaceful hamlet of Fox Bay after the fighting was over, with Argentine red crosses still painted on the roof of a house.

END OF THE WAR
Argentine prisoners of war lined up by sheep pens at Fox Bay waiting to be taken onto HMS *Intrepid*, for shipment back home.

FO5 saddling up for an operation. The "SOP loads", bergens and equipment weighing over 120 pounds, make it impossible to get up without help if you fall over. Captain Chris Brown (left), with a bearded Bombardier Oliver and Lance Bombardier Burke still wearing his anti-flash protection in the background. This very stong and battle-hardened team also comprised LBombardier Ferguson and LBombardier Muncer and played a crucial part in the Pebble Island Raid.

Battery Sergeant Major "Brum" Richards, who saved our lives on the Fox Bay raid, despatching FO1 on a parachute training jump into the sea. Brum's unparalled experience was to safeguard our lives and those of the other FO teams throughout the war. Behind him, Flight Sergeant Doug Fletcher, the battery's parachute jump instructor, who became our self-taught Thermal Imager expert.

FO1 and 3 SBS pose after a makeshift range day zeroing weapons near San Carlos before Operation Brewers Arms.

The author during Operation Brewers Arms, sitting at the entrance to his muddy hide. Having undertaken three operations back to back, FO1 are exhausted, and the extended misery of this operation is clearly visible. (Thick mist allowed limited daylight movement from their holes.)

SBS Lieutenant Andy "N" sees daylight during Operation Brewers Arms. The reality of war is short periods of excitement, and very long periods of deblitating, uncomfortable boredom...

Steve Hoyland packing up happily at the end of Operation Brewers Arms - just before we learned of Kiwi Hunt's death.

The main dressing station (surgical hospital) in the meat packing factory at Ajax Bay - nicknamd the "Red and Green Life Machine".

Beagle Ridge, as seen from Port Stanley.

Beagle Ridge looking toward Long Island Mount on the morning of the Wessex attack on the Police Station.

The view from Beagle Ridge across to Port Stanley.

11 June. Nick Allin on radio "stag" in the OP on Beagle Ridge. The aerial is bent backwards to avoid it being silhouetted on the skyline.

2 Para assault Wireless Ridge on the night before the ceasefire, 13-14 June. A shell is exploding and lines of machine-gun tracer come towards our OP on Beagle Ridge.

Steve Hoyland, Nick Allin, Tim Bedford, an SAS friend, Des Nixon and Hugh McManners celebrate victory precariously in a howling gale with a Union Flag on the summit of Beagle Ridge.

Front to back: With an SAS chum, Hugh McManners and Nick Allin stand up in the OP for the first time as the cease fire comes into force. Note the author is wearing every stitch of clothing he possesses, including his arctic quilted "Chairman Mao" suit trousers; and a first field dressing taped onto the stock of his AR15 Colt Commando rifle.

FO1 waiting for a helicopter (to the north of Beagle Ridge) at the end of hostilities. Hill 500 is in the background.

The helicopter arrives. D squadron SAS and FO1 get all the unused equipment ready to load (mostly crated Milan missiles).

Argentinian PoWs being airlifted by Sea King onto HMS *Intrepid* from Fox Bay.

Government House, the main Argentinian helicopter park, and the hospital (*left*). Military targets positioned next to the building marked with a Red Cross.

FO1: Gunner Tim Bedford, Gunner Des Nixon, RO1 Steve Hoyland, Captain Hugh McManners, Bombardier Nick Allin

Row one, left to right: Captain Harmes, Battery Commander Major Mike Morgan, Sergeant Major Malcolm  Row Two: FO1: Captain Hugh McManners, Gunner Bedford, Gunner Nixon, RO1 Hoyland, Bombardier Allin plus Sergeant Rycroft  Row Three: FO2: Captain Willie McCracken (who was awarded the Military Cross for his part in the campaign) Gunner Barfoot, Bdr Jackson, RO1 Hardy, Lance Bombardier Dunn plus RS Booth  Row Four: FO3: Captain Nigel Bedford, Lance Bombardier Leigh, Gunner Booth, Gunner Pennington, Sergeant Thomas and Bdr Tattersall  Row Five: FO4 Captain Kevin Arnold, Lance Bombardier Turner, Gunner Clifford, Bombardier Abbott, Gunner Bayliss and LRO O'Brien
Row Six: FO5: Captain Chris Brown: Bombardier Oliver, Lance Bombardier Burke, Lance Bombardier Muncer and Lance Bombardier Ferguson plus LRO Wilcox. (The author believes Lance Bombardier Burton is missing and possibly took the photo).

The wonderful welcome at Southampton.

Families and friends on the quay at Southampton.

Being a small rubber boat, we did not register on *Plymouth's* radar screens and we were too far away for her to see a light. We sent bearings from us to where, out to sea, we could see the muzzle flashes of her gun firing. The two heads looked large on either side and I sent bearings from us to the heads so *Plymouth's* navigator could triangulate our position.

From the shore, a thousand metres or so away, a 30-mm cannon opened up, the tracer looping towards us in the darkness and bursting over our heads with bright flashes and loud explosions that echoed round the bay. This gun was probably firing over our heads in desperation at HMS *Plymouth*, out of range, at sea. There was much machine-gun tracer being fired in what seemed like our direction. Our naval gunnery was going very well in spite of everything, with shells whispering in over our heads and exploding with deep, heartless report that reverberated in the surrounding hills. The flashes and brief frozen silhouettes of the slopes and buildings were enlivened by 'extra' detonations indicating ammunition and fuel dumps being hit.

At 0600Z there was a sound of a transport aircraft going overhead and it seemed that our part of the world was becoming impossibly busy. Later I was told that this was coming in from Argentina carrying an 'air defence expert' to Port Stanley. Six o'clock was also the latest time by which we had to be back safely on board *Plymouth* so she could steam flat out to the safety of the anchorage at San Carlo before the Argentine fighter bombers arrived.

Once our cut-off time elapsed, we had reconciled ourselves to landing on the east side of the bay, burying the boat and walking north up the coast to our emergency shore rendezvous. This had been arranged before we set off and a helicopter or boat would visit at a set time after so many nights. If we didn't turn up there, there was another spot even further away which would be visited every week at set times until we were picked up – or until it was proved that we were dead or had been captured.

However, Captain Pentreath had decided that he was going to stay and pick us up. He announced over the ship's tannoy that as far as he was concerned, we were part of his ship's company and that he was not going to set sail from Fox Bay until we were safely back on board.

Slowly and painfully we were making our way out towards the entrance of Fox Bay and the safety of the ocean. We had to put in a frantic burst of paddling to get around the East Head and avoid an involuntary landfall on the rocks. We flashed torches out to where *Plymouth* lay and heard on the radio that at last she had seen us. She launched her Gemini to meet us and tow us along the coast a little; to where she had moved once she had spotted us (in the lee of the East Head and away from the threat of any land based missiles).

Even with the Gemini towing, we had to continue paddling, as the RIB was so heavy and the seas so choppy. This last quarter of an hour or so, now that we knew we were safe, was exhausting and it was with relief and a little disbelief that we gazed up at the rusty sides of the warship as we came alongside. The way to the deck was up the scramble net slung over the side and over the rail. Thankfully there were a number of soldiers to help, for we were heavy with all our personal equipment (the ammunition, spare pistols stuck into holsters in the combat vests etc.) and it was an effort to climb from the heaving boat onto the net and clamber the fifteen feet to the deck above. Our inflatable, assault lifejackets would not have held us up with the weight of our equipment. In the water we would have sunk like bricks. Falling from the net did not bear thinking about at the time.

As we were helped by willing hands over the rail and onto the deck, the officer of the watch piped the news of our safe arrival to the rest of the ship. I was touched to hear a spontaneous cheer erupt from the surrounding decks. I felt pretty much like erupting too!

Once all were safely aboard and the RIB winched on to the deck, we went into the flight-deck hangar and stripped off our equipment, the rubber dry suits and the sodden clothing underneath. From bags stowed there before we left, we took towels, dry tracksuits, thick, woollen roll-neck sweaters, socks and white plimsolls (the last three items from the excellent Navy survivors' pack given to any sailor unlucky enough to be sunk). Already starting to feel warm again, we trooped below for a hot shower, huge breakfast, pint of beer and a deep sleep on the wardroom floor.

*Plymouth* steamed flat out towards San Carlos and gained the safety of the air-defence screen as first light dawned. We were completely knackered.

Captain David Pentreath had made a very difficult and brave decision in staying to pick us up, a decision which despite the obvious risks, his ships company clearly supported, judging from the way they had helped us. Had *Plymouth* been Exoceted when he brought the ship in to get us, or had his remaining beyond the cut-off time led to *Plymouth* being bombed in Falkland Sound en route to the safety of the air-defence screen at San Carlos, his judgement would have been questioned and he would have suffered the remorse of being responsible for any deaths and injuries that his sailors might have sustained.

There is no doubt that we were pushing it a bit with a heavily loaded boat. Pete E. said that if this had been an exercise he'd been running in Poole with a full peacetime safety back-up, he in fact would have called it off because of the bad weather. Because everyone did their best and were well prepared, it came off. And when the results came through, all our efforts were proved to have been worthwhile.

Part of my debriefing process was with the Force's top-secret signals intelligence office, which was manned by spooks from GCHQ, who were able to gather information from Argentine military radio transmissions. The Argentine military reports back to Buenos Aires revealed that we had done quite a bit of damage to the fuel dump and ammunition storage sites. There were three officers killed (they did not bother to radio back the number of ordinary soldiers killed or wounded). At the questioning of prisoners at the end of the campaign, it was also discovered that the commanding officer of the Fox Bay battalion shot himself on the night of our bombardment. If he had known the drama going on out in the bay so very close to his own trenches, he wouldn't have bothered – he might even have even seen the irony of it all.

We made it back on to Intrepid later that day (26 May). I heaved all my kit from the flight deck and up through the usual hatches and ladders once more to the wardroom flat. After a coffee (or maybe it was a beer) I went up to the Amphibious Operations Room to collect any signals that might have come in for me and to see how the war was going.

Meanwhile Nick Allin (the other half of FO1) was planning a raid similar to Fox Bay, but on the settlement to the north – Port Howard. After the excitement of our adventure, Sergeant Pete Y. of 8 SBS (who was in charge of Nick's insertion) had decided to take two boats, and rather than relying on anyone else's craft, despite the logistic complication of boating across the Yarmouth, we'd use our own Gemini assault boats. Their original intention was to go in and stay ashore for five days, but eventually simplicity overcame the complexities of a longer operation, and as I had done, they decided upon a one-night operation. I lost track of them once their planning got under way and I went off to Fox Bay – they having been initially warned off for the operation on 23 May, at the same time as me.

Nick and his SBS escort team waited 24 hours in order to debrief an SAS patrol that had juts emerged from hiding in the area of Port Howard for the last several weeks. They then transferred from Intrepid to HMS Yarmouth. The full team was Nick Allin, Des Nixon, Pete Y. and five SBS Marines, two coxswains, and three others in case they had to fight their way out of trouble.

At this point I'll let Nick tell it in his own words:

On HMS Yarmouth, we sailed from Bomb Alley at about 2100 hours (on 27th May) due to late air attacks from enemy aircraft. We arrived at our drop-off point, which was 3 ? kilometers south west of Bold Point at about 2330. In total darkness we launched the two Geminis and made our way to the east of Bold Point, scanning the area with the thermal imager and with the image intensifiers to check for the enemy – nothing was sighted.

From there we took a bearing north east to get our landing place, which was a little sheltered rock cove on the seaward side, all the time checking for enemy movement. We landed at 0015, secured the area and gave a radio check to the ship and were 'fives' both ways.

Then we made our way to our pre-arranged observation position taking great care walking up the hill to that location. We sent the machine-gun team to cover the northeast and we covered the southwest. I established comms with Yarmouth and informed them that we were ready. After a short delay, due to the ship turning around, at 0130 we started engaging targets from our prearranged fire-plan, that I had given to Sergeant-Major Richards, our liaison officer on the ship.

The first target was some tent positions and troops dug into trenches. We then shifted the shellfire on to an anti-aircraft position and store. The last target was the enemy headquarters. While firing again at the first target we came under fire from a gun battery. Its fire after a bit became quite indiscriminate, going over our heads, possibly aiming at the ship. Low-lying mist in the Port Howard area made visibility bad.

Nick was still firing at another target when the team came under artillery shell fire. Des Nixon had seen flashes earlier on, and when the mist closed in, had carefully noted the location. Des was able to produce the co-ordinates of where the gun battery was hidden:

This gun battery was about 1,000 metres southwest of the enemy Headquarters. I gave a correction from that, and the shells landed a bit short. Once the shells were falling in the target area I covered all along the ridge because the guns were spread out across about 500 metres. Using VT and covering the area very comprehensively we heard nothing more from the guns. We fired about 297 salvoes altogether, which covered the target area.

We left the observation point and made our way back to the Geminis very carefully, just in case. We started the engines and headed back out to sea to the ship – on a compass heading as the mist had become very bad. We had to get on the radio and use the ship's radar to guide us the last bit.

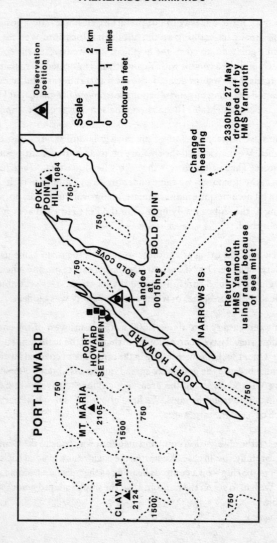

PORT HOWARD

POKE POINT HILL 1084

750'

750

BOLD COVE

BOLD POINT

Changed heading

2330hrs 27 May dropped off by HMS Yarmouth

Landed at 0015hrs

Returned to HMS Yarmouth using radar because of sea mist

NARROWS IS.

PORT HOWARD

PORT HOWARD SETTLEMENT

MT MARIA 2105'

CLAY MT 2124'

750'

750'

1500'

1500'

750'

750'

Observation position

Scale

Contours in feet

0      1      2 km

0        1      miles

On our return we had a debrief and sorted out a few problems. Afterwards we had a good breakfast and got our heads down.

The radio intercept messages that we saw when we got back to Intrepid said that there were two officers dead, two wounded, with two houses and a store room damaged.

With a heavy sea mist, the weather was quite calm in comparison with the two nights earlier at Fox Bay. Nick's operation was a textbook version of what I had been trying to achieve at Fox Bay, and could not really have gone better.

# Chapter 10
# Survival

Before I joined the Army I assumed that modern technology had revolutionized the soldier's life. The indescribable scenes of mud, water and cold in the trenches of the First World War, men soaking wet for weeks on end in the Crimea and epic paintings of armies huddled together wrapped in cloaks trying to sleep on the ground in the open the night before a big battle; I had thought these things to be purely historical.

When I arrived, naïve and young, at the Royal Military Academy, Sandhurst, I was surprised to find that we spent some of our time on training exercises digging trenches. They had to be deep enough for only the head to stick over the parapet and large enough for two, with an underground space for one to sleep under the claustrophobic protection of two feet of earth above his head.

As the course progressed, we learned to dig quite fast and, using the turfs we had carefully removed from the whole area, returf and camouflage the trench so that it blended in with the rest of the hillside. With night patrols to test our navigation, endurance and leadership, we lived for weeks (I cannot say happily) in these soggy, muddy holes. Trenches are one of the peculiar and inescapable norms (the lowest common denominator I should think) of military life – a necessary evil.

The chapter after this describes Operation Brewers Arms, which became, apart from anything else, an exercise in survival. We had to vanish by day into gently rolling moor land, which was completely waterlogged. Before I proceed with the narrative I would like to describe the mechanics of living under these conditions – when you are soaking wet and freezing cold, unable to move when it is light and with very little food. Indeed, such is the backdrop to everything in this book. These aspects of war cannot be altered by technology and this is why ultimately it is the quality of the soldiers that decides the outcome and not the degrees of sophistication of their equipment.

Eating, next to being dry and clean and sleeping, was the most enjoyable and so personally important activity. Because eating is 'normal' there was, for us, an element of escapism in it.

On the ships you could get two hot meals on most days throughout the fighting. These meals, breakfast and dinner, were served during the hours of darkness when the air raids were not coming in, and were fairly normal, if a little tinned and dehydrated. Because of the danger of fire from hot ovens and chip pans there was no cooking during the day and we lived off "action snacks", eg. Hamburgers, hot dogs, cheese rolls... washed down with countless cups of hot, sweet tea and coffee from urns that that did the rounds every hour or so. This was sheer luxury compared with the cuisine available when out on operations.

The British Army 24-hour ration pack – known appropriately as a 'rat' pack – is coveted by our compatriots in foreign armies, who will happily swap the most delightful delicacies from their own rations for a packet of 'Biscuits Sweet' or a small tin of 'Bacon Grill'. This astonishes the British soldier, who avidly collects the strange things that other armies eat. After a while one comes to realize that their food is not nearly so good as ours. The Americans eat a strange mixture of cocktail snacks and kiddy food, the Danes change their menus every few months and the Dutch simply provide too much (which you then have to carry).

The Brit 24-hr 'rat' pack comes in a plain, unmarked, brown cardboard box containing Breakfast and a Main Meal, plus several packets of plain ships' biscuits (Biscuits AB) and Garibaldi biscuits (Biscuits Sweet AB). There are several brew kits providing tea, coffee, powdered milk and sugar enough for several 'wets', each of one pint so you can share it around several people (all drinking from the same mug). There is a 'sundries' pack containing a generous supply of hard lavatory paper, chewing gum (as an aid to tooth cleaning), salt sachets, a small tin opener, a book of matches and a copy of the menus provided in the four types of pack.

Each brown box is labelled Menu A,B,C or D, and soldiers know exactly what each contains, and which they prefer to reject, swap or dump. Breakfast consists of Biscuits AB, a tin of Bacon Grill or Bacon Burger, a tin of Baked Beans or Spaghetti and a block of Compressed Oatmeal. The main meal ranges from miniature steak and kidney puddings (nicknamed 'Babies Heads') to stewed steak, minced beef and chicken curry. I should add that the tins are all half the size of the normal ones that you buy in the shops. Dehydrated apple flakes or apricot flakes are included in the main meal and a tin of fruit pudding (heavy plum duff) or the universal favourite, fruit salad.

Fruit salads were the ultimate treat and people would horde them up in their packs until they needed cheering up. I very often returned from ops with several fruit salads because I just couldn't decide when to eat them. Des Nixon had a similar problem but he, with the inescapable logic of the Yorkshire man, overcame it by eating all his at once at the beginning. I even heard of one person who ate all his fruit salads before leaving the ship.

It is possible to create some quite remarkable dishes with the 24hr 'rat' pack, on exercise if you have the time. But when I tried this at home in the kitchen, the results were bland and not very nice. Out in the field in the fresh air, with hunger as the spur, 'compo' rations can seem to be rather nicer than they actually are, and can even be eaten cold. In more leisurely times, on long training exercises, I have created such delights as apple crumble, but in the Falklands we stuck to the classic British Army 'all-in' stew if we were in a position to heat our food.

Cooking is done in small mess tins or aluminium dixies and everyone has their own methods, utensils and preferences. I like to cook mine in a circular dixie with a lid, using a shortened wooden spoon. The wooden spoon is an essential bit of kit as far as I'm concerned. It serves both as a cooking and an eating implement, scraping the last of the burnt stew from the bottom of the dixie without adding any not quite nourishing aluminium, and also most importantly doesn't get hot and burn your fingers or lips (which may be chapped or wind-burned). I used the same dixie for making brews, which serves to clean and sterilize the container and save water. Again to avoid burning sensitive lips, I used a green plastic mug from which to drink. This mug got melted during the last fortnight of the conflict by being left too close to a hexamine cooker, but thankfully I was able to re-melt it and smooth hot plastic over the hole. It's not easy to get green plastic mugs in the South Atlantic.

In the cold and the high winds of the Falklands it was not possible to use the 'bluey' propane gas cookers that we all prefer, as they were simply not hot enough. The hexamine tablets, issued one per ration pack, are very hot and with appropriate shelter from the wind, worked very well. The main problem was getting the 'hexxy' blocks alight in howling winds. The Rolls Royce method of cooking was using a Coleman's petrol stove that was very hot and heated things up quickly - but you had to scavenge around the ship for suitable fuel.

The best 'rats' of all are the ones used in the arctic, which provide 5000 calories per day if you eat the lot, and have very adaptable, but mainly dehydrated menus. The great favourite, apart from the fruit salad, is the hot chocolate, which is virtually a meal in itself.

The main problem with dehydrated rations is that you inevitably never have time to soak them for long enough, assuming you have enough water. Improperly soaked, these arctic rations were crunchy, which was fine but they soaked up water from your stomach and made you very dehydrated. Even in the excessively wet conditions of the Falklands, there was often a shortage of pure enough water that was safe to consume. Quite often you could not find even a muddy pool in which you could carefully immerse your water bottle. Water purifying tablets were always used, and made everything taste of chlorine – like swimming pool water.

Dehydration was a great problem in the cold, wet, windy conditions. The wind tended to evaporate moisture from the skin very quickly especially when moving and perspiring heavily, which soon became dehydration, making you vulnerable to exposure. We always cooked just before last light and drank lots of wets to keep the body fluids up.

But drinking lots after a meal, then trying to get some sleep creates problems of its own. Getting up in the night for a pee is more difficult when you have to crawl over the top of your 'oppo' underneath a two-foot high poncho that is stretched tight with accumulated rainwater, and a camouflage net piled with turfs and grass. You then have to negotiate a muddy tunnel to the outside world. Many of us used the 'pee bottle' technique, which doubles up as a very welcome hot water bottle. The bottle had to be large, and there was the serious risk of miscalculation and a disastrous overflow.

The long days spent lying up waiting for nightfall, or in concealed observation posts on mountaintops, were bone numbingly cold. We could not move at all, and certainly not in order to generate some body heat. We would wear all our clothes plus arctic quilted Chairman Mao suits, then if the security situation allowed it, crawl inside our 'green slugs' and huddle together for warmth. Eating a chocolate bar seemed to release an almost instant glow of energy and perceptible warmth, and the value of a hot, very sweet cup of tea was unfathomable. We tended to keep bars of chocolate for after dark when we dared not light the cookers.

The meals that we produced under these conditions tasted marvellous even though they were monotonously similar. The best quick, hot meal was the 'all-in' stew, in which everything was mixed together, from the stewed steak through the powdered mulligatawny soup to the apple flakes and the mixed fruit pudding. You stirred in your salt, oxo-cubes, and broken biscuits, and afterwards had a nice cup of tea. The more sophisticated efforts took longer and could involve carefully boiling each tin in water to avoid sullying the mess tin. The biscuits AB were crumbled up into the stew and the soups were useful to thicken it up if you'd put in too much water.

Of course sometimes you dare not risk showing even the slight light of a hexamine block (like a firelighter), and so couldn't cook at all. Apart from the dehydrated stuff, compo can be eaten cold. The lunch or snack meal was chocolate and sweets with biscuits and a tin of meat paste. This was all right cold, but best with a brew.

In the cold, our chocolate and Mars bars, the wonderful fruit salad tins, and the meat paste very often froze, so you had to remember to put these thing in an inside pocket to thaw for a while before eating. Often the water bottles froze up and we knew from experience in the Norwegian arctic, that the metal ones would split, so we used the plastic alternatives. People often lost fillings and broke teeth on frozen rollos – which were part of the snack meal.

An interesting feature of compo rations is that they clog up the digestive system. For this reason you are supposed to have fresh rations every five days when eating the stuff continuously. We were understandably unwilling to attend to the call of nature on a daily basis – if at all! It was very cold. We wore lots of clothing, and undoing all the buttons with numbed fingers prior to exposing one's most tender part to the biting winds took far too long. Our trousers were very heavy; double thickness material that was wet, pockets filled with spare rifle magazines, first aid dressings and maps. Many of us wore braces rather than using a belt, which we knew from past experience would rub with the wet material raising unpleasant sores. Everything encouraged the postponement of the evil moment, further constipating an already unhappy system.

Expeditions at night with a shovel were therefore quite a performance. First you had to get your 'oppo' to come along as sentry, inform the rest of the team of your sudden task and the direction you were going out with your weapons and a shovel. The sentry studiously watched his arcs while you fumbled with your trousers in the teeth of cutting sleety wind. It is most important, in the darkness and urgency of the moment, not to mislay your weapon in any way. Our OP sentry would always keep an eye on things with the nightscope, an intimate but far from romantic task.

These expeditions were normally very fraught due to the pent-up nature of the business. They were however an animated source of conversation, recounted afterward in detail and with great satisfaction, because, like eating, they were a natural activity and had a degree of escapism about them. A perfectly acceptable opening gambit to a conversation, even with a stranger, was to say: "I had a fantastic shit last night." There was also another particularly important element to this very strange business – that of relief after the event, a catharsis, something that you'd endured or survived, that was almost allegorical. And most important of all, it was something personal, an event unconnected with anything military!

Clothing under cold, wet conditions is very hard to get right. If you wear full waterproofs then as you move, the perspiration builds up on the inside of the waterproof and you end up as wet as if you'd not bothered. I found Goretex equipment, very expensive and designed to let perspiration out but not let rain in, to be very good, especially the 'bivvie' bags in which you could sleep without bothering with a poncho or any overhead shelter.

The sudden drops in temperature to well below freezing (with strong winds creating a wind-chill factor that lowered the effective temperature still further) and equally sudden thaws, were very dangerous. At least when it starts to rain the temperature cannot drop below zero. We often ended up getting wet through, then the temperature would drop and the winds got up, creating the classic conditions for exposure (hypothermia) to strike. But the experience of winters spent on exercises in Norway stood us in very good stead, where just these conditions occur at the end of winter.

The layer principle of clothing, tried and tested in the arctic, is essential. You wear many thin layers rather than a few thick ones, to trap as much warm air next to the body as possible. I wore a Liefer thermal vest with a string vest over the top and string underpants and a Norge army shirt made of pile cotton with a zip-up roll-neck. I wore DPM camouflage double-thickness windproof trousers held up with braces, because with the pockets filled and soaking wet they become very heavy and chafe the waist. Over the Norge shirt I wore a DPM cotton shirt with lots of pockets, filled with food, first-field dressings, ammunition, a packet of loo paper, and pens and pencils. If we were moving I could undo all the buttons on the DPM shirt and unzip the Norge shirt to ventilate, with my DPM arctic waterproof smock over the top. The pockets in the smock were crammed with food, ammo and first-aid kit. The smock on its own weighed over 20 pounds.

When we stopped moving, I would put on the jacket of my Chairman Mao suit, sometimes over the top of everything else. In an OP I put everything on: Chairman Mao suit, windproofs and waterproofs. I wore a woolly mountaineering hat, with a black balaclava at night and a green arctic 'headover' around my neck. Wet feet were the great enemy, but could not very well be avoided. In spite of the military common sense of wearing boots at all times, even when sleeping (in case you are attacked) we very often removed boots and socks (putting on foot powder and dry socks, or arctic issue quilted bootees) when we were lucky enough to get into our sleeping bags. This became a very important ritual, so that our feet could recover a little by being dry and warm for few hours in every 24. It often took some time massaging, rubbing and tending to get the circulation going again, but the effort did keep trench foot, frostbite and other foot problems at bay.

Much later in the campaign, we acquired some Swedish Army ski-march boots which kept the water completely out, and with British issue white-pile arctic socks worn under a pair of the normal khaki socks, the foot problem was pretty much solved – provided you took enough time to powder and massage your feet each day. Wet socks could be dried to an acceptable sogginess by hanging them under your smock (over your shoulders), so you moved along like a mobile clothes horse.

With the large amounts of water about, we had to preserve every bit of our dry clothing jealously, and move terribly carefully. Getting wet was a serious problem, almost as bad as an injury. One SAS officer nearly died of exposure after getting wet while observing Port Stanley. He had tried to keep going by taking the risk of lighting a fire in a cave, but soon had to be evacuated. We would lie out in the driving rain, huddled under poncho shelters that were taut as bow strings from the weight of rain water, praying they wouldn't leak or collapse. The poncho slipping in the middle of the night, causing a deluge of water to cascade into the basha was a disaster that could rapidly lead to fatal hypothermia.

# SURVIVAL

The one thing you had to be able to do was put your hand immediately on any particular bit of kit. Thus you had to know exactly where in your pockets, webbing or bergen you kept everything. You also had to know where your 'oppo' kept all his bits and pieces, in order to make him a cup of tea or find his first aid pack. That is not as difficult as it sounds as certain things are kept by everyone in the same places, i.e. a first field dressing in a pocket over the heart (the left-hand side) or spare magazines in the left-hand pouch (so you can hold your weapon with your right hand and get a fresh magazine out with the left).

A soldier's time is spent struggling more with the elements than with the enemy. In surviving a hostile environment you have to work out a way of living and a routine for everything so that the uncomfortable circumstances do not take over and leave you unable to do your job. You have to be pretty stoical and a good, unshakeable sense of humour is by far the most important thing to possess. Operation Brewers Arms, our next task, might have been specially devised to test these sterling qualities.

# Chapter 11
# Operation Brewers Arms

Steve and I returned from Fox Bay (on 26 May) to *Intrepid* absolutely knackered, to have Jonathan Thompson summon us to the wardroom with his roll of maps laid out on the long, polished, dining-room table. He outlined a plan involving us going out again immediately. 'Our hearts died within us' (as I remember the Pacific island native saying when the District Officer tried to make him play cricket). There was a theory that the Argie air raids were being directed by someone with radios in the Mount Rosalie area, just across Falkland Sound to the west overlooking the entrance to San Carlos Water. We were to get across there, land, find him (with help from the TI) and either shell him, capture him or otherwise deal with him.

It was all to happen five minutes ago, and was a good example of how the Staff conceived what they thought was a good idea, immediately told us to do it, and thought no more about it, except to chide us for not getting on with it. After our two previous experiences I realized that if we were not to be given impossible tasks that would sooner, rather than later, lead to a disaster, then I was going to have to question closely everything I was told to do.

There were several things wrong with this particular idea, apart from our reluctance to rush off into something without proper thought. We did not know what was in the area. But we did know there was a long-term SAS patrol that had been there for several weeks, but they not communicating, so we did not know if they would be in our area of operations or not. Thus we could not open fire on anybody without the serious risk of getting close enough to be sure who they were. Our presence in the area would also be unknown to the SAS patrol, who would certainly shoot first and ask questions later.

Nevertheless in record time, we rushed off in a boat to *Fearless* ready to stay out for a week. After several hours getting cold and wet in an LCM, including the doubtful entertainment value of sitting out an air raid in the middle of San Carlos Water, it grew dark and the Mount Rosalie operation was postponed. We were left marooned on *Fearless*, which was grossly overcrowded, and had to sleep among the diesel fumes of the tank deck.

A little of the frustration that this sort of thing causes is evident in a letter I wrote home from *Intrepid* at this time (two days after the Fox Bay raid), whilst waiting and worrying about Nick and Des at Port Howard.

"Things are somewhat trying at present – mainly because nothing is definite and everything keeps changing all the time. It is quite a relief, in a funny sort of way, to get on with the job!".

It is hard to visualize 'normal' life at present, although I suspect that this is a natural defence mechanism. It seems to filter out all the unpleasant bits. I've just had a phone call from Tim Bedford – one of my hands – who has been given a very expensive bit of night observation equipment and wants to know who should 'sign for it'. I paused then said:

'Listen, Tim, you sign for it and we lose it I'll write it off.'

He chuckled at the other end and so I said:

'This is war you know, it doesn't really matter.'

Some people overheard this and burst out laughing, so did I. What a ridiculous thing to say!

As I was saying, we have no real worries out here – like mortgage repayments or trades-union disputes. Our funny little world starts in the morning and ends whenever bed is once again possible. Constant and unremitting chaos presents more of an intellectual challenge than most would realise, but provided you don't allow frustration and a sense of helplessness to get too strong a hold, you can always (a) carry on as you see fit regardless (b) obey the last order or (c) do absolutely nothing.

Any one of the three seems to work!

I referred to my younger brother Peter, a lieutenant in the parachute engineers, also in the Falklands.

"Typical of Pete to get on to *QE2* rather than one of the tramps that I came down on. I went on *Canberra* for a few nights at Ascension and it was really strange. They were all drinking exotic cocktails and there were stewardesses and all the normal cruise trappings, interspersed with phalanxes of troops running round the promenade decks and duty sergeants in fiercely pressed denim uniforms.

We are just reading the detailed Pay Review document – I think I get about £2 extra per day plus £1.70 and 50p for the privilege of being here! Except they will dream up some reason to take some of it away, i.e. because we are enjoying ourselves too much or something!

Well, I hope all goes well and that our bloodthirsty press and TV are not continuing to exaggerate things as they have done so far. Some of the stuff I've seen in our out-of-date papers is truly horrifying. It's not at all like that here. It really is infuriating the rubbish they write and print in order to sell copies! Don't worry too much about us (there aren't any cars to get run over by).

The next day, having survived a very noisy and fumy night on *Fearless*'s tank-deck, we got back to *Intrepid* to hear that a TI-scan flight in a Wessex had shown up nothing on Mount Rosalie. There was no air raiding in San Carlos either. But the Mount Rosalie operation was still on.

At sea, the fleet were attacked by Super Etendards and *Atlantic Conveyor* was hit by an Exocet. A second TI scan by helicopter still showed no enemy on Mount Rosalie but nevertheless we spent another day rushing around preparing to go up there to take out the mysterious forward air controller.

We had no idea where the SAS patrol had gone. They would not communicate unless they had important information, so this was not a surprise. I said that this mission was too dodgy a mission until radio contact had been established with the SAS patrol, and refused to go. Communications with the SAS team were never achieved, so the idea was shelved.

The Mount Rosalie op did keep cropping up for others at various times, and at one stage an SAS patrol did go out, spotted two men and put in an attack. But on searching the area, whoever was there had gone.

Thus ended two days of that most classic of military activities - being buggered about. At one stage we had been given just ten minutes to get totally ready for a full two-day operation!

There were also plans afoot to dump all special forces ashore complete with our mountain of special equipment, in order to clear the ship for 5 Infantry Brigade's arrival from the UK. This wonderful staff idea was just a total logistic nightmare. The detailed planning and mounting of special operations cannot be done adequately from slit trenches in the pouring rain.

The solution to this last problem was to pack up all our gear in waterproof bags and arrange it in the sort of order in which we thought we might need it, which was impossible as we had no idea what ops would be planned. In the end we pre-empted this dilemma and planned ops that would get us off the ships and into the field for as long as possible, pushing forward in front of 3 Commando Brigade as it broke out of the beachhead.

Outside of my little word and all its problems, other people were extremely busy. 2 Para were still fighting at Darwin and Goose Green, 45 Commando were getting towards the end of their long yomp to Douglas, and 3 Para were going very fast towards Teal Inlet Settlement. The future plan was for 3 Commando Brigade to move to Teal, and already an SBS team had completed their beach recces and were moving back westwards to meet 3 Para and guide them in, or tell them where the enemy were so a battalion attack could be made.

The SBS were very busy too. Lieutenant David T. was getting ready to move his complete troop in Rigid Raiders to Green Island at the southern head of Salvador Waters, to prepare for a move of the entire 3 Commando Brigade eastwards, eventually going overland to Port Louis Settlement (linking up with what we were to do). David's operation deep into the northern flank was a masterpiece of watermanship and navigation, being achieved without detection and moving through very tricky waters at night.

Another SBS troop were warned to start the lengthy preparations needed for the mounting of attacks on shipping in Port Stanley harbour. This is a more traditional SBS task, involving a drop-off from ship, submarine or canoe, a long, approach swim by compass, then a long underwater swim again on a compass bearing, to place limpet mines on the hull of the target ship. This is done at night and requires very great diving skill and tremendous stamina, as well as precise navigation and single-minded courage.

FO1 were to accompany Lieutenant Andy N. and his troop of three four-man recce teams and a small HQ. We were to prepare for an operation lasting a minimum of ten days, in which we would infiltrate into the Mount Brisbane area and clear it south to Berkeley Sound. Once done, the way would be clear for crossing the water and getting on to the high ground north of Stanley. This was to be called Operation Brewers Arms.

The crazy idea of putting all our stores ashore was still hanging over our heads, like an unthinkable nightmare. In the end, the orders to actually do it were ignored, because it was just too difficult. We had over two tons of fragile gear, plus a huge pile of many different types of ammunition. The gear alone less ammo, was 130 pallet loads. Without being on the ship, our casualty evacuation and radio communications problems would have been insurmountable. We had to have a secure base from which to plan, monitor operations and recover to afterwards to prepare for the next mission.

And so we made a firm decision to ignore the problem and disregard the order, and lo and behold, nothing happened and the problem went away.

On shore there was great activity, much shifting of kit, trench digging and confusion. The Argies managed to put a bomb into the BMA (the Brigade Maintenance Area) killing four, and injuring others. Another bomb went into the meat-packing factory being used as the MDS (the Main Dressing Station or hospital), which thankfully failed to go off. The surgeons continued operating and the bomb-disposal man, to aid morale, set up his sleeping-bag next to it, to convince those who doubted him when he declared it safe.

Once we had been warned for Operation Brewers Arms (so named after Andy N.'s favourite pub in Poole) the mucking about stopped. We were even able to go ashore for a rather congenial range shooting day zero'ing our weapons.

We left Intrepid in an LCM, on a beautiful, sunny day – although it was very cold. As we motored through the calm waters of San Carlos, the coxswain received an air-raid warning over his radio. We cocked our weapons and angled them 45 degrees upwards against the side of the landing-craft and watched the horizon. The Argie jets screamed in over the hillsides, skimming the water and desperately dodging the missiles and gunfire from the ships. All the helicopters, busy ferrying supplies ashore, had gone to ground in valleys and re-entrants around the anchorage and sat tucked into the folds in the ground as far as they could go with engine and rotors 'burning and turning'. Our coxswain, who by this stage had spent several days going from ship to shore during air raids, grinned at us and steered even closer to the shore than before. This time we did not manage to 'bag' anything.

We landed at the rickety-looking jetty at San Carlos Settlement, which was a hive of activity. Lines of muffled troops with rifles and submachine-guns slung over their shoulders, were carrying rolls of barbed wire up the very muddy farm tracks that ran between the weatherboard farmhouses. Others carried filled sandbags to the trench positions that were being constructed everywhere. Near the water's edge a series of elaborate entrenchments with sandbagged roofs and galvanised-iron sides had been constructed and bristled with GPMGs.

## OPERATION BREWERS ARMS

We waded through the thick mud past tractor sheds and the low palisade fences of the corrugated-iron-roofed houses. Tractors with trailers piled high with barbed wire, metal picket stakes and cheerful muddy soldiers hanging on to the sides, moved busily to and fro in the mud. Behind the settlement the hillsides were dotted with soldiers, stripped to their vests and shirts, digging into the peat. There were many friendly faces, begrimed and sweaty. They had spent their first day ashore being moved from one defensive position to another, having to dig in afresh each time. Their bergens, left on the ships during the initial landings, had failed to reach them and they had spent several very cold nights out without sleeping-bags or shelter. It was not surprising that everyone was keen to get on with the war.

I spoke to some of the Falkland Islanders, shy people with a rather outmoded look to them that reminded me of the Mennonites of Belize, (an ethnic group of farmers who seek remote parts of the world to raise crops and live unmolested). They had been delighted but not surprised to see us, and were quite sure that in a very short time they would be able to shop once again in Stanley. One chap said he hardly ever went there, but that he would make a point to visit this next time.

After announcing our presence to the HQ of 3 Para, who were ensconced with their radio-sets in an unused outhouse of one of the farms, we were shown a small valley near the water's edge where we could fire our weapons.

It is essential to 'zero' a weapon, by adjusting the sights so that what you see through the aperture when you pull the trigger is what you hit. It had not been possible to do this accurately on the ship, and even a small knock can upset the fine adjustment. The high-velocity armalites that most of us carried are not really so critical, but the snipers, with their heavy, wooden-stocked rifles and telescopic sights, needed to spend some time on this task. The process of firing and then adjusting (with a fine screwdriver) was repeated until perfect, and then each sniper carefully put his weapon back into its wooden case and we left our makeshift range.

On the way back down to the jetty I bumped into a familiar figure who regaled me with the story of how he had gone out with shovel and rifle to attend a call of nature, but while so doing had heard some strange noises, and finished up by capturing a stray Argentinean officer. He confessed that this had not been achieved without a little initial embarrassment.

It was a day out for us, beautiful, sunny weather and a couple of carefree hours on the range. On returning to *Intrepid* in the LCM, getting wet as the wind had got up and waves were breaking over the bow and drenching us, I went up from the fume-laden darkness of the dock to the AOR to find out what was going on.

Up in the nerve-centre of the ship, just below the bridge, the gaunt steel bulkheads are slightly softened by the polished oak handrails and brass fittings. The narrow passage to the AOR (normally 'bumpered up' to shine like glass) was littered with hooded sailors, drinking tea and reading books and newspapers, lying on the floor at their action station. With an apologetic grin I stepped over them and entered the AOR.

Inside, the large map display on the wall was marked with chinagraph arrows showing the attack on Darwin and Goose Green by 2 Para. The radios were blasting out crackles and sometimes unintelligible transmissions and everyone was riveted to them. The Paras were tied down by Argie artillery and mortars and, on the green, open moorland, were unable to move without being fired upon by enemy machine-guns.

This was turning into a potential disaster. The fleet were at anchor in San Carlos and *Canberra* was daily escaping being sunk by what seemed like a string of miracles. The attack on Darwin was the first test of our enemy, one that we had to win in order to 'encourage' the rest when the time was ripe. A failure by the Paras, our 'mailed fist', would be catastrophic. The day wore on. Reports came in that the Paras' CO, Colonel 'H' Jones, had been killed. The Staff carried on with their work, the atmosphere was tired and sombre.

It gradually became clear that something extraordinary was taking place to the south of our anchorage. Before last light Captain Kevin Arnold, the calm reflective boss of FO5, brought in an air strike of three Harriers on to the eastern end of the Goose Green Peninsula, a deliberate demonstration of fire-power directed at anti-aircraft cannon and gun positions. FO5 spent an uneasy night amid the smouldering gorse grass.

Early the next day (29 May) reports were received that the enemy were asking for a formal surrender, with an officer of equivalent rank to their commander to be produced by us at a formal parade. Jokingly we said that a lance-bombardier should do – who probably outranked the Argentinean colonel. This insistence on a formal parade seemed bizarre and ludicrous.

Personally I know that had the Paras taken a hammering with heavy casualties, or even needed to be reinforced to take their objectives, our morale would have suffered a very a severe blow. The enemy's morale would have received a reciprocal boost.

The Para's attack had bogged down, it's vital sense of momentum blunted into a stalemate, which H' Jones' sacrifice had succeeded in breaking. This very near disaster was the result of the numerical inferiority of the Paras, and an inadequate allocation of the fire support upon which such a fast-moving, lightly equipped attack would depend. The gun ship HMS *Arrow* could not remain on station beyond daybreak, because of the risk of air attack, so at daybreak on 28 May, the attack was left with just mortars, whose explosive force was mostly absorbed by the soft peat, and just three 105mm Light Guns, a single troop from 8(Alma) Commando Light Battery, my old unit. With insufficient helicopters available to fly more guns and ammunition south to support the attack, the Paras were on their own.

'H' Jones would have known full well how important it was that his attack succeed – that would be why, in the traditions of the Parachute Regiment, he was up front in the battle, where he could have the most influence and give the most encouragement to his 'Toms'. His decision to take out the machine-gun nest would have been taken in this context and with a very clear idea of the risks involved. He would also have been sure that his battalion would carry on regardless. His self-sacrifice was an action of the moment, taken deliberately and for the common good. He was a very brave man.

The packing for our Operation Brewers Arms involved a lot of kit: ten days' ammo and food in our bergens, plus a further seven days' worth carried in sandbags, to be buried in a cache once we got ashore. This cache also contained a very large ammunition resupply, as we were expecting quite a lot of 'business,' and had to be completely self-contained.

Our task was quite simple: the clearing of a large amount of real estate of enemy, without tying down units from 3 Commando Brigade. Our patrols had been in the area before the landings and regular enemy activity had already been noted.

We were to land in troop strength (about twenty of us, consisting of three teams with FO1 and a small HQ), then establish ourselves in the Volunteer Lagoon area, dig into underground hides, bury and 'cam' out the cache and send out patrols to locate the enemy. Once the enemy positions were located, we were to attack and eliminate them, supported by my NGS (Naval Gunfire Support) – to compensate for our lack of numbers. These attacks would have to be done at night as the gunships couldn't leave the safety of the air-defence screen around the *Hermes-Invincible* group until after dark. The Chatelaine (the thermal imager) was also to be taken along.

Our insertion was the most exciting part of Operation Brewers Arms. It had been arranged for us to be taken out to the *Hermes* group by *Plymouth*, to fly across to *Avenger* who would take us near enough to fly us into the LS (Landing Site). Previous patrolling had shown the surf in the area to be too rough and unpredictable for us to use our boats, so the ship's Lynx helicopter was going to have to make several trips.

Once we had struggled from *Intrepid* to *Plymouth* by landing-craft, been steamed out to the fleet (lying 100 miles or so north of East Falkland) and cross-decked on to *Avenger* we realised that we were being given too much to do in one night. My time appreciation gave us only 30 minutes to dig in the cache and hide ourselves away before first light – which was far from acceptable.

I had met the captain of *Avenger* Captain Hugo White the previous Christmas whilst in Belize doing some naval firing. I had spent several weeks with the ship and had very much enjoyed their company. It was very good to see them again. Hugo White is the nearest thing to a heroic pirate captain that they have in the Royal Navy, completely relaxed and friendly, never put out and always amused and amusing. And always the complete professional.

When the difficulty of our situation was put to him, Captain Hugo agreed that we should not go in that night but should wait 24 hours. It was a very great help to have his backing in going against our orders, and, although it was not required, he offered to countermand our instructions himself.

Our many movements from ship to ship, with no notice and very often without knowing where our ultimate destination might be, were confusing to us, and certainly impossible for anyone else to follow. There were many other lost souls like ourselves being shuttled around the fleet, leaving a trail of belongings behind them. The men of the ship's companies, who crewed the ships and had sailed them down to the South Atlantic, did not move about the fleet, but on any one day might well be on another ship collecting documents or stores and doing business. Thus when a ship was bombed or sunk it was extraordinarily hard to get an accurate list of the casualties and decide who was missing and killed.

Every 24 hours each ship was obliged to send a 'Souls on board' signal to *Fearless* saying exactly who was on the ship at a particular time. Of course if you left the ship five minutes after the signal was sent you might end up on the casualty list if that ship was sunk in the next 24-hour period. You might even end up on more than one 'Souls on Board' signal.

The long pauses that occurred after such disasters as Bluff Cove, before the names of casualties were released by the MoD, were caused by the desperate tracing of everyone who had, like us, been moving around the Fleet, to ensure that only those who were actually killed, injured or lost were named in the list. It is amazing really, under the circumstances that errors did not occur, that people got lost or were reported lost when they were safe and sound elsewhere.

In spite of very bad weather and *Avenger* rolling heavily and quite sickeningly I managed to write this letter home and posted it on the ship before we were flown ashore:

Nothing particular to report – I've been on several different ships and life continues in its now normal way. I'm on *Avenger* at present, which was the ship I went to Belize and New Orleans in last Christmas. There are many friendly faces on board, including the captain who is a particularly cool and capable customer. He greeted me on his bridge as one of his more unusual lieutenant-commanders (remembering the masquerading in naval uniforms that I had done at several of his ship's cocktail parties – having only combat kit of my own to wear!).

We have just heard the announcements about the surrender of Goose Green on the World Service – after a fairly canny pause by the MoD. I am really hoping that this will be the start of a 'house of cards' collapse by the Argentineans. I say this because the prisoners we have taken are all convinced that we were about to murder them and so they had been fighting for their lives. This misinformation system drums it into them that although we are signatories to the Geneva Convention we don't abide by it and don't take prisoners. Hopefully the public surrender ceremony, etc at Goose Green, will remove this barrier to surrenders and make our job a lot easier.

I have the feeling that this will be the last letter I will write before this entire nausea is over – I am optimistic, but with the time it takes the get mail back to the UK and also because I will be out of contact for a while, I am hoping that my next letter will be in a relaxed post-crisis mood and that even by the time you receive this – in several weeks' time probably – it will have come to a conclusion. Now that these idiots have decided that their pseudo-Prussian military code does allow them to surrender they might start being sensible. Wars certainly are different but really they are something one can do without! Not even the astonishingly helpful mask that quartermasters wear in war-time justifies all the nausea! I suppose as soon as the dust settles they will all revert back to normal and ask pointed questions about where exactly did you lose this, or that, and no, you cannot walk in here and help yourself even though you did so yesterday.

I had an excellent fillet steak on HMS *Plymouth* last night! [This refers to events that were in fact four nights previous. I deliberately wrote vague letters.] Apparently, their supply officer was telling me, they acquired half a ton of the stuff and are having steak sandwiches as snacks and getting a little fed up of it! He was also telling me that they carried some [SAS] troops to South Georgia and said jokingly that they wanted a reindeer. The next day a helicopter arrived and dumped one, suitable gutted on the flight deck. They hung it and ate it. The head and skin were a nuisance though on the upper deck. At night in the dark a cold, wet, gory nose is most unpleasant! Hope all goes well and that the nice summery things are going well. I hope you don't run out of summer before I get back.

May 30 was a very bad day, and sharing it with the crew of HMS *Avenger* was just about the only good thing about it.

It was rough weather and the narrow Type 21 frigates move very sharply up, down, and side to side. I was seasick and spent most the time horizontal on a spare bunk.

Throughout the day there were the usual air-raid warnings 'Red' and as we had left our lifejackets, anti-flash gear and once-only suits on *Intrepid* because of the operation, we felt very vulnerable. We were out in the Total Exclusion Zone with the *Hermes-Invincible* group and would leave them after dark to make our way to East Falkland and down to our fly-off point.

In the afternoon, after several air raids, we went to 'Red' yet again. This time the navigator Peter Hatch (whom Captain Hugo laconically referred to as 'Pilot') said calmly over the tannoy that they'd picked up the signature of a Super Etendard doing a single sweep on his radar. This needed no further explanation, as by now we recognised the textbook indication that an Exocet is about to be launched; the single sweep being to acquire a target without giving away the position and intention of the aircraft.

The next pipe announced that the radars had detected an Exocet launch on a bearing heading for us. By this stage Andy N. and I were on the wardroom carpet along with the emergency medical team who had their action station there.

Immediately the ship swung violently into a series' of dodging manoeuvres, and the guns pumped off round after round of silver foil 'chaff' to confuse the radar on the incoming missile. This is a carefully practised drill designed to 'convince' the Exocet that the image of the chaff is the ship, and to attack that instead.

The Super Entendard had launched the Exocet at 28 miles range and then turned for home. There were, however, what seemed to be two A4 Skyhawks in front of the missile 'riding' it in. This added to the confusion.

At Mach 1.2 it doesn't take long to travel 28 miles and so the next pipe was the horrifying:

'Impact imminent 12 seconds. Brace, brace, brace.'

We examined the weave of the wardroom carpet in some detail and tried unsuccessfully not to think of the *Sheffield*.

Exocet is programmed to hit the image on its radar screen amidships, nine feet below the top of her silhouette – and the missile launched at *Sheffield* hit her in exactly that place. How far was the wardroom from the ops room, which was in fact the target point? Not far enough.

I have never been as frightened as at that moment. The rest of my team had gone up to the flight deck with their machine-guns, because they wanted to do something - anything at all, rather than go down doing nothing. The imminent threat to life, and ones inability to do anything at all about it, made these moments so terrifying. Other dangerous moments, probably more dangerous than this, were not at all frightening at the time because we were in our own element on land, and could do something about it. But in a warship, even one as rigorously capable as *Avenger*, you are totally dependent upon others. My most fearful moments have all been in aircraft as a passenger or as a passive participant in air raids.

From the wardroom carpet we counted off the seconds, hearing the roar of the Sea Dart missiles bursting out into the spray, the high-pitched chatter of our machine-guns, the deeper, slower rhythm of the Oerlikon AA guns and the pounding shudder of the big 4.5 inch gun.

Then came Hugo White's pipe:

'This is the captain speaking. We seem to have splashed the Exocet with our gun. There is a nasty oily mess off our starboard beam, which seems to be the remains of a Skyhawk that flew over us and was splashed as well. You may be interested to know that the Exocet was only 9kms out when we hit it. I don't need to tell you that at Mach 1 that is not very many seconds. I told you when we left Guzz that I was lucky, well here's proof of it. Well done to you all for a very cool and professional effort.'

'Boat crews assemble at the starboard waist. We are going to investigate the wreckage.'

After such episodes everyone breathes out heavily and starts talking absolute rubbish in an animated way. I lit a cigar. Andy and I shook our heads at each other.

Another pipe:

'D'yer hear there. This is the navigator. We have just recovered our boat and crew, along with several bits of what is confirmed as wreckage of an A4 Skyhawk. A document box has been brought back and will be stored in the seamen's mess-deck. A leg complete with flying suit boot and a book in the pocket was also recovered. That is all.'

Before we set off on Operation Brewers Arms, Jonathan Thomson (the OC of the SBS) had confided to us that when we returned it would probably all be over. (We were always kept away from any planning about other ops that were not relevant to ours, especially future intentions, so that if we were captured we would not actually know too much.) This little hinted detail was a great help to us in the days ahead.

We also knew that the Paras had now taken Darwin and Goose Green, that Teal Inlet was secured and that 45 Commando had marched to Douglas cross-country and although suffering quite a few injuries en route ready to move on again.

Air attacks were still judged likely, though at ships and large formations – not us. Special Forces were deployed well forward to clear enemy OP's (Observation Points) and the flank areas. We were part of this effort.

The last intelligence report that we received indicated a platoon (of around 40 men) in troop strength on Mount Brisbane and in the Eagle Mount area. There was a radar on Dutchman's Island to the north, and a good deal of helicopter activity in our area. Generally the enemy seemed to be withdrawing to Port Stanley, and their defensive positions seemed to be shallow lines of trenches that should be easier to infiltrate, rather than being spread over larger pieces of ground, with any depth. There was a counter-attack threat, especially as there were still several large helos available for an enemy rapid-reaction force to use. C130 Hercules transport aircraft from Argentina were thought to be flying in supplies at night, using the Stanley landing strip.

On the night of 30 May, *Avenger* left the Hermes group and steamed south on her own to put us ashore. We had on board the Lynx and crew from HMS *Ambuscade* (another Type 21), as *Avenger's* helo had gone unserviceable. They unfortunately had no PNG (Passive Night Goggles) – for flying in pitch darkness so strictly speaking we would have to turn on lights to land. As it was an enemy-occupied area I was not too happy about this.

As we steamed down the coast of East Falkland, I decided to bombard the suspected enemy on Macbride Head and the radar on Dutchman's Island. This had been done by gunships on the previous nights, and if *Avenger* continued down the coast shelling sporadically, she could also fire on Mount Brisbane without exciting any particular suspicion. This fire on Mount Brisbane would be very carefully timed to come down as the helo got close to the landing-site and so to mask its delivery runs.

It was most interesting to be in the ops room during operational firing, without any of the safety restrictions of peacetime. Without having one of us on the ground adjusting the fire onto the target, a ships radar could instead be used to confirm the line along which the shells were going and roughly where they were landing. This was most

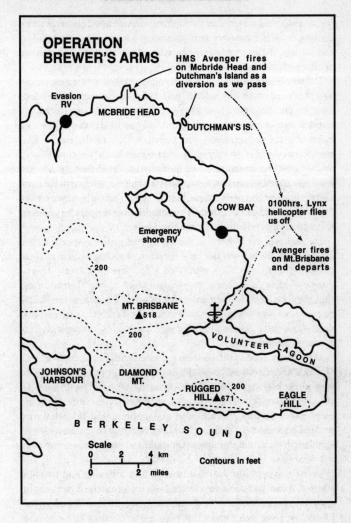

**OPERATION BREWER'S ARMS**

HMS Avenger fires on Mcbride Head and Dutchman's Island as a diversion as we pass

Evasion RV

MCBRIDE HEAD

DUTCHMAN'S IS.

COW BAY

0100hrs. Lynx helicopter flies us off

Emergency shore RV

Avenger fires on Mt.Brisbane and departs

200

MT. BRISBANE ▲518

200

VOLUNTEER LAGOON

JOHNSON'S HARBOUR

DIAMOND MT.

RUGGED HILL ▲671

200

EAGLE HILL

B E R K E L E Y   S O U N D

Scale

0   2   4 km

0   2 miles

Contours in feet

inaccurate, and like the philosophical debate about whether the cannon fired in the desert actually makes a bang if there is nobody there to hear it, there was no way of telling if you were hitting anything at all – but I'm bound to say that really.

The whole ship shuddered as each round crashed off into the night. The darkened room was hushed, with only the gunnery orders being audible. The green glow from the radar screens illuminated the white-hooded figures crouched over them. Andy and I stood, our rifles in hand and faces completely blackened, watching the scene. The computer-operator on a Type 21 frigate punches in the coordinates and the type of ammunition, then the gun trains on to the target, holds itself on target by constant adjustment despite the heaving of the ship and the imprecision of its course, then fires itself off. When the man on ground has sent back a correction over the radio, the operator punches it in and the gun reloads itself and fires again.

The real skill lies in keeping the highly mobile firing system at sea locked accurately onto the land which is standing still, a serious problem that field artillery simply does not have to address. This is done by keeping a radar fix on a known point of land then ensuring that the fix on this known point doesn't slip. The navigator has to calculate his position very carefully, monitor it and calculate his tidal drift – as a check on the computer which should be taking it all into account automatically.

At 0100 on 31 May the LS securing team, with Jim Y. and me, and our TI scanner, took off from the heaving flight-deck of *Avenger*. It was pitch black, the moon obscured by cloud. The Lynx was completely stripped of everything except for two crew seats. We hung on grimly in the back, to each other and to the mound of kit that was wedged between us. The doors had been removed so we sat with our legs dangling alarmingly out into the darkness, numb fingers grasping our weapons.

We flew in very low and fast in spite of not having night-vision goggles. As we came in over the land the moon emerged from cloud and, very cautiously, the pilot was able to land without using his lights. I heaved a great sigh of relief, as our LS was overlooked by Mount

Brisbane, the prime enemy location, and any lights would have been easily visible from there.

The helo landed, we jumped down, and Jim and I ran away into the darkness with the TI scanner to check that the area was clear of enemy. Wally P. and the protection team took up fire positions near the aircraft and unloaded all the kit. The shells from *Avenger* were pounding down rhythmically on Mount Brisbane every time the helo appeared and were accurate enough for our purposes. This was being timed in the ops room, by the ship firing every time the helo crossed a line on the radar that had been determined earlier by me, and stopping when the helo recrossed on its return trip.

It took six Lynx lifts to get us in with all our kit, and the cache came in as a separate under slung load in a large net. Jim and I moved forwards to Mount Brisbane to get a better look, but I could not really scan well enough to be certain of anything. I did not break the radio silence to the ship as the shells were accurate and also because we were close enough for the enemy 155-mm guns to fire at us from Stanley. We knew that they had radio direction-finding equipment and I was very keen not to advertise my presence by sending HF transmissions unless they were absolutely essential.

Some people did not properly understand this, and when the need to minimise transmissions was accompanied by meteorological difficulties that made it impossible to get through, there were further misunderstandings and gunships risking themselves steaming to gun lines for nothing. I was surprised, and at times angry, at the lack of understanding back in the headquarters responsible for co-ordinating this effort. Sometimes it seemed that the consequences of being extremely isolated and vulnerable, 20 miles behind enemy lines were just not appreciated.

The night was very clear and very cold. FO1 formed part of the perimeter security, whilst the cache was being dug in and cammed out. We lay in the mossy grass with the ice crunching under our knees and elbows, occasionally having fits of teeth-chattering and uncontrollable shivering. From the moment that we had clambered aboard the helo back on *Avenger,* every weapon had been cocked ready to fire and the safety-catch applied. Then one of the blokes accidentally fired a shot, with a shocking and frightening suddenness. I ascertained that no one had been hurt, and we waited. If there was an enemy patrol nearby, they would most certainly investigate. Also the main body of our patrol, digging in the cache, would now be at maximum alert in their fire positions, ready to deal with any movement – and we were out in front of them. If I attempted to go back and tell them what had happened, I'd probably be shot. Eventually Andy arrived, having realised what must have happened, and the work on the cache continued.

These 'negligent discharges' (as they are described in military law manuals) normally lead to the culprit being charged with an offence, then punished hard. As were going to be out for at least a week and the guilty man was not only aware of the possible implications of his error but was disgusted with himself, I told him to forget about it. Under these worrying circumstances an extra, small worry can be one too many, and tip you over the brink. He still owes me a drink...

We spent what remained of the hours of darkness digging into the side of a peat bank, then spreading our ponchos and cam nets across the hole. With our peat walls built up and covered with turf, we disappeared into the moorscape.

The next day was bitterly cold, spent shivering and shaking in the peat bank, not being able to emerge from our cold, wet holes until after dark. Under these circumstances time passes very slowly and having to get out of your sleeping bag to crouch in the mud every few hours as a sentry is a bore. At last light, after stand-to we packed up and moved towards Mount Brisbane. The team that was to OP the enemy position moved off up the mountain, where they would, with infinite care, dig in so they could observe the Mount all the next day, before returning to us to say that it was either clear of enemy, or with enough information for us to be able to attack the next night.

It was even colder the next night, and here the ground was completely frozen. Steve Hoyland and I tried to dig a two-man hole but it caved in, so we had to start again. It is a completely hopeless feeling when little things go wrong – this failure felt pretty cataclysmic at the time. It was another very cold day in the peat bog.

That night we received a coded signal from our co-ordination cell on *Fearless* and decided to postpone further operations until we had decoded it. It turned out to be fresh info about the enemy in our area, and a warning not to touch any Argie kit we might find, as it may be booby-trapped. (Someone had presumably been blown up and this was a general warning.) The OP team moved off to a fresh position on the Mount.

The second of June was another very cold day with constant rain, which turned the peat bog into a riverbank. I felt like on of the characters from *The Wind in the Willows*. By this stage it was becoming very boring as well as cold. We decided to send all three teams out to recce all the remaining enemy locations simultaneously as we reckoned the Argies had probably been flown back into Port Stanley and our area was clear. Everyone was champing at the bit, and as we were now happy that Mount Brisbane was clear, we had eliminated the key piece of ground from our operation. We moved the patrol HQ to a position overlooking the LS for our eventual extraction and dug deep into the peat. We made a big four-man hole and pitched a two-man mountain tent inside, covering it over with turf so you could stand by it and not know what was there. This, with four of us inside, was warm and dry and we were able to spend the long day chatting and making brews.

Inside this snug hollow we manned the patrol radio in case the three sections reported up with anything. The weather outside alternated between heavy driving rain and sleet, or heavy mist. The cold was constant and all pervading. At night or during periods of heavy mist we crawled out of our holes to attend the calls of nature and squat close to each other and have whispered conversations.

In our four-man shelter we told stories about how we had spent the past Christmas, exactly where we were going to get drunk when we got home, what our most embarrassing experiences had been, and so on. I got to know every bar and pub in Middlesbrough from Steve Hoyland, so that I felt I could go there and recognise them without being told. The thoughts of home were the practised reminiscences of people well used to being away from home and family. These conversations were pure escapism with each person having their own say and being asked questions by the others (who had heard all the stories several times before) in order to prolong the illusion. The dripping walls of the tent and the sound of the distant artillery fire were at times completely forgotten.

At night we listened avidly to the World Service. The Argies or somebody seemed to be jamming out the news, except at ten o'clock at night. This strange period in our lives coincided with the Task Force's news blackout, which was imposed while the supplies were being flown from San Carlos into the mountains in preparation for the final assault on Stanley.

Night after night we waited for news of the big push going in, but heard only that the positions on Mount Kent were being consolidated, and that messages were being dropped by canister on the Argie troops urging them in Spanish to surrender. We would debate every night (as we had done continually throughout the campaign) as to when they would finally see sense and give up.

(I spoke to Rod Bell, the Spanish speaker, afterwards as we sailed home, and he said that the leaflets that had been dropped by the Harriers were in 'BBC' Spanish which none of the Argie soldiers would probably understand – and those that did would find the phraseology amusing rather than awe-inspiring and morale-sapping.)

We could hear continual shelling, day and night, and it seemed as if the enemies' big 155mm field guns were pretty active. There was also a lot of aircraft activity, with the sounds of jets and anti-aircraft fire coming from Stanley (which we knew was caused by Harriers) and helicopters flying by day and night in our area (which we knew were enemy). On several occasions the enemy 155s pumped a few shells in our direction, presumably homing in our radio using their DF (Direction Finding) kit. None of these were near enough to cause us much concern.

We had lost radio contact with everyone. We knew that our patrols could talk to us but were remaining silent – that was OK because they would not transmit unless they had something to report. We could not communicate back to *Fearless* even using CW (Carrier Wave, using morse), because the local conditions were bad and the operator on board could only get bits of our messages. We spent night after night wandering around trying from different positions.

With HF radio it is purely luck when you happen upon a place where you can get through. Twenty paces in another direction might be the difference between loud mush and clear bell-like conditions. We were on one net working back to *Fearless*. The land-based radio nets, which were much closer to us than *Fearless*, were using the same radio sets as us and we knew where (roughly) they were so could orientate the radio antennae. They were much clearer and we finally succeeded in getting through. Unfortunately we did not have the correct codes for their set-up but they did send our coded messages on to the ship. By this convoluted method we were able to hand on the information that we thought our area was probably clear to enemy and that, when we were certain, we would report.

The patrols were finding absolutely nothing, so we called them back in, assuming that the Argie helos we had heard must have been withdrawing their troops into 'fortress Stanley'. The patrols came tramping in the next night, and having run out of food ransacked the cache. Our message, that we had completed our evolution and the area was clear, was coded up and sent along with a request to be extracted.

Such was the pressure on helicopters (being used to lift stores, mostly artillery ammunition), we had to wait for three days before they came to get us. We had eaten all the food and were having visions of hot showers and food on plates while we sucked our last Rollos and nibbled biscuits AB. When the helos came it was to a grid 1500 metres too far north. When we failed to appear, they went away and it was only through having firm words on the radio with the helo tasking agency, and messages back down the tortuous route back to the ship, that we persuaded them to have another ago at picking us up. Thankfully the same helicopter sortie returned, having refuelled in the interim, or we could easily have spent another three days waiting. As soon as their engines were faintly audible, we abandoned caution and any attempts at concealment, letting off orange smoke-canisters to ensure their attention.

Two Sea Kings arrived, one carrying the OC, SSM (Officer Commanding and Squadron Sergeant Major) and various other members of the squadron. Andy and a few others, less their bergens, were mysteriously taken on board and without explanation the Sea King took off. The rest of us started loading kit and men on to the second aircraft, which lurched upward and shuddered off at shoulder height, hugging the ground.

I clambered on to the third Sea King, which took off and screamed northwards very, very low, following every valley and hillock. We had no idea whether we were going to a ship at sea or in Bomb Alley, or a trench or tent in San Carlos or Teal Inlet. Someone attracted (very carefully) the pilot's attention. He said San Carlos, so we all hoped that meant *Intrepid* and a shower, dhobi and hot food. I was most pleased to see the familiar dock and flat arse-end of the LPD, and the marshaller waving us down.

The flight had taken 30 minutes, over Salvador and Teal. When we had gone out on Operation Brewers Arms these areas were hostile, to be flown over only at night, at very low altitude. Now they were clear of enemy, and the helos flew over by day. So although clearly the war was not yet over as we had hoped it might have been by now, clearly we had progressed.

The same familiar friendly faces were as usual at the Flyco window over-looking the flight-deck. Roy Laney waved, and welcomed us back, but our happiness was short-lived.

The mysterious extra Sea King that had taken Andy and some of the boys off first, had been going to San Carlos Settlement with a coffin on board for a funeral.

'Kiwi' Hunt, one of the SBS' most experienced recce team leaders, had been killed during another operation, and they had picked up his closer friends to take them to the sad ceremony. It was a bitter moment, particularly as we discovered that Kiwi's team had been dropped off in the wrong place by a Navy helicopter, and while trying to locate themselves, they'd been ambushed by an SAS patrol.

That night, in the ravaged gunroom-cum-operating-theatre on *Intrepid*, we tried to have a wake for Kiwi. It didn't really work. We were all too tired to do more than drink a can or two of lager each.

Andy asked for silence:

'I don't know how to say this.....I've never done this before, and I hope I don't ever have to do this again. A toast please...an absent friend, Kiwi Hunt.'

There was complete silence for twenty seconds after this, and someone said to me, 'Well, which ship are you going home on then, boss?' I said, in the silence, '*QE2*. No doubt about it.'

As I said this, and it was a real wrench to try to make a feeble joke, the talking burst out spontaneously around us.

# Chapter 12
# Beagle Ridge

After returning to *Intrepid* at the end of Brewers Arms, Roy Laney had greeted me in the wardroom with the news that I had just missed seeing my younger brother Peter by 24 hours. Lieutenant Peter McManners at that time was troop commander in 9 Parachute Squadron Royal Engineers and had come south on the *QE2*, before transferring to *Canberra* at South Georgia. He had spent the last night before being put ashore at San Carlos on board *Intrepid*. His troop had originally been attached to the Welsh Guards, but had been transferred to the Scots Guards, with whom he remained.

Roy had recognised the family similarity and introduced himself. I had heard of Peter from several people throughout the campaign but we never actually met whilst in the South Atlantic.

Friends who knew that my brother and I were both on Operation Corporate were very good about passing on messages that we were well. It was rather a strange feeling to know that Peter was so close and yet out of contact. There was no reason or likelihood that we would meet in the normal course of events. I knew he would do his job well and could only hope that no dreadful twist of fate would intervene. There was no time for me to worry – but my mother, having her two sons bobbing about in the South Atlantic involved in mysterious military activities, had all the time in the world. It was very hard for both my parents, especially when the landings started and news and information dried up. All relative were told, at that point, not to expect to receive anything from us, as we would no longer be able to write. This very sensible advice brought to those at home the enormity of the transition from preparedness to actual combat.

While we had been ashore on Brewers Arms, the air raids had stopped, the Argie Air Force having seemingly run out of steam. Everyone was much more relaxed on the ships, and *Intrepid* had been busy ferrying 5 Infantry Brigade ashore, who had just arrived from the UK. They had put the Welsh Guards ashore at San Carlos, and then a few days later had picked them up again. My friends in the Wardroom were confused, nonplussed and in some cases angry after sheltering the Welsh Guards, and because I was an Army officer, wanted to tell me about what had happened.

The Navy are well used to having the Royal Marines and other green beret wearing members of Commando Forces on board. They therefore assumed that the Welsh Guards would be the same – if not something similar. However it had rapidly become clear even to the saltiest of sailors that the Welsh Guards were nothing like as well prepared as they needed to be. After confusions and difficulties, *Intrepid* had put the soldiers ashore, only to be recalled back to pick them up again. This entailed quite a bit of work, with the LCMs ferrying the troops back on board, and much disruption of a ship that was difficult to operate under normal circumstances. The sailors were shocked at the condition of the Welsh Guards when they returned after just a night or so ashore, wet, filthy, miserable – and obviously ineffective. Their yardstick was the Royal Marines, who come back on board after arduous exercises in good order, even if they do leave muddy boot prints throughout the nice clean ship.

With six hundred demoralised, dirty troops all trying to shower, wash clothing, eat and rest, the ship was in chaos. Then military equipment and personal belongings went missing. One of my friends complained to the Welsh Guards hierarchy after their military stores were raided, to be told there was little that could be done. A senior officer said ruefully: "Taffy is Welshman, taffy is a thief." Helping yourself to other people's cassette-radio players was clearly stupid, particularly as the Welsh Guards were only to stay on *Intrepid* long enough to get dried out, rested and re-organised. The sensible man carried extra hand grenades rather than a stolen boogie box. Intrepid's crew were very relieved when the Welsh Guards moved out – into the two ill-fated Royal Fleet Auxiliary ships *Sir Tristram* and *Sir Bedivere*, that were so soon to be bombed at Bluff Cove.

The day after our subdued attempt at having a wake for Kiwi Hunt (8 June), hung over in spite of having drunk very little, washed out physically and with all our clothes dhobied, wet and drying out in front of a warm air vent, Bob Harmes arrived with the news that we were going immediately back out into the field that same night, to a position overlooking the final objective, Port Stanley. Nicky and I just looked at each other and sighed wearily.

We were to join D Squadron of 22 SAS, who had a four-man patrol in the area. As they were all residing in the RFA *Sir Lancelot*, we had to change ships at once.

Getting ready to move across the RFA *Sir Lancelot* the day after we got back in after Brewers Arms was not easy. All our clothes were wet, having been washed by us in the heads as soon as we got back on board. I had completely dismantled all my webbing and emptied my bergen to clean out the mud, the soaked rations and spare ammunition (that was going rusty). I was cleaning my armalite and pistol when Bob Harmes came on board, and the bits were spread out all over the cabin.

Bob did not know, and neither of us could guess for how long we were required to go out, nor did he know exactly what we were supposed to be doing. I was told initially that my task was to get on to Beagle Ridge with the aim of hitting the Hercules supply aircraft that the Argies were running in and out of Port Stanley at night, as well as observing and sending back information.

The brigade planning staff, who were developing plans to attack Port Stanley from the western, landward side, wanted to get us into an observation position overlooking Port Stanley as soon as possible. It looked as though once there, it would be up to us to do what we thought best to support this plan – even though we would not know anything about this plan. All this quite understandable uncertainty

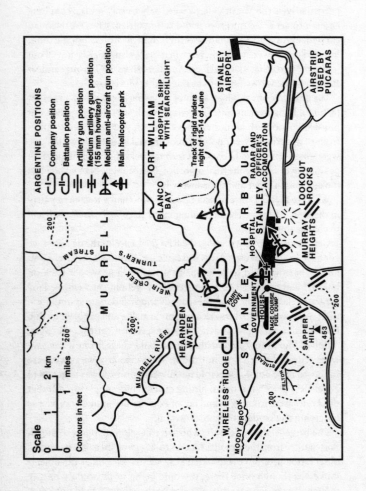

added to the tension of the desperate rush of getting ourselves together and on to *Sir Percivale,* in less than two hours.

As usual, having rushed around the ship like headless chickens to get our wet kit more or less dry, radio batteries recharged, weapons cleaned, codes and maps prepared, rations packed and webbing and bergens packed and balanced... we had to spend the rest of the day waiting for transport across San Carlos Water to the RFA. The well-known military motto 'Rush to Wait' is particularly applicable in war.

As we sat in the cold on *Intrepid*'s flight-deck waiting to move to *Sir Lancelot,* the mail arrived. We all got letters except Des, who hadn't had one for a while and was very fed up about it. We read him bits from ours to cheer him up. Then some one gave him a thick envelope – the long awaited letter from his wife. He said he hoped we wouldn't mind if he read it through on his own – and moved to the other side of the crowded deck.

Eighth June was a very bad day for air raids and the fleet was constantly being stood to, and then stood down. Our trip to *Sir Lancelot* was delayed until late afternoon, and as we finally set off, we were caught out in open water between the two ships in an LCM when two more raids came in. The landing craft could do nothing except heave-to until the strike was over.

After an hour and a half in the cold LCM, we came alongside *Sir Lancelot,* which was rolling in quite a stiff swell. There were only Chinamen who spoke no English on the rail, and so a 'white man' was summoned! The stern ramp was broken and could not be lowered to allow us to unload directly into the hold. We had to climb from the heaving LCM up a rope scramble net on to the upper deck, then pull the heavy bergens up by rope.

I made my way to Lancelot's wardroom to find the SAS squadron commander. It was getting late in the afternoon and the SAS' evening orders, known as 'Prayers', were in progress in a makeshift office, with maps around the walls and ashtrays full of cigar butts. I had missed a lot of it, but they sportingly went through it all again.

*Sir Lancelot* had survived several air attacks, being strafed by cannon, and straddled by bombs. Like all the RFAs, she was a sitting target, and had actually been hit by an Argentine iron bomb. Thankfully the bomb had not actually exploded, but it had done considerable damage, which under less extreme circumstances would have required immediate and extensive repairs. The bomb had been dropped at very low level, and had been lobbed into the port side of Lancelot at the top of her superstructure. It's weight and momentum had penetrated diagonally all the way down through the centre of the ship, then out through the other side just above the waterline.

The bomb hole was large, and the its wide, jagged trajectory had smashed walls, equipment and steel decks. Looking from the top of the ship, you could see all the way through to the choppy grey waters below; and from the ships' usually dark lower decks, you could see the sky. But *Sir Lancelot* had been got back into action with very little delay. Splintered fittings and wall surfaces had been ripped out and shoved to one side in a pile on the upper deck. The main passageway through the ship, the 'Burma Road', and the entire main galley with its fixed tables and plastic chairs, were a couple of inches deep in dirty looking sea water. It was bitterly cold and everyone wore duvet waistcoats and pile jackets, and the lucky ones had Wellington boots.

The hole caused by the passage of the bomb was utilized to provide an extra route through the ship. Ladders and rope handrails had been lashed up through the hole to the next deck, and the worst of the holes covered by planking cat-walks. I dumped my bergan gear in a cabin to one side of the bomb hole, which looked as though it had escaped damage. Its outer wall had a formica surface which was cracked and damaged, and when it got dark I understood why. I returned from a convivial evening in the wardroom, to discover strong, werewolf inducing moonlight shining through a colander of ten pence sized holes made by a strafing Skyhawk's 20-mm cannon. The wind also whistled in – a healthily ventilated cabin.

I made my way up to the stern of the ship and the wardroom, to find several friendly faces grinning at me from behind beards and long hair. By this stage we were all beginning to look like bandits and it just didn't seem sensible to scrape faces with razors. The Chinese barber was far too preoccupied with the war to do haircuts. Some people had come directly from other jobs for which a non-military appearance was an advantage; we looked more like Knebworth survivors than Sandhurst graduates.

An old friend, Captain Roger Dickie, was waiting in the wardroom. We had been in the same platoon at Sandhurst ten years earlier, and our paths had not crossed since. Roger was also a Royal Artillery Officer, an air defence expert, and he commanded and coordinated Sir Lancelot's successful anti-aircraft defences. He had a contingent of shoulder-held Blowpipe missiles, and is job was to shoot down as many enemy aircraft as he could when they attacked the ship. Roger had been on board when the ship had been bombed, losing everything except the clothes he was been wearing. He was given a shipwreck survivors pack, and wore the distinctive white plimsolls and blue shirt provided with a huge grin and a cheerfulness that was undiminished by all this chaos.

In every air raid, Roger stood on deck to organize his missile operators and machine-gunners. He wore a camera slung around his neck, and was determined to take a dramatic photo of a jet screaming in at 20 feet above the waves. This potentially prize-winning picture had now presented itself to him on several occasions, but every time, he had completely forgotten about his camera. He was ruefully wondering if he could ever manage to press the shutter button.

The Chinese crew, caught up in a war that had very little relevance to them, were confused and far from happy. They shuffled morosely around their wrecked ship like oriental Michelin Men, wearing large orange lifejackets, steel helmets, anti-flash gear and all their clothes.

The Royal Fleet Auxiliary officers were not terribly happy either. Both they and the Chinese crew were contracted in, and being well paid for the dubious privilege of being in 'Bomb Alley'. They complained loudly about having to stay so long in such a dangerous place, and questioned why the ground forces were delayed marching on Stanley. They had no idea of the vast amount of equipment and supplies, in particular artillery ammunition, which would have to be flown into position before a final assault could begin. To be fair to them, the Royal Navy did not always understand this either, so the rather bitter conversations that I heard in that wardroom, although disappointing, were also predictable. Furthermore, being on board ship – even one so badly damaged - they could not possibly imagine the atrocious conditions in which the troops were living ashore. If they had, they would have realized that no one was delaying for one second more than necessary.

The RFA officers were especially scathing about the way *Fearless* positioned all the ships during the raids, feeling that they were being put in unduly vulnerable positions. In fact it was quite clear that the RN escorts, the 'goalies', were in the most vulnerable positions of all and as a result had suffered the most. Of course, if you have only a few machineguns and Blowpipe missiles with which to defend yourself you feel terrible exposed wherever you are placed. Had all the equipment on board the RFAs not been needed, they would certainly have departed to the relative safety of the Hermes group at sea. However, all these rather bitter discussions suddenly became shockingly relevant, because that night 8th June, the two RFAs at Bluff Cove were bombed with tragic loss of life.

There had been a lull in air attacks for the previous week, and so 8 June was a major effort of whatever strength the Argentinean Air Force could still muster. At the end of that long day they had lost twelve aircraft, but scored one of their greatest successes.

There had been a steady series of air raids all evening, but we carried on planning and working regardless. There was vague news of an RFA being hit in the south and this was followed by a hint that our operation might be postponed. Food and drink on board *Sir Lancelot*, courtesy of the Chinese cooks and stewards, was excellent – a serious complication. After all our adventures, a relaxing evening was required – as opposed to the potential nightmare of the insertion. Nothing was certain and I was caught on the dilemma of remaining teetotal in case we did go in after a good dinner, or having a few much needed beers and quite a lot of wine. Tough decisions, trivia mixed with tragedy.

Steve Hoyland arrived with some mail that had somehow found its way to us, which I read, then readdressed to myself and posted on to

*Intrepid*. There were music cassettes from home, and some quite old letters sent before the hostilities had commenced. One of these was a much-forwarded, final rates demand in red printing which seemed absolutely ludicrous, and from another very distant world.

As we sat down to dinner, it became clear that the news from Bluff Cove was very bad and that all the helicopters were likely to be used rescuing the injured. I decided that our op had become too difficult, and would certainly be cancelled. The duty free wine beckoned. When it became clear that the Welsh Guards had suffered the most casualties, I could only hope that my brother Peter was all right (I hadn't yet heard that he had been moved to be working with the Scots Guards, and so was not involved in the disaster).

The food was superb; a choice between excellent Chinese dishes and steaks, fish, cheese and pudding, with very good duty-free wine. Needing to build up the calories, we waded through a full five-course dinner with coffee at the end. Under the circumstances this seemed completely bizarre, but we required no persuasion at all to make the most of it. We had clam chowder, escargots, steak, pudding and cheese with wine, plus a couple of beers afterwards. The operation was then formally cancelled, and we had a good night's sleep and the next day were able to have a leisurely and a comprehensive sort-out of our kit.

Looking back now on that night, when the Argentine Air Force struck perhaps its bitterest blow, I'm struck by how little we knew of what was going on at Bluff Cove, and how little it distracted us from what we were doing. We heard snippets of information from time to time – one report of how the Sea King pilots were performing miracles blowing the orange survival dinghies away from the burning ship, and conflicting reports of the numbers of casualties. I was beyond the stage of each fresh disaster making me sad, sickened, angry or worried. The five of us were living in each other's pockets and keeping our minds firmly on what we personally had to do. There was no time to consider anything else. As the news of the tragedy at Bluff Cove filtered through, it was yet another sadness to absorb.

It was not our responsibility and there was nothing we could do. The casualties would be looked after as well as could possibly be managed, and so we made the most of the extra 24 hours breathing space that Bluff Cove had given us. I was very grateful for this extra time. Life on the front line is very much about living now; sadness and the dead are put to one side until it is all over.

Ninth June was a relaxed day on *Sir Lancelot*. I spent some time trying to clarify what I was to be doing once I got on to Beagle Ridge. My prime role had been to shell the C130 transport aircraft that seemed to be landing and taking off at night from the airport. Then this role was changed to that of gathering information and engaging any targets that I could see. This presented me with a dilemma that was never resolved. Did this mean military targets only, outside Port Stanley, or military targets in the town itself? We were not supposed to engage targets near any settlement. Firing near hospitals was totally banned, and as they were protected by the Red Cross, firing near them would also be a serious breach of international law. So how close to hospitals could I fire, and what were the targeting priorities? As I pored over air photos and town plans I realised that the Argies had interspersed their radar sites, troop accommodation and helicopter landing areas, with civilian houses. All their Chinook helicopters were parked outside the town hospital, and as these medium lift aircraft were the means by which they could launch a surprise counter-attack on our vulnerable rear areas, this helicopter landing-site was an exceptionally high priority target.

Beagle Ridge is part of the line of hills to the north of Stanley, about 6kms from the town. The ridge rises fairly sharply from the Murrell River valley and is pitted with steep rock outcrops, which provide protection and cover. It is the coldest, bleakest place imaginable.

We would be just about as isolated as it was possible to be, deep behind enemy lines, far from any help or reinforcement. The enemy were known to be on the surrounding features, with an observation post 1000 metres to the north, and on Mount Round and Mount Low, as well as the twelve thousand or so troops thought to be in Port Stanley, on Wireless Ridge, Mount Longdon and on the Two Sisters. The nearest friendly forces were 19kms to the north west on Mount Kent, and the Paras about 13kms away on Long Island Mount.

# BEAGLE RIDGE

I was worried about getting us into place on Beagle Ridge without being spotted. However, once we managed to insinuate ourselves on to the Ridge, we would certainly be very hard to find. Provided nothing happened to draw attention to us we should be able to remain undetected. The ridge was easily within the range of Argentine medium and field artillery massed in and around Stanley. Intelligence reports indicated that in addition to the enemy positions surrounding Beagle Ridge, helicopter patrols kept the area under regular surveillance.

My evaluation of the operation was very positive. The value of having one of our teams on Beagle Ridge far out weighed the risks involved, and I was in no doubt that once there we could justify our pay and allowances. I was happy with our prospects once we got our feet on the ground, but the night helicopter insertion was rather an unknown factor. After the Sea King crash that killed eighteen members of D Squadron SAS, I was uneasy about helicopters. I knew that I would not feel entirely confident until the Sea King had flown away and we had waited the necessary half hour or so to ensure that a curious enemy were not coming to investigate the engine noise.

At dinner that night we were joined by Lieutenant Martin Eales, a Sea King pilot from *Fearless*, who was to fly us in. Martin was a really first-rate pilot – I had been able to get to know him a little on *Canberra* and *Fearless* on the trip down, and his presence cheered me up greatly. He looked drawn and tired having been flying all the hours the aircraft could stand. He was equipped with passive night goggles (PNG) and so darkness was no problem. These goggles intensify tiny amounts of ambient light (on what appears to be a completely dark night) to give a green image. The pilot has only narrow 'tunnel' vision and has to constantly move his head from side to side, and up and down in order to see to fly. The weight of the goggles (about 3lbs) and his flying helmet (3 or 4lbs) and the consequent eyestrain, produced splitting headaches after half an hour or so. It also meant that he had to fly round the clock, resting in snatches whenever he could.

The overwhelming need for helicopters required pilots to ignore peacetime rules and flying regulations in order to get the many vital tasks done. Each aircraft has very precise tables that stipulate the maximum number of men and weights of equipment that can be carried. These figures had rapidly proved unrealistic in wartime, because of the vast amount of ammunition we needed to carry. On the Fanning Head operation we had carefully loaded exactly the right numbers of men into the aircraft, and it had been able to leave the deck. The risks were not so great when taking off, because when the pilot applied maximum power and lift the aircraft remained on the deck. The dangerous bit was landing, which needs more power than the takeoff. If an aircraft was too heavy to land, it would be unable to stop itself in time to make a sideways hover, and would instead crash into the flight deck. However, as these overloaded flights were usually travelling some distance so as the fuel was used up, the overload would be reduced, so the landing at the other end would be all right. In emergencies, aircraft would have to dump fuel and load in order to land.

Sergeant O. and his four-man SBS team arrived on *Sir Lancelot* that afternoon to accompany us onto the ridge. They had been given the unenviable task of trying to infiltrate south, to the Murrell River, which they would swim, in order to hide on Wireless Ridge - a hair-raising prospect and they were clearly concerned. As with all special operations, the onus is very much on the men on the ground to do what they think is best, and Sergeant O. was going to stay with us for a day or so on the Ridge to assess the possibilities.

Just before dinner I was introduced to a Naval Wessex pilot (I think from *Fearless*). He was quite small, bearded and disarmingly cherubic, and wanted to fire his SS11 rockets at Government House in Stanley with a view to killing General Menendez. SS11 rockets can only be fired from the hover and have to be guided every metre of the way to the target. Whilst this is going on the helicopter cannot move, and so is extremely vulnerable. He wanted to make his approach over Berkeley Sound at first light then hover behind our position – as this would be the safest place for him, guaranteed to be clear of the enemy.

It certainly was the safest place for him, but I did not relish the attention of every single Argentine soldier on Port Stanley being focused on my bit of real estate. We had already experienced the hail of spent rockets, AP (Armour Piercing) bullets and cannon shells that fall in the wake of departing aircraft, and I had no desire to compare Argie anti-air ordnance with our own. I also wondered what would happen if the Wessex got shot down in our area and the enemy sent out a patrol to investigate the wreckage. Anyhow, it was important for us to know about it, if only so as not to shoot him down ourselves.

After dinner on our second and last night on *Sir Lancelot*, we humped all our gear up on to the fight-deck and lined it up beside the fire extinguishers. As the sun went down over Bomb Alley and its sombre green hills, we loaded the bergens into the Sea King and Martin wandered around it doing his checks. We waited until it was completely dark then climbed in and strapped into the net seats. The generators started their gradual whining crescendo, the two engines started, and then with a rhythmic rocking the rotors engaged and turned.

In the cockpit Martin and his co-pilot were checking dials and switches, talking to each other through their helmet microphones. Except for a few crucial dials which were fully dimmed, all the lights were covered over with black masking tape. The flight-deck crew operated in complete darkness, and only when Martin flashed a light from the cockpit to indicate that he was ready to take off did the marshaller light his two neon wands plus a dim horizon-indicator on the flight deck, so that Martin had enough information for a safe take off.

We flew first to *Fearless* because someone had forgotten something, then waited, burning and turning, until they came running back with whatever it was. We heaved up into the darkness for a second time. The indicator lights on *Fearless* and the marshaller's wands went out, leaving us in the blackness of a cloudy, moonless night.

As soon as we got clear of San Carlos Water, Martin dropped down to about fifty feet. I could see him sitting with his back very straight and the PNG covering his face. His head bobbed up and down and side to side continually. He could only look out and not down because even the dim light of the dials would 'burn' into the PNG image and make him blind. The co-pilot handled the navigation and read the dials, and they were continually muttering to each other. I knew from experience that this was not worth listening to; a particular brand of black humour featuring crashing and air disasters in general, so I was quite happy not to listen.

As we hunched in the back of the Sea King, screaming along in total darkness veering from side to side, pulling up suddenly and swooping down to avoid hills and follow valleys, the perspiration caused by the loading of the bergens became a chilled dampness. The cold began to permeate the layers of clothing.

The rear side-door was open and the wind swirled and buffeted. The darkness outside suddenly became a hill with sheep running in all directions away from the sudden presence of the helicopter. The crewman sat on the sill with his foot braced against the jamb and his safety strap flapping violently in the downwash. Occasionally he would murmur into his throat-mike or flash his teeth in response to some joke from the cockpit.

We cut north over Douglas Settlement and flew down Port Salvador. The moon came out briefly and lit up the savage monochrome scene of smooth water and sharply indented coastline. We then cut up north again over Port Louis Settlement and along Berkeley Sound. The crewman held up two fingers to us and we grasped the quick release catches on our safety harnesses. As Martin turned sharply right and came in very low and fast to the east of Mount Round and its enemy position, he tucked into a fold in the ground, slowing down sharply. Ahead from the darkness winked the coded signal from the muted torch of the four-man SAS team that had been in the area for the past week. Martin flared backwards and landed; we got out fast with the gear. After a quick shouted conversation with the reception team, I waved the aircraft away. Martin pulled off, the crewman waved out the back and gave a thumbs up and they flew north towards the black water, very low and very fast.

It was suddenly still and quiet, and as we waited, lying in the wet tussock grass hills, heels touching and weapons pointing in a circle outward, we were on our own again.

We lay quietly for about three-quarters of an hour, getting colder and colder. There was no sound apart from the wind. Scanning with the NOD (Night Observation Device) revealed nothing and so we struggled to our feet with our bergens on our backs. I couldn't lift mine so the only way I could stand was to put the straps on whilst sitting on the ground and then have two people pull an arm each to get me to my feet.

We tottered off in a long 'snake; with a scout at the front and 5 metres between each other. Although dark, there was no cover and very little shadow. Frequent stops were made to scan ahead and to the side. There was one very exposed part across a wide, flat valley immediately behind Beagle Ridge, but the moonlight, such as it was, was from the south and cast a shadow to the north. Once we reached this shadow we felt safer.

The walking is hard at night, with tussocks, bog and holes in which to stumble. With the heavy bergens it was difficult to avoid falling. Our progress was punctuated by breathlessness, silent cursing as we fell and were helped laboriously to our feet again like turned-over turtles. The sweat began to flow inside our clothes and down our brows, necks and chests. When we stopped, the inevitable chill rapidly set in. My bad back was also starting to feel the strain, being very painful and turning these long deliberate progressions into real ordeals.

We moved along Beagle Ridge, on the north side, until we reached the western end of the rock outcrop. There was an obvious summit about 600 metres further along and I did not want to go anywhere near that. If the Argies were able to get a bearing on our radio transmissions, then they would inevitably shell the ridge, going initially for the summit (that is what I, in their place, would do). I wanted to be tucked away in more of a random position.

We dumped the bergens in the shadows and Nick Allin and I went to search for an observation post. We found a suitable flattish bit with a rock outcrop to the rear as well as a deep gorge on the forward slope edge. The rocks to the rear would give protection and I hoped that the angled rock cleft on the top would be deep enough to get at least two of us into a position from which we could work. I crept up to the top of the ridge and the slab of outcrop, and carefully looked over the top. There I was below for the first time the place that we had come all this way to recapture. There below me lay our final objective, Port Stanley.

I was very surprised at what I saw. All the streetlights were switched on, tiny stars of normality burning brightly as if none of this was actually happening. The town's layout was revealed, showing the grid of streets, the blocks of houses and the line of road along the edge of Stanley Harbour. In that bitterly cold night, the air was so clear that the lights seemed to be very close indeed.

To the right of the beaded necklace of the town, the shape of Sapper Hill loomed large with a saddle to the right leading up to Mount William and Tumbledown. The outline of Cortley Hill and Wireless Ridge occupied the foreground and the bends in the Murrell River glinted greasily in the pale moonlight.

In the very far distance I could see the silhouette of Mount Kent (to the far right) where the rest of the brigade were getting ready for the final push. In front of us, on Wireless Ridge, and below us on the northern slopes of our ridge, there were the tiny flickering lights of Argentine fires, around which, no doubt, shivering sentries were warming their hands and trying to dry out chilled feet. The nightscope and Swiftscope revealed countless additional fires all over the hills around us, like tiny glow worms in the darkness.

We had a gunship actually on the gunline waiting to fire should we need it. (This term gunline dates from when ships lined up to bombard a besieged port and then sailed back out to the fleet to get more powder and shot – a fairly similar situation to ours). I decided, however that I could not fire on the very sketchy information I had gleaned from my map and air photos, the intelligence briefs and chatting to the SAS patrol who had met us.

I wanted to be absolutely sure of the ground before I started shelling near the town. The streetlights would be an invaluable aid, but I needed to confirm their location and numbers in daylight before using them as markers at night. The Argies might well be leaving sectors turned off in order to confuse. I also expected that once the shells started coming down they would turn off all the lights – at least I would if I were them.

Even firing well away from the town would involve a risk. The first round of a shoot can go anywhere and is nicknamed 'the navigators round'. Once the fall of shot has been spotted and an appropriate correction made, the naval gunnery system is extremely accurate. But the big danger of firing at night in unfamiliar territory, is of that first critical first round being 'lost' in dead ground.

'Dead ground' is ground that the observer cannot see because of the folds, valleys and hills, so that the shells can drop away and explode without being seen or even heard. The first thing you do when setting up in a new observation position is ensure that you have identified all the dead ground in your sector, and thus be able to predict when rounds are likely to be lost. Having thought this through, you can then work out a strategy for how to avoid losing shells into dead ground, so that you can get the next rounds moved out and on to a bit of real estate that you are certain *can* observe.

So, if the initial salvo, the 'navigators round', is lost it may be in dead ground near the target, but it could be just about anywhere else. If you apply a correction to bring it out from where you think it went, you may be moving it into some quite different area, and it may remain lost – and perhaps fall on something that was not a target. I was not prepared to run this risk so near to Port Stanley, and so I released the gunship once I was happy that we were not going to need it for our own protection.

Nick Allin and I would man the OP during the day and Des, Steve and Tim would provide our rear protection. They set about digging themselves into the turf at the base of the rock outcrop to the north, behind us, and Nick and I set about digging into our rock cleft. We were able to suspend a poncho at an angle over the lower bit of the cleft to keep the rain off, and we put a camouflage net and some turf over the top, to blend in with the surrounding outcrops. The cleft was about 9 feet long and between 2 and 3 feet wide with a 30-degree slope to it (that made us slide down very slowly in our sleeping bags as we slept). We wedged the bergens into the holes in the sides, into which the wind whistled, and carefully arranged our webbing and weapons so that they were close to hand. I put my pistol on the ledge close to our heads.

Nick and I took it in turns to observe, the other sleeping or making brews in the shelter while the observer sat out in the open, behind the rock parapet, with binoculars, Swiftscope and nightscope, several maps, the town plans and some photos of the main buildings. The HF radio, with its aerial bent backwards to as not to stick up over the silhouette of the skyline, sat on a rock ledge with its telephone handset and morse key. Our spare water bottles were kept handy to make brews and fill from a brackish puddle that Des had found further along the ridge. (It was very necessary to filter and sterilize this water as I discovered to my cost later).

It was just possible, in the lower shelter part of the OP, to snuggle both in together – although one person had to sleep on his hip while the other was on his back. There was one strategically misplaced rock in my bit that meant I could not stretch out fully, or lie flat.

We did not cook at all during the night, but I did smoke the odd cigar under the cover of the poncho – fumigating Nick, who did not smoke. Map reading, radio tuning, etc., was done using a carefully shielded and much dimmed torch. (A red lens completely covered by black masking tape with a single very small pinhole to allow only a faint glow of light to show.)

We were just on the forward slope of Beagle Ridge which meant we could not move at all from the OP during the day. Because of the Argentine positions to our rear (on Mt Round and Hill 500 – just 1km away), Steve, Des and Tim could not move either. They took it in turns to keep watch and came over to see us at night. They had to dig what can only be described as shallow graves, with a hole at one end from which they could observe. The sharpest wind came from the north and so they were permanently chilled. They could not, however, be seen, even in daylight, by someone standing a few feet away. Their discomfort was all the worse for the utter boredom of having nothing to do but keep watch during the long, cold days.

As it got light we came carefully out of our shelters to check that our camouflage looked all right and make a few additions and adjustments before the growing light of dawn made it too dangerous. The early morning was the best time for surveillance. The morning sun was soft and the air was clear (as photographers know, the quality of light is best in the morning or evening). The sun, coming up over our left shoulders, but still low in the sky, cast shadows that sharpened the outlines of the landscape.

Just after first light was also a time of activity in the Argentine positions. Figures would emerge from the rocks and gullies, some walking across open ground carrying their mess tins, going for breakfast. Groups of grey-clad figures would stand in circles with hands in their pockets stamping feet and slapping sides to get warm after a night in a cold sleeping bag.

On that first morning, 10 June, a light helicopter took off from the main Argie HLS (Helicopter Landing Site) in Stanley and flew in a methodical manner along the northern shore of the Murrell, up all the creeks and then onto Beagle Ridge using Turner's Stream for cover. The aircraft was two hundred metres too far west to actually fly over the top of us, and went north toward Mount Round. He then clattered along the coast (presumably searching for any signs of landings having been made during the night) then, after a look at Mount Low, returned to Port Stanley.

Nick and I spent the morning matching the information we had with what we could see on the ground. We ended up with six enemy positions that we could identify and locate. They were a medium artillery battery, a troop defensive position, a fuel dump, eleven helicopters in a field beside the hospital and two targets close to ourselves that we would register to use as protection if we were attacked, on the most likely enemy approaches into our position. In extremis, forward observers usually bring down fire on themselves, on the premise that you know it's coming and can maybe survive, whereas it will certainly take the enemy by surprise.

Nick set our target list in code, we sent them down on the HF radio to the SAAC (Supporting Arms Coordination Centre). As we were having an 'appetizing' breakfast of baked beans, bacon burger and biscuits AB washed down with a huge mug of hot, sweet coffee, two

Harriers appeared overhead, circled behind the ridge, and then went, one behind the other, to make a bomb attack on Sapper Hill. The bombs landed some 500 metres east of the gun battery and there was so much flak being fired up into the sky that a re-attack would have been very dodgy. I tried to speak to them on our UHF radio, but even if they did hear us they were fully justified in ignoring a strange unauthenticated voice purporting to be in a place where no one was supposed to be.

They over flew a second time, this time high above the maximum altitude of the enemy's Roland anti-aircraft missile defence system, then flew north back out to *Invincible*.

We coded up another message to add to our target list indicating where their bombs had exploded, because the pilots would certainly have had their hands very full avoiding flak and releasing their bombs – to the extent of not being certain where the bombs had landed. We also asked the SACC for guidance about firing at the helicopters near to the hospital.

I had carefully measured bearings from the targets to points on the ground that I knew I would be able to see at night.

The street lights of Port Stanley were a very great help, and the silhouette of Sapper Hill and the curve of the Murrell River were also points from which locations could be determined. The brief flash from the shell gives a quick burst of topographical information – a silhouette of a hill or ridge if it has landed in dead ground, or a frozen black-and-white image of the target.

The ships did have star-shell that would float down under a parachute and light up a very wide area. The high-explosive shells could then be adjusted onto the target whilst the starshell was still burning. The firing of the different types of ordnance on different bearings and elevations gave the gun end added complications and made things difficult for them, although the computer easily managed. The benefits did not always justify the extra trouble; for example it was no trouble to adjust on to point targets without star-shell, and secondly – and more importantly for us – the use of star shell tells the enemy that an observer is adjusting the targets, whereas shells coming down at night and happening to hit targets, might be fired purely from map data. Star-shell also completely destroyed our highly tuned night vision which would take time to reacquire.

Our first night's shooting was not entirely successful, but we did manage to set fire to fuel on the aviation-fuel dump to the west of the racecourse, as well as upsetting one of the gun batteries along Felton Stream, to the north-west of Sapper Hill. It was a confusing shoot, as the shells did not seem to obey the corrections I gave, and none of the usual remedies or ploys seemed to work. I discovered afterwards that the ship had got her own position slightly wrong, her radar having been surreptitiously moved from the correct point to another datum point, which put the entire system out. As so often in the campaign, human common sense intervened with the technological complexities, and the next night the ship was firing quite excellently.

Nick and I had, by this stage in the campaign, evolved a system for night firing. He would work the radio, establishing communications with the ship by morse and then going to voice as soon as she was close enough to do so. We would start off with a target that I knew would be easy to adjust, with as little dead ground as possible and well away from inhabited areas. I used my binoculars to scan the ground and to measure the bearings and distances. They had graticules marked on the lenses for this purpose.

Nick was constantly checking the tuning of the radio and referring to his code book so his night vision was impaired by his using a torch, albeit with only the faintest red glow. He would also use the nightscope to observe, which was also quite a bright light source, allowing my night vision to remain intact.

The firing took quite some time, as we were extremely careful and methodical. It was bitterly cold sitting out in the cutting wind, not being able to move to keep warm.

Tim crawled over from the rear sentry positions to see what we were up to. He casually mentioned that it was his 21st birthday today (it had just turned midnight).

What can you say? We both wished him many happy returns.

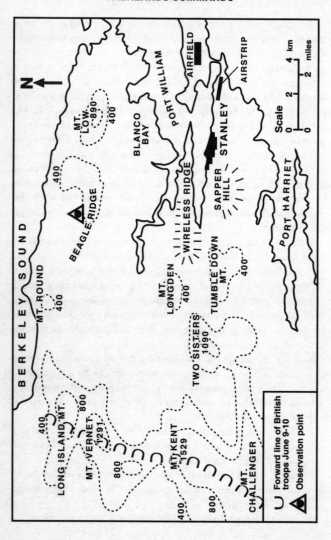

242

240.3   3.3714   5505 2044
579.4522

25 1082 .. 357 724   3 M110
87 - 359741  TPS
90 - 371725  FUEL
91 - 398727  11 Helos
92 - 372812
93 - 396798

AIR STRKE 500m E of guns.
91 HAS HOSPITAL 500m INTERROGATIVE
94  364 760
95  413710 ... want to use DFs, ... 'DF'
(ximnmk)
288.8  96 391745
330.0  LH Beagle ? 604 MISSILES.

RV Blancos Bay 0700
Air Aslt Wpn
415784  Mor
40 75 ASSY (TBD)
415744  landing Area
45 mins OT
896738  Gun
No FIRE E of 41 Easting
OB Gun C HILL  40 to 41E

*The first page of my notes from Major Cedric Delves (OC D Squadron SAS) Orders Group on the afternoon of 13 June, prior to the SAS diversionary raid in support of the main brigade attacks on Wireless Ridge and Tumbledown that night.*

*The first target list as transmitted by FO1 from Beagle Ridge on 10 June. This includes information on the effectiveness of a Harrier bomb attack and a query about opening fire on military targets near the hospital in Stanley.*

The gunline from which our ships fired, was back out to sea behind our OP position. We could hear the ships fire in the distance and then hear the shells as they screamed in over our heads. Once we were on target the ship would pump shells onto the enemy position, one every three or four seconds with a most distinctive, hollow, booming explosion from far out to sea. We ate Rollos, bars of chocolate, and nuts and raisins from our ration packs like squirrels, in order to keep warm.

We spent the next day with binoculars and telescope giving ourselves eyestrain trying to assess the results of the previous night's firing. Our picture of enemy dispositions was growing steadily. It is surprisingly difficult to determine whether the infantry trench position that you are looking at is a platoon with some 30 members, or a actually a company of around 100, or even a battalion position with 300 and more, until you have begun to recognise people's faces and actually count reach one of them. Soldiers dressed in drab dark green clothing look the same.

Gun positions are hard to see and very often it is only possible to locate one or two of the guns and perhaps one of the command posts. I was looking through the telescope at one of the 105-mm guns we had already spotted, under its camouflage net, when smoke came from its barrel. To my amazement, five other smoking guns appeared in the same small area – it was a battery position. Once we had seen the position, the rest were easily picked out.

The lines of Argentine soldiers wandering about at first light, gave us a good indication of their defensive positions and the equipment they were manning. To avoid missing things you had to let your eye 'walk' very carefully and slowly over the ground, pausing to look into the rock clefts around the buildings. At high resolutions, the slight shake on the telescope, and the need to hold your breath when looking added to the fatigue caused by eyestrain. We had to have regular breaks from surveillance.

Having 'stagged' each other in the OP hall all day and added to our target list, we had a very good night's shooting. I had spotted a radar dish antenna behind some prefabricated huts that intelligence reports had listed as Argentine officer's quarters. There had been a lot of soldiers going in and out, which confirmed this. There was also a 155mm howitzer in a gun pit to the east of Sapper Hill.

We had a good go at the radar and the officer's quarters using the streetlights to line up the fall of the shells. We must have hit part of the electricity system at one stage because sectors of the town kept going out then coming back on. We were able to set the ammunition piled around the Howitzer alight, and it burned suddenly and with an extremely bright, fierce flame. We also set some fuel on the racecourse alight.

At dawn the next day we crept out as usual for a quick check of our camouflage, to find one of our Wessex helicopters making its way laboriously along the edge of Berkeley Sound. It came up towards our position and hovered in the lee of the ridge. There was a tongue of mist that spread down from the west of Beagle Ridge to the Murrell River and along the surface of the water, like a grey curtain about 100 feet high. It was another very bright, clear day, with the rising sun gradually shortening the shadows with its golden light. The pilot of the clattering helicopter was presumably the small, bearded naval officer I had met on *Sir Lancelot* and, as he had promised, on this beautiful, bleak morning, was going to try to kill General Menendez - or at least give him something about which to think.

The Wessex came over the top of the ridge and down, following the tongue of mist along the river, getting closer and closer to Port Stanley. Nick and I just held our breath. He hovered virtually over the top of an Argie anti-aircraft gun position we had spotted the day before. I was wondering whether they had a sentry who was awake and, if not, how long it would take them to get out of their sleeping bags and run to the guns.

He fired the first missile with a loud bang and held his hover while the co-pilot guided it on to the target. There was an explosion as it hit the upper storey of Stanely police station, where Menendez was said to be based. He fired the second missile, guided it onto the same target and then dipped sharply to the right and down into the mist to fly flat out northwards.

As he did so, the AA guns burst into life and within seconds, the stunned silence into which the two rocket explosions had echoed, was shattered by every anti-aircraft gun in the town blasting away at imaginary targets for several minutes. Happily this time, none of the residue of this firework display came our way, but we kept our heads down just in case. The engine noise of the Wessex died away to the north-west.

Our SBS colleagues further along the ridge had decided not to attempt to move south and were staying put. The SAS patrol that had met us on the LS had been recalled to *Sir Lancelot,* and a Sea King had picked them up from a site well away from the ridge. We were very much anticipating the start of the final attack on Port Stanley, but the security isolation system of only telling us what we needed to know and no more, meant that the date of the big push was a matter only for conjecture and great interest.

We were next told that the bulk of D Squadron 22 SAS were coming to make a diversionary attack to complement the main effort. Des and Tim trooped off that night to secure and mark out the LS then lead them back to our positions, as Nick and I were busy firing. It was a real relief to know that the end was nigh and that we were to be stiffened up so considerably on our lonely ridge.

We had yet another day getting headaches peering through the binoculars and telescope. The BBC World Service to which we were listening with rapt attention was saying no more than 'Our forces are continuing to consolidate their positions and move forward equipment. The Task Force continued its bombardment of military installations.' The last sentence referring to our efforts.

The results of the night's firing were very good. The 155-mm gun had been hit and knocked over, defying the daylong efforts of the crew to get it turned the right way up again. There were huge holes in the roofs of the officer's quarters, and the large seaward-facing radar dish that I had spotted behind these buildings was not to be seen. (Much later, back in England, I attended an intelligence debriefing in the MoD at Whitehall. A colour slide taken by someone after the fall of Stanley showed this radar dish turned over and broken. On Beagle Ridge, I had suspected the dish was something to do with the land-based Exocets that we knew to be in Port Stanley – or was a low-level radar to give early warning of incoming aircraft. My suppositions turned out to be broadly correct.)

D Squadron arrived that night by helicopter, carrying a mountain of equipment. The bulk of it was long, wooden crates holding Milan anti-tank missiles. They also brought the sad news that Captain John Hamilton had been killed when his four-man patrol had been discovered in an OP near Port Howard. I had met John a year or so earlier when we were both doing a course at Hereford, and he had just joined the SAS. He had a great love of mountains and an almost mystical interest in exploring the outer limits of his own endurance. He had lived for some time next door to me on *Intrepid,* and his quiet sense of humour and gentle manner were welcome in those anxious early days.

The manner of his death, surrounded by enemy, gravely wounded and giving covering fire to allow the other 'brick' (one pair in his four-man patrol) to get away and then his own 'oppo' to escape, was entirely in the character of the man. We had all brooded long and hard about what we might do if one of our patrols went wrong. John did what I hoped I might have the courage to do if the nightmare of compromise and ambush had happened to us. I very much liked him.

D Squadron also brought some extremely disturbing news, delivered to us in true SAS style. A voice from the darkness: "Hello lads, is Captain McManners around?" "Hi Boss, how's the Butcher of Beagle Ridge then?" We didn't laugh, and once the newcomers realised we hadn't a clue what they were talking about, their mickey taking stopped. Just as well, as we wouldn't have put up with it for long once we knew what they were talking about.

It seemed that on one of the previous nights, naval shells had killed several civilians in the town. The information was simply that; with the possibility that two of them were women. This very upsetting news was not something that we could joke about in order to reduce its impact, but it was not something that we could afford to let get the better of us, so we simply tried to forget about it. Also it might not actually be true.

In fact it was all too true, and swiftly an Argentine communiqué was issued:

*Communiqué 150.* The Joint Chiefs of the General Staff communicate that yesterday, 11 June 1982, English forces began an indiscriminate bombardment of the town of Puerto Argentino, killing two women, aged 46 and 30, and wounding another two, aged 30 and 35 respectively, and two men of 32 and 35 years. All those concerned are residents of the islands (Kelpers) who were surprised in their homes by the naval bombardment.

In relation to the event described, those Joint Chiefs of the General Staff point out with particular emphasis that, during all the naval bombardments performed by the English forces until now, the civilian population, who in this case were converted into a priority target, have never been attacked.

It must be stated that modern firing systems that the enemy employs, as well as his training and experience, eliminate the possibility that what happened could have been an error.

This attack, executed against innocent civilian townspeople, together with that carried out by English aircraft on the hospital ship *Bahia Paraiso* draw grave attention to the lack of respect for human rights shown by Great Britain, an attitude that leaves no doubt in constituting an affront to the western world.

All the above is in visible contrast to the performances of the Argentinean forces who have acted throughout with maximum restraint and humanity, as is proved by the fact they took the islands without producing casualties among the English forces and the inhabitants, nor damaging their goods and properties.

*Communiqué 153*....English naval units......the following casualties:

Killed:
*Susan Whitley*: Aged 30 – British citizen.
*Doreen Boner*: Aged 46 –Citizen of the Malvinas, born

24/10/35. Passport No. 323490

Wounded:
*Mary Goodwin:* Aged 82 –Citizen of the Malvinas –
very serious.
*Veronica Fowler:* Aged 38 – married – teacher – British
citizen born Scotland 18/10/44
*John Fowler:* Aged 39 – father of two children: Rachel
aged two and another born recently – seriously
wounded.
*Steve Whitley:* Aged 35 – British citizen –
Superintendent of Education – seriously wounded.

The health services in the zone are doing their utmost in their efforts
to save the lives of the four wounded people.

These citizens, British and Malvinenses, killed and wounded by
British weaponry, are the very same that the British government is
claiming to protect and in defence of those whose interest it says it is
waging this struggle for a land that it had usurped and therefore
doesn't belong to it. *

The next day, 13 June, the Ministry of Defence announcement was
made:

"Argentine sources have reported that two civilians were
killed and four injured during the course of recent hostilities
around Port Stanley. We cannot be certain about these reports
but sadly there is some evidence that they are true."

Argentine communiqué number 152 alleged that because of the
accuracy of the naval firing system and the expertise of the operators,
the fatalities and injuries caused that night by NGS were a 'deliberate
attach against innocent townspeople'. Nothing could be further from
the truth.

When we received the sad news several nights later, it was not possible for me on Beagle Ridge to decide exactly on which night the tragedy had happened.

The peculiarities of the first night's shooting (11/12 May) seemed the most likely. The shells had not done what they should do, and when I had told the ship to check their system they had been unable to find anything wrong. I had 'lost' several shells in dead ground which should have landed well away from any houses. But if the tragedy had not occurred on that night, then I was extremely worried, as every other shoot had seemed to go well.

I could not afford to entertain such doubts. Since it was I who controlled all the shelling around Port Stanley, the airfield and the hills to the west and north, it was definitely one of 'my' shells – which was deeply upsetting.

Once hostilities ended, 148 Battery gathered on HMS *Fearless*. One of our liaison officers, who had been on board the gunship on that first night, made a point of telling me what happened. He said that when the firing system had been checked, nothing was amiss and they assumed I was mistaken. I had then told them to 'Check Solution' a second time, and an impasse was reached when still they could find nothing wrong. At this stage I terminated the shoot and ordered them to leave the gunline.

The next day, worried by my insistence, the gunnery crew made a complete check of the computers and firing system. They discovered a small deviation on one of the tracking radars that would produce the error that I had estimated the night before. To be proved correct after the event was a small comfort, but I was very grateful to have been told.

Such a comprehensive check would not have been possible on the night of the firing. On the gunline, a few miles off Port Stanley, the gunship was well within range of the land-based Exocets. (Later that same night, HMS *Glamorgan* had been hit by one of two Exocets launched from Stanley while she was on the gunline). All the ship's company were fully occupied with the gunnery and defence of the ship. They were over a hundred miles from the Task Force and the safety of the integrated defence of the missile-carrying destroyers and the carriers. It was the conscientiousness of the crew, checking in spite of believing themselves to be right, that unearthed the fault, hidden away in the complexity of the computer system.

It was a tragedy, part of the comprehensive tragedy of war.

Up on Beagle Ridge in the biting wind, it just seemed to be yet another sadness to have to absorb. The SAS reinforcements, fresh from *Sir Lancelot*, who had brought the bad news, had no details other than the fact that two or possibly three civilians had been killed. I swore a bit. Then I carried on with the job. It had happened and there was nothing I could do about it. The only response was to do as best we could to get the whole cruel business over with as fast as possible.

Later that evening, one of the D Squadron hierarchy (a rather officious officer or NCO) appeared in the darkness demanding for some reason, to know why we hadn't got a rear sentry. He only narrowly avoided being shot by both me and by Steve Hoyland – who was the sentry in question. Steve heard this man's bad tempered question, and hissed that he was just a few feet away from treading on him. Nick and I were firing and not in exactly the best of tempers, so we told him to piss off, and he retreated in some surprise.

I also had a very strange conversation with one SAS trooper from G Squadron, who told me about how Kiwi Hunt had been killed. This guy really wanted to talk about it, as if he had to get the thing off his chest. The conversation started with him asking me a question: had I ever been wounded? When I answered "No", he said that he'd been wounded several times and it really hurt. I didn't know this guy at all, and had never actually seen him as it was dark and we were together in a hole in the rocks. He told me he'd been the machine gunner in the SAS patrol that had ambushed Kiwi's team. He said they'd spotted the SBS team a way off in their night scope, and had lay in ambush for them. He'd wanted to open fire with his machine gun, but the squadron commander had ordered him to hold fire until they were only ten yards away. The squadron commander then challenged the SBS in English. Kiwi behaved perfectly, freezing and holding both arms out to his side. The two behind him also stopped, but the man at the end, 'tail-end-Charlie', who might not have heard the challenge, tried to sneak off into the darkness.

Tail-end-Charlie was thought to pose a threat to the SAS patrol, and the squadron commander lost the battle of wills so the machine gunner opened up, killing Kiwi Hunt. The machine gunner told me that his abiding memory of this was of the ammunition in Kiwi's combat vest exploding in the darkness. He was clearly quite badly affected by this incident – which had occurred very suddenly and shockingly at just a few yards range. He was derisive of what he said was the SBS patrols' reaction to this, singling out 'tail-end-Charlie' for breaking down in tears and pounding the ground with his fists. It was their fault as they shouldn't have been in the SAS area; having strayed in, they got what they deserved.... And so on.

This was a very uncomfortable conversation, which rapidly became a one-way monologue, delivered as if I wasn't there. I got the impression that it was one of those things that had to come out, but only to a stranger. This person sounded lost and very lonely, so I hope telling me eased his pain a little.

We knew that the big attack was probably going to take place on the night of 13/14 June, with the initial push forward on the night before. Our friends were going to be in those attacks, in teams like ours, out in front of the units, bringing down the NGS and artillery fire. We all checked in on the radio twice daily, the voices on the radio net enabling us to keep abreast of who was with which unit, and how they all were.

Our own commando artillery batteries were now moving up to within range of some of the targets we could see, and we started to use them during the day. That night gunships were allocated to each of our fire-control teams but with stringent ammunition restrictions to save resources for the big attack. As we were still well behind the front line with plenty of high priority targets, we carried on as usual, and had a good shot, hitting enemy artillery positions and troop positions to the east of Sapper Hill.

On the afternoon of 11 June, our Naval Gunfire Control Net was very busy as all our teams made radio contact in readiness for the first big push, which I now know was to be a series of battalion attacks on

Mount Longdon, the Two Sisters and Mount Harriet.

It was a dark night, very cold and quiet. Crouching in our OP, Nick and I listened in to our radio net, as the other FO teams started moving towards their start lines. They made their routine reports over the radio, their breathing becoming laboured as they moved quickly across the rocky ground. 'Tich' Barfoot reported that his unit had crossed their start line and were moving towards their objective. A very fit long distance runner, Tich was breathing heavily and whispering into the headset. They started climbing the hill and under the weight of their heavy bergans, breathing became even more laboured and their sentences truncated.

Then came the chilling message, between gasps, 'We have come under fire and are taking casualties.'

One by one, the FO teams with various commandos and parachute battalions crossed their start lines. They were the same voices saying the same things as on countless training exercises. But this time they were our friends, whom we might not see again. After half an hour another call-sign asked the question that Nick and I had been dying to ask:

'Zero this is Zulu 41 Echo, are you in contact with 41 Bravo?' (Call-sign 41 Bravo was Tich Barfoot's team).

'This is Zero wait, out to you, 41 Bravo this is Zero over.'

'41 Bravo over' – a breathless voice.

'This is Zero, give Zulu 41 Echo a call. Out.'

'41 one Bravo roger out to you, Zulu 41 Echo this is 41 Bravo over.'

'Zulu 41 Echo, can you please confirm that all your own call-signs are OK?'

'This is 41 Bravo yes, I say again yes over.'

'Zulu 41 Echo roger, Golf Lima, out.'

The latter was one of several little messages that were sometimes slipped into radio transmissions by individuals to a pal. "Golf Lima" was simply 'Good Luck.'

By this time there were lines of red tracer screaming out in long angry curves, some concentrated on particular places, some curving into the mountain and ricocheting upwards like sparks. The artillery of both sides were firing and the sound of shells whistling from right to left (ours going over) or left to right (theirs) was punctuated by the phut of a star-shell bursting and the wavering light, swaying under its parachute and making the shadows of the moonscape underneath elongate and deepen as the flare fell slowly to earth.

The enemy's medium artillery were putting up star-shell too, but thankfully they were unable to adjust it properly, so either the phosphorus burnt out on the ground or ignited too high to be of use. The same was true of their mechanical time air-burst shells which all went off too high, and were alarming but not lethal. The bang was a shock, but the fall of shrapnel too spread out and dissipated to be effective. Knowing the science of artillery can be very reassuring on the battlefield. If airburst shells explode directly overhead, the shrapnel will fall well to the rear because of the shell's trajectory, and shell case design. You take cover and start praying when airburst goes off in front of you, around fifty feet high.

Nick and I were very much spectators, listening to our PRC 320 HF radio and watching the flashes and lights of the battle. Hitherto silent radio nets became suddenly alive with fire procedures, and it was impossible to work out what was happening. We were tired, and so despite men dying and history being made in the darkness outside, we got our heads down to sleep. The noise of the naval shells whispered overhead, their dull crump echoing across the dark hills below us.

The next day, D Squadron, led by the ever-resilient and resourceful Major Cedric Delves, the man in charge of the Pebble Island raid, decided to take out the enemy on the two features near to us; they were a distraction we could do without. So just after first light the Squadron advanced in a most unusual SAS operation – a conventional infantry company advance to contact. They had one troop forward, two troops behind in an arrowhead formation, and advanced steadily toward Hill 500 and the enemy OP position one thousand metres to the north. They found a few empty tins and some rubbish, but the position was unoccupied. They then came back, had a cup of tea and set off eastwards to clear our ridge, Twelve O'Clock Mount and Mount Low.

The enemy on Twelve O'Clock Mount saw them coming and fled, ditching weapons, rations and equipment. There was a degree of disappointment at this, as D Squadron hadn't even been able to loose off any mortar rounds, as the range was too long. (And so the mortar team had to hump the heavy cases all the way back).

By this stage we were running short of food, and we found the Argie rations from Twelve O'Clock Mount both useful and appetizing. There was stewed steak made in Argentina courtesy of Fray Bentos, and roast beef made in England.

The shelling from both sides continued all day, interspersed with bursts of machine-gun and small-arms fire. We knew from the radio net that our units were in their positions and consolidating. They would be digging trenches, cleaning weapons, recharging magazines and replenishing ammunition. The sergeants-major would be listing the names of casualties and determining kit losses, and the commanders would be going around talking to their men and planning the next stage of the operation. The boys would be tucked away into the rocks, brewing tea and munching biscuits AB, with sentries manning the GPMGs and anyone not actually doing anything, taking what rest he could in the cold and the constant noise of the rather desultory firing that persisted.

We could see artillery shells exploding with large, white clouds of smoke against the hillsides. It was not really possible to see what the targets were. The larger sized clouds were the Argie medium artillery positions, which because of their great destructive force, were very much a priority target.

The Argie enemy gun positions that we could see in front of us were in action, their cam nets partly drawn back and white smoke showing up the gun barrels as they fired. I was delighted when our CO Colonel Mike Holroyd Smith came on the Naval Gunfire Control Net and told me that I was to do something about them and that I had priority use of all our artillery. Nick established communications with the regimental fire-control centre who allocated one of the commando gun batteries to us. We settled down to capitalize on our ideal observation position.

It is simply not possibly to destroy anything with artillery unless you are lucky enough to hit a key position, for instance the command-post tent of a gun battery, thus destroying the radios. Destruction shoots can be attempted using medium or heavy artillery but large amounts of ammunition have to be used. Our naval shells were large enough to be able to do this, and the small spread of the rounds (all being fired from the same gun) made it possible to concentrate on single objects like a bridge or building.

The destruction of a gun position would be very difficult because the guns themselves are very robust and each battery's various components are spread out over quite a large area. But the battery's operational efficiency can be drastically reduced by killing the men that serve the guns. Once the gun layer and the Number One (the man who sets the gun to fire in the right direction and at the correct elevation, and the NCO in charge) have been incapacitated, that gun will either not fire or be inaccurate. Gun ammunition can be set alight and be made to explode, which is dangerous for the crews and depletes their stocks.

In the Royal Artillery the firm rule is that if a gun battery is 'in action', i.e. firing in support of the infantry, then it continues so to do in spite of the fact that it may be under attack or being shelled. If the attack is likely to succeed, the GPO (Gun Position Officer) may decide to dedicate half his gun crews to fighting off the enemy, but the priority is to continue providing fire support, come what may.

In the days before artillery had the range to be 'indirect', i.e. they could not be sited behind the protection of hills and fire over the top, the guns were deployed in front of the infantry and to the flanks. This put the guns in a very vulnerable position and they were often attacked, with many heroic and classic actions fought to get them back again. In the smoke and confusion of the battle the gunners more often than not had a clear view of what was going on, and the infantry looked to them for moral support (and still do). To infantrymen in their squares and lines, flustered gun crews suggested a successful enemy assault, and gunners running from the guns could be a trigger for general panic. The tradition arose that although gunners run to their guns when the cry 'Fire Mission battery' is shouted, when the mission is over the crews will form two ranks behind the gun, about turn in unison and march away from the gun, regardless of the situation. Our gunners did this in the mud and driving rain of the Falklands, in exactly the same way as they did in Korea, the World Wars and before.

The Argentine gunners were not so determined nor so dedicated. As soon as they felt that incoming shells might be intended for them, they fled the guns and ran for their protective holes in the rocks. After about half an hour of quiet, their sergeant-major or officer would emerge to scour the rocks and get them back onto the gun position.

Nick and I had worked out eight-figure grid locations for all the targets. This meant that guns firing on this data were accurate to ten metres (i.e. within a ten-metre square). Rather than adjusting targets with single rounds, I would have all guns in the battery allocated to us fire three or four rounds as fast as they could on an eight figure grid reference, so that the enemy would not have the benefit of the warning that adjusting rounds give.

We used proximity fuses when these were available, which are able to sense the ground and explode the shell twenty metres above it, creating a similar shot-gun effect to the naval VT fuse settings. Thus the Argie gunners were subjected to a furious hail of shrapnel, an aerial ambush, without any warning, which lasted about half a minute. There was no point in firing any more shells, as after 30 seconds, the survivors would have gained the safety of the rocks, fear lending wings to tired feet. The horrifying severity of these sudden attacks clearly affected them because there was a very marked reluctance to come out of the rocks. Whenever they heard any shells landing in the general area of batteries that we had already attacked, the crews dropped everything and ran, and the time interval between us shelling them and the battery going back into action lengthened.

I wrote in my diary for 13 June:

> Shelling a gun battery when it is in action firing at your own troops is actually quite satisfying.

We were called up on the regimental net by [Bombardier] 'Blodger' Green (who was in [Captain] Nick d'Appice's OP party) who, with 2 Para on Wireless Ridge, was under heavy artillery fire. We could hear the noise of it over the radio. He was wondering if we could do anything about it for him. We had a quick look and none of the enemy positions that we had tagged seemed to be firing, but there was a position that we suspected. We got 79 Commando Battery on to it, giving them an eight-figure grid reference and an order to fire 4 rounds fire for effect. As the shells came down, we could see men run for the rocks and a bright flame as an ammunition dump exploded. Blodger came back up on the radio to say that the fire had stopped, that they were able to move on, and thank you.

I wish they had gone ahead with the plan to get guns forward and within range earlier. We could have done much damage. (I understand that the guns were no problem, but they would have needed a rifle company each to help protect them, plus a large number of helicopter flights to fly them and their ammunition into positions, when helicopters were in very short supply.) However, one must not indulge in this sort of criticism because decisions in battle are made in a very different environment and with far from perfect information.

By concentrating artillery fire on the enemies' gun positions we were able to overturn guns, set fire to ammunition and vehicles, and keep the crews away hidden in the rocks for long periods. The 155-mm howitzer position never seemed to fire at all, its gun pointing skyward in the same position that our naval bombardment had left it several days earlier. There was also enemy artillery firing from the south-east side of Sapper Hill, over the top and out of sight to us. We wondered if this was part of the 'dead' 155-mm howitzer's battery and we 'walked' a few shells over the top of the hill and into the dead ground beyond out of sight, to see if that would silence them. The results were inconclusive so I did not waste any more ammunition on it.

According to the handbook, artillery shooting is supposed to be a snappy, tense affair with the officer barking orders to the bombardier who queries them in certain specified instances, then the signaller sends them. In our case the signaller was freezing quietly to the rear doing sentry duty – and could not fit into our hole in the rocks anyway. I was on one radio and Nick was on the other, often doing different fire missions or 'phoning round' the frequencies to get a gun battery that was spare. We were very tired and cold so were making mistakes (like saying left when meaning right) and the other would interrupt and correct. We would argue and contradict each other, take short cuts to speed things up and get angry with people on the net. We would tell jokes while waiting for the gun battery to process the data and fire the first rounds. We would daydream to each other about what we were going to do when we got home (to the perfect world that we had left behind) whilst waiting for our battery to finish off a fire mission for someone else.

During the shoots, our gun batteries were often reporting to us on the radio that a particular gun was 'out', meaning that due to some problem it would not be able to fire. After some twenty minutes or half an hour the guns would report 'Number Three In' and that gun would fire again with the others. I only found out afterwards the reason for this. In the soft, wet ground, the recoil progressively dug the trails backwards into the ground until the breech was recoiling in the quagmire and the layer was sitting with his bottom in the water. At this point the crew would declare the gun out of action and get spades to dig it free. Every available person would then help pull it out of the hole and onto to a fresh gun platform where the same process was repeated. The gun crews were working extremely hard, carrying the crates of ammunition from where the helicopters had dumped them to the guns, breaking the seals and laying the shells and cartridge cases out ready to fire, then heaving them to the guns, loading and firing. The guns themselves would have been dug into pits for protection and then when the firing caused them to bury themselves more labouring was required to get them out again.

When a battery is in action, actually firing, its location is obvious from the smoke and noise. Camouflage in between times had to be of a very high standard, and this meant constant work replacing dead foliage on the cam nets, rigidly enforced rules about not moving from under the nets by day, and track plans to prevent tell-tale wheel marks and footpaths developing between guns and command posts. Nick and I found that the Argentine failure to observe these basic rules made our observation post work very much easier.

The most dangerous threat to ground troops in general, apart from enemy artillery, were the Argies' turbo-prop Pucara counter-insurgency aircraft. The fast jets from the mainland (the Skyhawks, Daggers and Mirages, etc.) were better against the ships and could only hit easily seen ground targets, if the cam was very poor and it was a major installation, like the main dressing station at Ajax Bay, which was bombed. Our own artillery positions must have been superbly camouflaged in the bare-arsed terrain in order to have escaped being bombed.

The Pucaras were highly manoeuvrable and carried a nasty weapon load. On the morning of 10 June, Nick and I watched three of them take off from the very short runway in Port Stanley itself, just after first light. They split up and flew very low westwards towards Mount Kent and Long Island Mount. They could not be heard and even from our ideal position were hard to see. We heard distant explosions as they dropped their bombs, and heard the clatter of our anti-aircraft machine gun response. Minutes later they reappeared and calmly landed just out of our sight.

By the afternoon of the 13th the intermittent sleet had come to say, the sky was clouding and the driving wind was cutting even through the many layers of clothing which we were wearing. I had a thermal vest, string vest, Norwegian army shirt, cotton DPM shirt, arctic windproof smock, my quilted Chairman Mao suit and waterproof trousers and jacket, with a pair of fingerless mitts plus normal woollen gloves, an arctic head-over, a black balaclava and a grey woollen climbing balaclava. I was still cold.

The sleet was horizontal and gathering in rock crevices. More SAS had arrived during the night, with yet more equipment. There were bodies encased in 'bivvie bags' strewn in every sheltered cranny on the reverse slope of the hillside. Familiar faces kept peering over our parapet and asking how we were. It was quite a sociable day really.

Late in the afternoon of 13 June, Cedric Delves called an 'O' group (Orders Group) for the operation that night. I called the SACC and asked for an indication of whether we were likely to get a gunship allocated. I knew that as our op was a diversionary raid we would be at the bottom of the list of priorities. I made the case that we should have a ship on call and was told that we were not to be given one – as I had suspected.

The 'O' group took place in a small, clear area between the rocks in a snowstorm. Cedric knelt on a sleeping-mat and tried to keep the wind from blowing his notes and map away. We had all emerged from holes in the rocks and were blinking like badgers caught in car headlights. The people fresh from the ship had smooth faces and rosy cheeks, while the remainder of us were sallow faced and sunken-eyed, with bearded faces smeared with old cam cream and dirt.

My biro ran out halfway through the giving of orders, and I had to press hard on the paper with the useless pen to make an impression that I could re-inscribe later. The proceedings were punctuated with pauses while Cedric tried to light the stub of a badly rolled cigarette.

He went through the plan, to move south down to Blanco Bay and meet up with a group of Rigid Raiders from *Fearless,* which would take a raiding party across the mouth of the Murrell River and land on the north-eastern end of Cortley Hill. This party would be supported by a number of GPMG (SF)s and mortars – from the high ground between Blanco Bay and Weir Creek.

The aim was to give our best impression that the main attacks from the west were being bolstered by large sea-borne landing, which would push up Wireless Ridge and link with the Paras. There were at least two anti-aircraft batteries, a gun position and an infantry company on this feature – so there was no question of our actually attacking it. This was similar to a raid carried out by the SAS some four long weeks ago, on the night of the official landings at San Carlos. With the two FO teams, the SAS had successfully created the impression of an attack on Darwin and Goose Green. The Argentineans had been absolutely convinced that the main landings were taking place there and not at San Carlos, a few miles to the north.

When we reached the fire support part of the Orders, which people had learned to take very seriously indeed, I had to interrupt with the very unwelcome news that there was unfortunately no NGS available to support the raid, as it had been allocated to the units actually doing the main assault. I could feel the mutterings and disappointment, which was understandable especially in view of the huge success of the previous diversionary raid in which NGS had played so important a role.

I had to make the most of a bad position – for the first time in the campaign, very suddenly finding myself no longer a top priority player, and decided that if we came to need NGS to bail us out of trouble, then it was vital for me to have the best radio communications possible. I reckoned I would be best placed on Beagle Ridge, and not down on Cortley Hill where radio communications would certainly not be as good. If we got into trouble, I was going to have to lobby for a gunship being used by somebody else, who would either be part of the plan, or have equally pressing needs, so after some thought I decided to remain on the ridge. This turned out to be a very wise decision. We decided that Cedric would ask for fire if he needed it over the radio, and I gave him some target reference numbers to use instead of complicated grids.

After this disappointment, Cedric got on to the 'Timings' paragraph of the orders format. Behind us, over the hill, there was the constant boom of artillery, the sound of the shells spinning across the front, and the distant clatter of sporadic machine guns.

'At eight o'clock there will be...'

Cedric never got the chance to tell us what would happen at eight o'clock because at that moment, there was a very loud explosion very close by and a whooshing, roaring noise. The 'O' group vanished like rabbits, diving into holes in the rocks.

Cedric remained unperturbed, kneeling on his sleeping-mat, trying yet again to get one of his appallingly badly rolled fags going. We stuck our heads out to see what was happening.

'What the hell was that?'

'Oh I'm sorry, didn't I tell you? I was on my timings paragraph. I will resume. At eight o'clock there will be a test firing of a Milan anti-tank rocket. I see from my watch that it is now just after eight o'clock.'

All the other NGS teams were clocking in to the SACC on the radio in the same way as last night. They had virtually all been reallocated it from the units they'd been with the night before to other units. This was because, wherever possible, fresh battalions were being brought up from being in reserve, to take the lead. We only had five teams so our people had to move on to whichever unit was leading the attack.

I got onto the radio to Mike Morgan and lodged my point about NGS for our attack. I was told that if the need for fire arose I would be treated sympathetically, which was the best I could hope for. The shellfire and small arms were very much closer than the previous night and the Argentine artillery seemed to be much more active. Both the medium and 105-mm howitzers seemed to be at work, and there were quite a few mechanical time rounds going off over Wireless Ridge, mostly too high to be effective.

D Squadron left just after last light, laden with GPMG ammunition, mortars and boxes of Milan, wire-guided anti-tank missiles. Des, Steve and Tim had popped their heads over the parapet for a chat, and Nick and I settled down to another cold night in the OP.

We had been listening to the shelling, the muffled boom of the guns firing, the pause and the whistling shimmer of the rounds spinning across our front toward their targets. Then another pause, and the hollow thud and echoing crump of the rounds landing. But this time, the sound was different from the usual noise; we both noticed it and came to the same conclusion.

Nick was in the basha, our improvised shelter, on the radio and I was up in the OP. He scrabbled right down as far as he could go and I was half into the basha as far as I could go.

'That one sounds like it's coming in!'

The first shell was short by about 100 metres and crashed into the forward slope of the ridge just below us. The other shells were in the air at the same time and the space between the rounds exploding was filled with the whispering whistle that large calibre shells make when they are coming for you. The next round landed a few feet below the parapet of our OP and filled the air with a peculiar humming sound. Metallic ringing sounds made us realize this insect-like noise was shrapnel spinning through the air and ricocheting off the rocks around us. Jagged shards of hot metal, the size of a hand, cut into the moss all around us.

There was a pause while the Argie gunners adjusted their dial sights, and the next lot came down, bang on line. Thankfully, the unlucky one that comes right into the cleft never arrived; instead the shells either plunged into the forward slope a few feet below or went over the top and into the peat valley behind us. I tried to get closer to the rocks and peat, desperately moulding myself to the shape of the ground.

There was another pause and we muttered at each other:

'Bloody hell, I hope there's not much more where that came from.'

'They seem to have got us located all right.'

'That's bloody annoying. You spend bloody days keeping your head down and being careful. Then the other buggers come along and wander about the place so that the Argies see what's going on, then they thin out leaving you to get this.'

A head stuck itself over the top of the parapet and a voice said breathlessly, 'Well booger me, that were bloody close. Are you two all right?'

Des stuck his head over the top of our OP, thinking we'd had a direct hit and concerned about what he was about to find.

'Oh thank fook you're all right. That were bloody close.'

I stuck my head back up to listen for any more incomers and said, 'We're OK mate. Still it makes a change from slaving away over a hot radio all the time.'

'I'd best nip back in case there's some more on the way. Keep your heads down, for fook's sake.'

The shells stopped coming, the strong smell of RDX/TNT – High Explosive (HE) faded and the lines of red, curving tracer fire started below us, showing us how far the attacks had progressed. We could just see tracer strike on the black hump of Cortley Hill, which was almost certainly the support group of D Squadron opening up with the SF kits (machine guns on tripods, for giving accurate sustained fire), from above Penarrow Point. The SAS assault group were on their way down to meet the Royal Marines Rigid Raider assault boats at Blanco Bay.

That same area then became illuminated by enemy para-illum flares, fired by their artillery. This was, for a short time, interspersed with mechanical-time HE, as always bursting too high to be effective. (The D Squadron boys, on their return from Blanco Bay, said that nevertheless it had been an alarming experience, particularly before they realised the bursts were set too high.)

In addition to all this attention, there seemed to be searchlights coming on from time to time, down in the Port William area, off Doctor Point. These lights were being shone due west and turned out to be the Argie hospital ship lighting up D Squadron's area of operations. This was a very serious breach of the Geneva Conventions. A hospital ship is neither Argentine nor British but neutral so long as it wishes to be exempt from hostilities. It should certainly not have attempted to use its searchlight in that way, thus abandoning its neutrality. In view of what happened to D Squadron on the way across the river entrance, the hospital ship was a far from innocent party, and when things became desperate for D Squadron the very serious idea of putting down a couple of warning salvos of Mark 8 4.5 inch naval gunfire would have suggested itself, had there been a gunship available to me.

The SAS raiding troop, having split from the two groups with the support weapons, had made its way down to Blanco Bay and met up with the Rigid Raider boats.

Rigid Raiders are flat-bottomed dories that are able to skim across the surface of quite rough seas carrying up to eight fully laden people, who sit on inflated rubber sausages that absorb the impact of the flat bottom bouncing along the surface. The coxswain stands behind the upright steering column against which he is able to brace to avoid being thrown overboard. 'Raiders' are very fast and manoeuvrable but tiring (from the jolting ride and the need to hang on grimly to avoid being thrown out) and very wet.

The other two troops in D Squadron had moved on to the high ground to the west and were preparing the GPMG (SF)s, the mortar base plate and a line of Milan missiles to fire across the water in support of the raid. The mortar line was in the rear. All this heavy equipment had been carried down the hill from our location.

Nick and I sat chatting, shivering and watching. Tracer from further down the hill was streaming forward in long bursts onto Corley Hill. Our radio link with Cedric came to life with a request for help. The raiding troop was under heavy fire and having to withdraw. We got onto the NGS control net and asked for a gunship. Our request was immediately granted and we were told to contact Bob Harmes who was the LO on board. At this point things became very difficult because the gunship was out of range and Bob could not tell us when he would be ready to fire. This was of no use to us at all.

The next three-quarters of an hour were filled with frustration and anxiety, but no NGS. After half an hour of the ship being 'ready within a few minutes' I called Captain John Keeling, the adjutant of 29 Commando Regiment RA and asked him if he could help me out. We had also received a few more shells in our direction, and as they came in I reckoned I could see a flash from behind Cortley Hill, above Fairy Cove, where we had for several days suspected the location of a gun battery. I had an eight-figure grid of this to hand and gave it to John Keeling who promised to do what he could. All the guns were tied up with firing for the main attacks so I was not too hopeful.

John came back very quickly and said that there was six rounds fire for effect (from 6 guns – totalling 36 shells) coming down any second now on the target, and that he was sorry he could not do more for us. I was greatly heartened, keenly appreciating the problems of getting heavily committed gun batteries to fire an extra six rounds per gun onto a new target in the middle of a complicated fire plan.

The rounds came down beautifully; the grid reference was spot on and they were bang on the data, and there was no more firing from that enemy gun battery. Cedric Delves told me later that the rounds had come crashing in at a most opportune moment and had suitably quelled the opposition. John Keeling came back up on the radio a little later on to check that all was well – another nice touch, as I might have asked him for yet more fire, further complicating his already over-loaded existence!

Things now became very confused whilst D Squadron were extricating themselves from this exposed situation, getting safely back onto the shore, and back up the hill to relative safety. They had sustained a casualty and were arranging a casevac flight for him. However the injuries turned out not to be serious, but nevertheless, swathed in bandages, he was evacuated to the MDS (Main Dressing Station), and then on to *Canberra* at sea.

When the raiding party returned we were able to piece together what had happened. My suspicions about the Argie hospital ship were well founded; it had indeed been scanning about with its searchlight, and may well have picked out our raiding party as they crossed the harbour. As the Rigid Raiders approached the far shoreline they had come under heavy fire from three 20-mm anti-aircraft guns, small arms, mortars and heavy .50-calibre Browning machine-guns. This fire was accurate, leaving splinters in the hulls and engines being hit. The Royal Marines coxswains behaved immaculately, swerving and dodging the red tracer that curved out through the darkness at them. They had very swiftly become adept at steering crouched behind the steering-wheel console.

It became impossible to try and get all the raiding party ashore and carry on as planned, so the Rigid Raiders made their way back to Blanco Bay, running the gauntlet of what was clearly a strong Argentine defence. To everyone's great relief only one man was hit, and although damaged, all the craft managed, one way or another to get back to safety. The 36 rounds that John Keeling had organized fell during the withdrawal of the squadron back up to our location, and gave the Argies suitable distraction at a most opportune moment.

The weather was taking a turn for the worse, dull cloudy skies, very cold bitter winds and sleet driving into our faces, and the next day was a tired anti-climax. D Squadron made little pretence at camouflage, moving openly about the ridge even in daylight the ridge. The ground was strewn with brown, 'bivvie' bags and recumbent figures covered in snow, bashas and even neat little camouflage tents. Figures huddled in the rocks making brews, and people wandered over to see us and tell us more about the last night's excitement, which everybody agreed had been a very frightening experience, particularly as sitting in the Rigid Raiders, they had been unable to do much except pray.

In the hills to the south of us, the commando and parachute units, joined by the Scots Guards, were once again going firm on their objectives (having all been successful), digging in, collecting captured weapons, shepherding prisoners away, making brews, sitting in groups muttering to each other and doing ammunition resupply. The FOOs (artillery Forward Observation Officers) would be on the headsets bringing down artillery fire onto the next lot of Argentine positions. Sentries would be sitting beside GPMGs with yards of carefully folded, shining, brass-linked ammunition, whose cleanliness contrasted with the accumulated dirt, damp and grime of everything else.

Nick and I cobbled all our resources together for a breakfast. Food was running out. We got everything out and shared it with the other three who were in the same state. The boys who were fresh from the ship gave us some tins and we were also given the casualties' food. (It is customary when casualties are evacuated, to take only their weapon and some ammo – if they are well enough to carry it – with the rest of their kit being left for everyone else to use.

Below us in Port Stanley we could see a fairly normal amount of activity; vehicles and men moving about the town, and the overall scene was much the same as usual.

The first indication that the war was drawing to a close was the establishment of a 'No-Fire' line beyond which we could not engage the enemy, and then, a little later, the order 'Weapons Tight' and 'No firing unless in self-defence'.

We were now just sitting around rather aimlessly freezing, and the rear protection group came over to spend some time chatting with us. These chats were largely conjecture about exactly when it would all end, and were not unlike the interminable sitting about that is usual towards the end of a big training exercise.

We could see groups of Argentine soldiers on the eastern slope of Sapper Hill beginning to wander aimlessly eastwards, and there gradually developed a movement toward the airfield. The soldiers from the various Argie gun positions were joining this exodus, which seemed to gather a strange, listless momentum as the day progressed. We presided over this scene, sending the odd report to the SACC to keep them in the picture.

A Gazelle helicopter appeared, coming towards us over Berkeley Sound. It landed to the rear of the ridge and Captain Rod Bell, the interpreter from the Fanning Head raid, and Lieutenant-Colonel Mike Rose, the CO of 22 SAS, clambered out. They explained that they were going to try and land on the Argie hospital ship and parley with Menendez. Rod had apparently been able to speak to them on the radio. Their aim was to try to speed up the inevitable surrender. We briefed them on what we had been able to see and offered advice about flying so as to avoid anti-aircraft positions. They clambered back in again.

The Gazelle pilot had in the meantime attached a wire cable to the lifting eye below the aircraft, and as they took off this wire lifted a large boulder, which kept the cable taut under the helicopter. From the cable flew a large white flag. The Gazelle made its way slowly round Beagle Ridge to the east and towards the hospital ship. We heard no more until half an hour or so later when the Gazelle returned, landed and Rod and Colonel Mike got out again. They'd had a favourable response to their suggestions and were going to organize a meeting between Major-General Jeremy Moore and General Menendez in Port Stanley. They loaded their ball and chain back into the Gazelle and flew off.

The NGS control net started producing favourable 'end of exercises' noises with the exception of one message, which was that everyone else was likely to be stood down except us, who were to be prepared for 'operations in the west'. This filled our hearts with gloom and I still wonder what the purpose of that message was – a deliberate security breach to pressure the Argies who we knew listened to our net very carefully? There was the danger that only the enemy in Port Stanley might 'wrap'. There was no certainty that the large garrisons at Fox Bay and Port Howard were going to follow suit, indeed the rhetoric from Buenos Aires had stated that these other outposts would be reinforced and continue to fight.

The idea of returning once more to those two places and doing further NGS raids really did not thrill Nick and me very much at that stage. We started thinking, as we had so many times before, about what we would have to do to get ready to go out again on operations, but this time it was with the hope that our efforts would prove unnecessary.

To the south, to our right, there was much helicopter activity as our Sea Kings and Gazelles took advantage of the ceasefire to bring up rations and stores, evacuate casualties and shuffle people round. We kept tuned in to the BBC World Service every hour to find out what was happening.

The programme was interrupted to go across to Parliament, and we heard the Prime Minister in the House of Commons announce that the white flags were now flying over Stanley. Nick and I checked the town very carefully with our telescope, and I assume that there was a degree of rhetorical license in that announcement, as at that actual moment we couldn't see any white flags at all.

At some stage in all this confusion Major General Jeremy Moore went to the Governor's house in Port Stanley and met General Menendez where they signed the Instrument of Surrender, with the word 'unconditional' struck out. The Paras were on the road 'tabbing' into Port Stanley and Chris Brown was on the radio giving a blow-by-blow description of the scene as they proceeded.

They went in through the old Royal Marine camp (once home of NP 8901) at Moody Brook and moved eastwards past gun positions that had received out attentions, and eventually past the racecourse. There were many more artillery guns than we had imagined, all virtually new and with unexpectedly large piles of ammunition around them.

As they passed various points along the way, whole blocks of target numbers that had become unsafe because of the advance were cancelled. The net became very chatty. Sgt John Rycroft, who had been on duty in the SACC command post during an air raid had been hit on the head by a neon light when a thousand pound bomb landed nearby. There was much solicitous enquiry on the radio as to his 'light injuries', was he making 'light of them?', did he feel 'light-headed?' etc. The teams that were in the advance on Port Stanley took orders for Colt 45's and sniper rifles. There were several questions about exactly what the situation was over the Argentine surrender, and amid all the *badinage,* a sense of wariness continued.

The surrender became official at 9 p.m. local time, which for us, on Greenwich Mean Time, was 2359 hours. At that moment I lit my last cigar (prior to giving up smoking) in celebration and somebody made a cup of tea. We made our weapons 'safe', i.e. took off the magazines, cleared the round from the chamber and applied the safety catch. The NGS control net closed down until the next morning, and suddenly it was all over.

The next morning we formally closed down the NGS net for good, having finalized the arrangements for the recovery of all our NGS teams as far as we could at that stage. As the stations were singing off for the last time, a voice with an Argentine accent came on the air:

'You may have won Puerto Argentino, but the war is not over,' said this voice.

There was a pause on the net, then quick as a flash everyone came up in order:

'41 Roger Out.'
'41 Alpha Roger Out.'
'41 Bravo Roger Out',
"41 Charlie Roger Out"    etc... in absolutely perfect radio procedure.

---

* All this information as supplied by the Argentinians, with their spelling.

# Chapter 13
# Waiting to Go Home

So after all this excitement, Naval Gunfire Forward Observation Team Number One were left stuck on Beagle Ridge in the driving snow without rations while the rest of the victorious troops were marching into Port Stanley, where no doubt they would be warmly welcomed. In lieu of this, we passed round yet another gungy mug of peat water tea. If you can't take a joke, you should not have joined.

The Divisional and Brigade Staff were now left with a new situation and a huge problem. They had gone from being completely dedicated to winning a war to an almost 'post-exercise' situation. 'End of exercise' had been declared and now all that anyone wanted to do was go home. There were the additional problems of the wounded, burying the dead, and the unknown number of prisoners of war. Units were spread out in the positions they had reached when the whistle blew. Stanley was the place with shelter and was the ultimate objective, so naturally the infantry units got themselves there as fast as they could.

The Staff also had to ensure that the surrender would hold. Mainland Argentina was continuing with the struggle and it was a fair chance that the air battle might continue. Mobility was severely hampered by the uncharted minefields, which continued to claim casualties for some time. Our regiment sustained such a casualty only hours after the cease-fire. Major Brian Armitage was coming up in the wake of the advance in his Over-Snow vehicle (a two-seater caterpillar-tracked vehicle that went very well over the boggy ground) and went over a land mine, which threw the vehicle up in the air and wrecked the rear, but thankfully not the cab. The driver was OK but Brian had several vertebrae damaged and could not move. He lay there with the driver keeping him warm for some thirteen hours before another vehicle happened upon them.

On Beagle Ridge the snow and wind-driven sleet continued. The next day it was rumoured that we would be flying out. We packed everything up except the shelter (promises of flights out being extremely fickle things). A large pile of the leftover missiles and ammunition was gathered and carried down the hillside to the flat area that would become the landing-site. We posed for photographs on the summit of Beagle Ridge (with a Union Jack Flag that someone had carried for this very purpose). The wind was so strong that it was very hard to remain upright. The release of tension that cessation of hostilities brought is evident in these photos.

The radio message came that we could expect a Sea King in the next hour, so we struck the shelter and humped the bergens down to the LS. There was a quite a considerable wait and it was very cold. When the distant engine noise was heard everyone was galvanized into activity, stores lined up on the correct side so as to be loaded straight on, and sticks nominated and grouped. FO1 were to be on the second stick. When the aircraft came into view an orange smoke-canister was thrown to indicate the wind direction and our location. The first lift went off and very soon we were clambering aboard the second.

The crewman handed round cans of beer – very magnanimous and very welcome. We thundered over the moorland moonscape to San Carlos Water and landed back on *Sir Lancelot*. The SAS got out and I negotiated our flying on to *Intrepid* where we could marry up again with the SBS and our equipment.

When we landed back on *Intrepid*, Roy Laney was in the glass-fronted box in 'Flyco' and gave us a huge smile and wave of welcome. We were now on our home base and reunited with our baggage. It was also lunchtime so we split rapidly to our respective dining-areas to eat about three lunches each.

It was lovely to become a gentleman of leisure. *Intrepid*, however, was far from being able to take it easy. She was due to sail for Fox Bay to pick up the Argentine garrison there and transfer them to *Canberra* for the return trip to Argentina. In the meantime we boxed up all our gear and packed our personal belongings. The squadron were due to go home on the RFA *Fort Austin*. We loaded everything except our personal kit on to the LCM that arrived to make the transfer. As far as we knew, we would shortly transfer with it. No one was answering my signals asking for firm instructions, so it was a question of doing what we thought best.

Des, Tim and Steve were offered a helicopter lift into Port Stanley and so they went off sightseeing. They came back with some interesting 'gizzets' (the name for war booty – you see something lying about that you want you say 'give us it'), and tales of absolute confusion. I had no desire at all to go, having become so intimately concerned with the place through a telescope and especially after the tragedy of the civilian deaths in Port Stanley. I think that Nick felt the same way. We sat down on his mess-deck wearing our 'Survivors' Kit', drank a few cans of beer whilst the boys were away and reflected on how well our 'scratch' crew had done.

The accumulation of souvenirs was getting a little out of hand. There were so many brand-new weapons lying about (some still wrapped in their original greaseproof paper) that everyone had acquired something. The most flourishing trade was with the sailors who were very keen to get their hands on a pistol to show off at home. We realized that before we would be allowed ashore in the UK, all these souvenirs would have to have been either handed in or thrown into the sea. Consequently, the pistols and weapons that had been gathered by us in the normal course of the operation were sold to willing matelots who were delighted – until, presumably, they had to throw them over the side.

*Intrepid* sailed for Fox Bay to pick up the Argentine garrison, arriving at night and putting a prisoner reception party ashore to meet up with a similar team from *Avenger* – who were already there. The following day, once the prisoners had been organized, they would be flown on board and incarcerated in the lower tank (where for three weeks before the landings, on our sister ship *Fearless*, the Blues and Royals had been living – I mention this in order to show how very socially acceptable the lower tank-deck can be).

Lieutenant Paul Humphries, who had been the co-pilot in the Sea King that had crashed, offered to take me along in the co-pilot's seat, to fly the PoWs on. [Although escaping from the sinking helicopter (through the front windscreen) with only scratches, Paul had been shaken by the accident. However, after a few days he was back on the job again.] It would be a long and rather boring shuttle run for him and we could chat away. We took just after first light and as we flew in, Paul showed me how to handle the helicopter using the dual controls. I flew the long runs in and out and the easy turns, and Paul did the landings and take-offs. A real treat for a simple soldier!

*Avenger* was stationary, anchored in the centre of Fox Bay, not far from where we had been in such difficulties in our rubber boat a few weeks previously. The LS from which we would collect the PoWs was on the periphery of Fox Bay East. It was a lovely clear day with the occasional sudden rain squall. The spartan beauty of the two small settlements was revealed and the weather-board houses with their red, corrugated-iron roofs and palisade fences looked very peaceful.

The LS was a large, green field with Dusty A. (the Quartermaster of the Special Boat Squadron) standing at one end, hands outstretched to wave us down. There were also two naval officers, in that incredible garb that naval officers affect when they leave their ships. The black, leather gaiters, blue, waterproof jackets and big, blue, dustbin-sized berets make them look like building-site foremen crossed with members of a field-gun racing crew. Their pistols and rifles, carried rather ostentatiously, seemed an incongruity, for the prisoners were lined up smartly and quietly in the gentle drizzle. The bulk were under cover in the sheep-shearing sheds, but there were several lines of fifteen sitting on the kit bags waiting to be picked up.

There were also four Royal Marines, from the landing-craft detachment on *Intrepid*, with their officer; just six soldiers and two naval officers supervising and organising over 1,000 Argentineans who were anxious to be moved. A few Falklanders stood by quietly watching it all. On a couple of occasions, before getting into a helicopter, one of the Argentine senior NCOs or officers would step forward and offer his hand to them, and pat the children on the head. There were farewells, and what I imagined to be promises to write being made in a strange and somewhat poignant scene.

Some of our prisoners did not seem to have been in a helicopter before, having to be told to put out cigarettes and shown how to fasten the seat belts. The crewman had a rotten job heaving them up through the door and stowing the kit bags which they were clutching – which turned out to be filled with tins of food. We took off with the first load, and as we got about halfway to the ship, with the doors shut, a strange and very unpleasant smell began to accumulate, a combination of wood smoke and dysentery – from which a lot of them seemed to be suffering.

On *Intrepid* they were put straight down on to the tank-deck and fed immediately with traditional Royal Navy corned beef stew. They weren't exactly delighted with this, presumably preferring pasta, but the ship just did not have that sort of food. The stew was nutritionally good, and we ate it too, so it wasn't all that bad. Despite their moaning, it was all eaten.

Unfortunately our prisoners also made a disgusting mess, which was probably the result of their officers not bothering, or not being able to exercise any control. Back on land, there had been trouble with some of the Argentinean officers who attempted to insist on retaining their pistols – because they were frightened of their men.

The Argentine officers seemed to have been looking after themselves quite well. A naval officer at Fox Bay appeared at the LS wearing an immaculately clean, dark-blue greatcoat and peaked hat with gleaming gold braid. Their officers seemed clean, shaved and dry, whereas the soldiers were sallow-faced, wet, unshaven and filthy.

The dentist on *Intrepid* told me of one prisoner who complained of toothache and was delivered by Royal Marine guards to the sickbay. After his initial trepidation, this chap realized that that he was going to be treated and became very pleased with himself. Once the treatment had been done, the dentist had to escort the prisoner back to the tank-deck. It was late at night, the lights were dimmed and the corridors deserted. The prisoner decided that the dentist was a kindly soul and started larking about, running off down the corridor and pretending not to understand. The dentist was carrying a sub-machine gun, and when he got fed up with these antics cocked it. His charge, like a naughty schoolboy, put his hands up in acquiescence and behaved perfectly thereafter.

I finally received an answer to my various signals requesting instructions, and was told to get across to *Fearless* as soon as possible to join the rest of the battery. This was a pain as we had sent all our equipment off on RFA *Fort Austin* with the SBS. And so, once *Intrepid* returned to San Carlos (from Port Stanley), we picked up our remaining bits and pieces and changed ships yet again.

We were the last of the FO teams to make it to *Fearless*. The one outstanding member of was WO2 'Brum' Richards who was away with HMS *Yarmouth* in the extreme southeast of the area of operation obtaining the surrender of South Thule (the final Argentine outpost) to wind the whole thing up.

It was great to see everyone again, and there was a lot of teasing and jocundity. Captain Kevin Arnold was complaining that he hadn't had any mail for weeks so we wrote him a very fruity letter from a girl describing a torrid and most gymnastic love affair. Captain Chris Brown had his leg pulled unmercifully over the newspaper reports about the 'cool, calm voice of the Royal Artillery captain on the Pebble Island raid'. Captain Bob Harmes, having been sunk three times and bombed on several other occasions, had now become the Jonah of the fleet. Ship's captains went pale whenever he darkened their gangplanks. We hoped his luck had changed. I spotted a familiar bearded pilot and complimented him on his dawn rocket raid on Port Stanley police station (he had destroyed the building). He smiled broadly saying he was delighted to see me, as I was the only person who had seen his attack and could corroborate it to his friends for him – which I was very pleased to do.

There was no space in the wardroom for the large number of officers congregating in *Intrepid*, so we took over the smaller gunroom mess (usually reserved for the midshipmen's use) and spread sleeping bags everywhere. The boys were ensconced down in the lower tank-deck, and every night, armed with bottles and beer cans, we gathered down there and recounted our tales and caught up with each other again. A guitar was borrowed and singsongs developed.

Some of the boys had collected some splendid 'gizzets'. There was a really handsome, polished-wood sniper rifle with telescopic sights, and even a .50 Browning machine-gun that Bombardier Jackson had carried for miles because 'You never quite know when it might come in handy'. (All these things were duly listed and collected, ending up in the UK with whichever unit could make best use of them.)

There were several video-cassette machines around the ship, and news and other TV programmes from the UK were beginning to arrive. The first one I saw was of the aftermath of Goose Green. It was very strange and puzzling to see the home reactions. These old tapes were not really very popular with us, though I suppose we enjoyed chuckling when they got it all wrong, more especially if there was an element of punditry in their pronouncements. The fact was, they scarcely seemed to be related to anything like our actual experience. As things became better organized, we started to receive cassettes dropped by the long-range Nimrod surveillance aircraft, giving news that was only 24 hours old. This was rather more satisfying. And above all, we enjoyed catching up on the sport we had missed – Wimbledon, the cricket and the athletics had all been taped for us.

'Now I feel that the war is at last really over – The RAF is here!' announced someone in the wardroom one night. He was not referring to the RAF officers who had been on *Fearless* all the while, or to the heroic Harrier pilots, of course, but to the influx of new faces in connection with the reopening of Stanley airfield. The situation was an interesting example of how bad feeling between branches of the Forces can arise. Everyone was now yearning to be off home and if an RAF Hercules transporter could have landed we could be away in no time – yet the RAF announced that it would take weeks to get the runways repaired.

Unworthily, we suspected that they dared not declare the airfield open to traffic too quickly as this would admit that the Vulcan sorties from Ascension Island had been a failure. We forgot too easily how those very Vulcan sorties, prodigious efforts as they were, had been a great boost to our morale at the time. We failed too in rational appreciation of the strategic position. The great objective could not be our speedy repatriation – that could wait; the vital thing was to repair and improve the runways so that the all-weather Phantom air-defence fighters could operate. Once the Phantoms were on station, the Argentinean Air Force could not restart the war.

We were very impatient to be on our way, and when we got the buzz that *Canberra* was going to be sailing soon, we thought that we should go on her. There was no one who either could (or would) say yes or no to this suggestion, so we put into operation the military ploy of inventing orders that suited us, and then carrying them out.

Thus we announced our intention to move on to *Canberra,* and made the appropriate arrangements. Bob Harmes knew all the purser's staff on board from the trip south, plus having passed through *Canberra* three times as a survivor of the three ships that had sunk while he had been on board. Survivors went to *Canberra* before returning to the UK. And so when we arrived on Canberra with our gear, he was able to get cabins allocated with our names firmly printed onto the manifest. The officers' cabins were already occupied by people like us, who had eased themselves in and were hoping not to be dislodged. But they had not approached the problem in quite the same underhand, well organised fashion. We sat down in the cosy coffee-annexe at the end of the corridor and waited, while Bob Harmes pulled strings at the other end of the ship. After a few hours, we were delighted to see the "squatters" moved out – with much understandable gnashing of teeth and chuntering at our presumption.

We were billetted in 'Canterbury Court', a private cul-de-sac used normally to house the purser's own staff. We had our own cabins with double beds, showers and loos, desks and radios. It was ridiculous luxury and we simply could not believe our good fortune. We kept our fingers firmly crossed that we would not be evicted.

The first thing that I had been looking forward to doing once I got safely on board was to go for a run. We had all become very unfit, having taken no proper exercise for over a month. The interminable sitting about in wet ditches, smoking the odd cigar to calm the nerves, the occasional bursts of activity and long and tiring moves at night laden with ludicrously heavy packs had been wearying and exhausting, and had made our condition far worse - rather then any better. The unhealthy diet of constant compo rations - not enough when out in the field, sometimes too much back on ship, stocking up while we could – had further weakened us. We were all mildly ill – digestive systems not functioning properly, with sore feet, backs and knees – and run down.

I dug out my running gear and went up to the cold air of Canberra's quarter-mile-long promenade deck. She was moored off Port William, and I could see Port Stanley and Beagle Ridge very clearly. There were others doing the same thing, and I started slowly and carefully. As I trotted round, slowing past the flagpole at the bow and running carefully over the rough bit on the port side where the deck surface had already been destroyed by countless pair of boots, I came across other members of our little unit trotting round as well. At the stern you go through into a covered way and around the door to the crew's quarters, who by now were very wary about stepping out into the path of the thundering feet. By convention everyone went round the same way and, to avoid disaster, the direction was announced daily and was altered from time to time for variation. As it got dark the deck lights came on, more people came out to run and the pounding of feet became the dominant sound. The process of getting fit again was not really very enjoyable – but it was something to do.

Apart from running and sleeping, our main post-operational activity was eating in the palatial first-class dining room. The normal luxury-cruise waiters were in attendance, every day at every meal, each with a group of several tables to do. They were excellent. You could have the entire menu, with every alternative, plus seconds if you so desired. We established ourselves at the same table for every meal, and discovered we had a most wonderful chap as our waiter. He had been aboard for the whole of the crisis, coping while his luxury cruise ship became in turn, an ad hoc Aldershot military training area, the prime target of the Argentine air force, a prison transport for Argie prisoners, and a forwarding station for sunken sailors en route to Blighty. Quite understandably, he found the whole desperate experience a bit difficult to take and so helped himself along the way with a constant nip or several throughout the day. As a result his memory for food orders was unreliable. So to keep his diners happy and avoid embarrassment he got one of everything for everybody, and if you didn't want it, you left it. As far as we could observe, his sense of balance with plates was unaffected – unless he was responsible for the loud crashes heard occasionally from the kitchens. We were also able to work our way trough the rather splendid P&O wine list (at a very modest expense), which was most educational.

We did try quite hard to get stuck into the excellent cocktail bar – because we felt we should. But regrettably, to the chagrin of the bar tenders who were keen to show off their drink building skills, we were not really up to it. In the evenings, after a couple of pints, then wine with dinner, I would quietly fade away to the quiet of Canterbury Court. My digestive system was distinctly unhappy, so I was laid low, on and off for much of the voyage.

I slipped into a routine of either staying in bed until after lunch then getting up and running – or of getting up for an organized 148 Battery exercise-period, which was available by mutual consent (of us all) every morning for an hour, going back to bed and re-emerging at tea-time for another run, then getting stuck into dinner. Some days I could not eat anything at all, and survived on kaolin and morph. I rued the days on Beagle Ridge when I hadn't bothered with water-sterilization tablets.

Over a period of days the units that were to return to the UK on *Canberra* came aboard and settled in. With a few exceptions they were the bulk of 3 Commando Brigade, most of whom we knew very well. It was a time for reunions, not only with people that I hadn't seen since the beginning of Operation Corporate, but with people I hadn't seen for years. There were the inevitable scenes of heartiness on some evenings – often as not led by Air Corps pilots – drinking around the grand piano which was very badly played and drowned out by even worse singing. I did not always feel sufficiently enthusiastic; it seemed like the sort of thing that is *de rigueur* in Air Force messes in war films. But, along with the drinking, there was also a good deal of serious talk – indeed, there was an almost constant analysis and comparison of notes during the voyage back to England.

The afternoon before we sailed, Major Brian Armitage, with a bad back injury from his serious encounter with an Argie landmine, was flown on board and incarcerated in the sickbay. He looked well but was in pain. He could not laugh without discomfort and was trying hard not to appear worried about how good a recovery he would make. Brian faced weeks of complete immobility in bed, followed by six weeks in a cylinder of plaster to allow the bones to grow back together. We understood that he was concerned about whether all his natural functions might be impaired, so a couple of copies of Mayfair magazine were rushed to the Sickbay. The regiment was gratified when Brian let it be known that he was now one worry less. *Canberra's* own sickbay staff, aided by RAMC and RN medical staff, provided lively and kindly care for the dozen or so wounded who came back with us. We tried to get down to the sickbay at different times to see Brian every day. There always seemed to be a good crowd around his bed and I think I was more entertained by him, than he by me.

We established a daily routine of PT at 0830 for an hour, which would be running round the flight deck and a series of exercises and games on the upper decks. Sweaty in ragged tee shirts and dirty shorts, we repaired to the aft concert room where coffee would be served out of an urn, in plastic cups with biscuits. Next door the souvenir shop continued as normal, selling *Canberra* tee shirts, hat, ashtrays, expensive silk scarves and perfumes. Further along there would be a queue for the ship's barber who was fighting a losing battle trying to cut everyone's hair. He was more used to doing expensive ladies' styling than hundreds of military trims.

We also had to get down to writing our comprehensive 'post-operation' reports, to be completed by the time the ship docked. This was a bore but necessary, and kept us busy and out of trouble.

Everyone had been doing their own thing for four months, and we were all by now very independent. It was important that the unit be reintegrated by the time we got home as the first stage of our 'normalization'. We could no longer indulge our preferences and idiosyncrasies. This change caused friction. We were also not prepared as a small unit to be inconvenienced by the central organization of the ship, which started out trying to control aspects of life that didn't really warrant controlling. In short, we were a prickly group of people, very united against the outside world and also pretty fractious within our own ranks.

Bob Harmes' cabin was directly under the promenade deck along which the running took place. There was a rule that you were not allowed to run before and after certain times. Someone regularly ignored this rule and to make matters worse, wore boots. I went into Bob's cabin one evening to find him lying on his bed with his pistol in his hand staring intently at the ceiling.

'I'm going to get that bugger the next time he comes round. He's woken me up for the past three mornings and he's disturbing my beauty sleep.'

No doubt he was joking; but thankfully the phantom runner had been on his last lap and did not reappear.

When *Canberra* finally sailed for the UK, the officer of the watch announced over the tannoy the usual P&O details of where we would be going and how long it would take. The ship would sail to Ascension Island, where some would be helicoptered ashore to fly back to the UK by RAF VC10, and where others would be flown on, including an MOD equipment-evaluation team (better late than never, striking while our memories were fresh). But most importantly a complete cabaret troupe courtesy of the Combined Services Entertainment organisation, which was rumoured to include a number of females, and consequently generated much interest!

Canberra was not going to stop at Ascension but press on to the UK at best speed, with helicopters flying off and on along the way; with we hoped, a lot of mail. The days were made busy with various jobs and diversions, but as we all wanted to do was get home, the voyage dragged. Every night there would be figures leaning philosophically on the rail watching the wake – and other dark figures carrying sacks, throwing things into the water. The inevitable clamp down on 'gizzets' was still producing Colt 45s, grenades, overlooked ammunition (I discovered a full pistol-magazine in the bottom of my bergen the night before we docked) and other dubious things which people were quietly lobbing into the waves.

# Chapter 14
# Home

*C*anberra made her landfall with the coast of England off the Royal Naval Air Station of Culdrose in Cornwall. Sea King helicopters from the base flew out to the ship bringing various people, like Colonel Mike Holroyd Smith who had left the ships at sea, and flown back to the UK from Ascension. Several of the newsmen who had gone down to the Falklands on *Canberra* were flown on too; bringing videos of footage they had taken to show us.

We all assembled in Canberra's William Fawcett Room to hear from Lt Colonel Mike Holroyd Smith of the arrangements for the disembarkation on the morrow. He had some well-chosen words to say to us:

'There is no doubt that there is going to be a welcome for us at Southampton as you never saw before. There's been nothing like it since the end of the Second World War. I know for certain that several of you are being met by parents and girlfriends, and I'll give those people details afterwards.

'You should be aware that the folks at home have been under a very great strain, far more than you realize and in many ways a greater strain than we've been under. I arrived home last week, having flown from Ascension, and found my family looking very drawn and tired. You will all have to be very careful and aware with your families and go easy on them because they've been through a lot of worry.

"We've got coaches coming down from Poole with your families

287

aboard. Those not actually being met can travel to Poole on these coaches, but of course you are free to do what you like.

'I understand that several hotels in the city are offering free rooms, dinners, etc., for us and I've got the list here.

'Unfortunately, I'm going to have to ask you all to come back to work on Monday morning. There is an awful lot to do, as I'm sure you realize and I want to get it done in a week so we can get away on leave. Although we haven't worked it all out yet, you should get at least six weeks.

'I would also ask you to go carefully with the blokes who didn't come down with us. They will be feeling very left out of things. Just remember that it wasn't their fault that they didn't come along and that they are just as good as you lot, but haven't got the tales to tell.'

My parents were coming down to Southampton to meet me. All the arrangements had been made by our battery rear party who had been doing an excellent job keeping everyone informed, and had organized the coaches to bring the families down to the dockside. They had also been covering all our normal work and training commitments as best they could, in our absence.

The atmosphere on *Canberra* was expectant and pent up. Ever since leaving Port Stanley, each day had been endured as an inevitable delay to getting back home. From the moment that the surrender was signed we felt that our presence in the South Atlantic had become irrelevant and we wanted to get home and resume our normal lives from where they had been interrupted at the end of March. The idea of a huge welcome was fine provided it didn't hold us back from going on leave. Rumours of a big parade filled us with gloom, with all the rehearsals and inevitable preparation for something in which none of us was remotely interested.

In spite of these cynical thoughts, the welcome, its scale, warmth and emotion took us all completely by surprise. We were stunned, some of us into silence and retrospection. Someone murmured a snippet of that bitter Kipling poem: 'It's Tommy this an' Tommy that an' "Chuck 'im out the brute!" but it's "Saviour of 'is country" when the guns begin to shoot;' for we felt that we had really only gone off, as many times before, done our job as best we could, and were now, very thankfully, coming back to our homeland. Why was it that on this particular occasion we should be given such a tumultuous welcome?

Fighting the war meant missing seeing all but a few of the vast amounts of news films and documentaries that had been broadcast in our absence. It was impossible for us to perceive the scale of Operation Corporate and the national feeling that had been generated at home by it. We had developed a sort of tunnel vision – probably as a defence mechanism to get us through, and the extraordinary welcome was like this blinkered myopia suddenly being transformed into a blaze of full colour, 3-D glory.

The Sea King helicopters took off and flew back ashore to Culdrose, and then, in the violet evening mist, the coast of Cornwall first became visible. The officer of the watch piped the news to the whole ship, the one pipe that no one minded being disturbed by. The rails on the port side of *Canberra* were crowded as we watched the distant coastline grow out of the pale evening light. My thoughts were a peculiar mixture of contentment, melancholy, anticipation and impatience. I felt rather sad at the ending, but thankful it was all over safely. There was also sadness and reflection, the friends who would not be coming back and the futility of sudden death. This sadness and reflection – and with it a peculiar calm – sometimes returns to haunt me now. The rugged coastline was pale and ethereal in the summer mist, the stuff of all the dreams that we had not dared to allow ourselves. I thought at first we were off the southern tip of the Lizard and then realized I was looking at Carrick Roads. After an hour of gazing and thinking and talking quietly, I went below for a shower before a special dinner that P & O were putting on, to show us a little of their normal cruising style.

Our last night on Canberra started very appropriately with a Royal Marine Band concert on the games deck. They played marches, pop songs and classical favourites as we watched the south coast of England slip by. In spite of the gathering dusk, small boats came out from the seaside resorts as we passed, foghorns hooting and holidaymakers waving. As streetlights ashore came on, parked cars on the cliffs and beaches flashed their headlights at us. With the band playing all the good tunes, and the cliffs and beaches of home slipping gently past, bringing us closer to Southampton, it seemed that at last we had made it – and on *Canberra* too – just as Steve Hoyland had joked in our cold, wet LUP (Lying Up Position) just a few weeks earlier.

After a sumptuous dinner given by P&O, we had a party in Colonel Keith Eve's cabin. I, quite rightly, got a hard time from our colonel Mike Holroyd Smith, for the length of my hair and general scruffiness. In view of the media attention likely on the morrow I was not at my most presentable. I remember being ruefully aware that we were coming back to military normality.

The next morning, thick heads and furred tongues were widespread. Great inroads had been made into a cache of whisky put to one side over the last three weeks. We were, however, up in good time to hand over our bedding and pack our kit. *Canberra* was now steaming closer to the shore, passing the ports and resorts of Dorset, the low sand dunes of Studland and the entrance to Poole Harbour – our home base. Although early in the morning several welcoming craft were accompanying with us.

The 'gentlemen of the press' had somehow got on board to report our arrival. These were not the journalists who had sailed south in the very beginnings of the conflict, but a different breed. They suddenly materialised at our last breakfast on *Canberra*, and two things stick in my mind.

One was a table of these journalists, all very scruffy and tousled-looking, remonstrating with their waiter about some omission. For them the meal was free and they were very much interlopers. Their waiter, to whom they were giving the hard time, had spent weeks in the largest floating target in the world, and he now had the misfortune to be serving them on his last morning.

The second picture I have of this incursion is a lady reporter, dark and attractive, but at this moment also very rumpled and grumpy-looking, smoking cigarettes at breakfast while all around her were eating, and then stubbing out the ends in the remains of her food as there were no ashtrays provided in the dining-room, with its 'No-Smoking' signs.

There were radio and TV interviews going on in most corners of the ship, and people were being buttonholed at every step by pencil-poised journalists. The responses they were eliciting were not terribly useful and the enthusiasm of the media waned. Willie went round wearing a vest with 'Exclusive Interviews Here' written on it. It was probably just as well that no one took him up on it.

There were all sorts of arrangements being made. The Prince of Wales was to fly on board to meet us, or at least an unrepresentative selection of whoever might be deemed presentable, and then leave before we docked so as not to upstage or distract the welcome. The troupe of entertainers was to be paraded up near the bridge to sing along with the Royal Marine band. (I had visions of 'Land of Hope and Glory' ad nauseam, but they played the pop songs and tunes that we had enjoyed at their concerts.) As it turned out, at Canberra's terminal there was at least one band to the square metre, so this last effort was somewhat overcome by events.

As Canberra entered the channel between the mainland and the Isle of Wight, yet more pleasure-craft came out to wave and follow us in. It was a perfect summer's day, a little misty but sunny, clear and warm. Some of the craft were slow and could only just keep up, others went racing round the ship hooting and waving. There were expensive gin palaces and there were small family boats that merely pottered along.

As the channel narrowed and the sea room decreased, the craft became concentrated and were sometimes virtually touching. The fire service tugs were putting up plumes of water – and drenching boats to lee of them. One chap in a gin palace kept coming in very close and throwing cans of cold beer and lager to the troops lining the rails above him, most of which fell into the sea. There were welcoming banners everywhere, some with names and others simply 'To the Task Force'.

Rail-space on the ship had been allocated according to units – very military and very necessary. The rails were absolutely packed with waving, shouting and very happy soldiers. Any boat that came by with ladies on board was subjected to good-natured cries of 'Get your kit off'! One of the gin palaces had two blonde models displayed on its bow and when it came by the cries were deafening. It could well have been one of the newspapers doing a picture story. Whether cued or not, these two ladies took their tee shirts off and displayed their shapely charms.

They repeated this performance several times and it seemed to catch on. There must be some hormone thing about hundreds of mean shouting 'get your kit off' which is irresistible to female species, for every boat with ladies on board eventually followed suit. Even several ladies really too mature and sensible for this sort of thing! (Being sporting and gentlemanly, how could one be so rude and chauvinistic as to invite only the curvaceous blondes to 'get their kit off!).

Somewhat upstaged by all this, the gin palace with the blondes came by again and they took off *all* their clothes, to great whoops and whistles of delight.

There was one particular boat with two very prim ladies who seemed rather too sensible to get drawn into this silliness – and seemed destined to be the exception that disproved my theory. However later that week, when walking through Southampton I saw their boat pictured on a display board outside a local newspaper office. They were there, as naked as the day they were born. Their 'conversion' must have taken place on the other side of the ship. The urgings of so many men must have proved too much – it was merely a question of time. Hypothesis proven!

On every bit of hard standing there were cars parked close together and people waving. The piers and jetties were packed and the scene was incredible. There were banners everywhere and Union Jacks on virtually every craft. *Canberra* had to slow down to avoid swamping her escorts. Some of these craft broke down and other boats took them in tow or took on the occupants. Every ship we passed hooted and *Canberra* hooted in reply.

As we came round the final few bends in the river it was impossible to tell where our berth was to be because every bit of jetty and standing was crammed with well-wishers waving flags. I kept anticipating the terminal but as we swept onwards I wondered if we would ever get there. The clue was given when finally the team of tugs moved away from the starboard side and formed up to port to push her in.

The P&O terminal was absolutely packed, a band on the quay, every roof occupied, and the huge unloading-sheds crammed with relatives. They had organized our families in groups according to unit, so that we could find the friendly faces in the sea of smiles and waves. These groups were easy to locate as the banners being held up were much more specific and personal. One very well-endowed and shapely lady was quick to reveal all from the terminal roof – we had I suppose become adept at encouraging this commendable and public-spirited activity.

I scanned the crowd with my binoculars but could see no one, until someone came down from the bow to tell me they'd seen a banner saying "Hugh McManners 148". When I went down there and pushed through to a place on the rail, there was my sister Helen wearing a ridiculous 'DeeDee Bobbler' head thing with springs and green stars that bounced up and down. She struggled off through the crowd to bring my parents and younger sister Ann. We could do no more than shout the odd remark and wave, and it was lovely to see them again.

Once Canberra had tied up alongside and the gangplanks went down, there was quite a long and frustrating wait. By tradition and for the benefit of the media, the brigadier, Julian Thompson, went off first, with the COs of the Commandos and the Commando Logistic Regiment. The units then disembarked in order according to a schedule designed to avoid an interminable crush at the single gangplank. We retired to Canterbury Court and drank a bottle of wine.

When our time finally came several hours later and we were called forward over the tannoy, we found that the rest of the boys had snuck off early. The crowd, who had been clapping ecstatically for several hours, clapped us off and we were back on terra firma, in England, three and a half months after leaving.

The band played and the crowd clapped and cheered, and hopefully life was going to become normal and we could forget the military for a while. A huge dog leapt out of the crowd and on to Captain Nigel Bedford, licking him furiously, delirious with delight.

It was all rather a dream. Our quartermaster, Staff Sergeant Ivor Pothin, was on the quayside with a lorry to load our kit and take it back to Poole, so all I had to do was take a few things like toothbrush and razor with me. I had only the brand-new combat kit (that had replaced my ragged Falklands gear) for the walk down the gangplank. Reunited with parents and family, we walked up the road past smiling, nodding policemen and hundreds of parked cars. I was at last away from soldiers and military – although I had no civilian clothes or money, and nothing but the combat kit I was wearing.

The complete transformation from the military environment to sudden and delightful normality made homecoming easy for me. It was a dream and a complete change. It was difficult however for my family who were suddenly confronted with this person they had worried so much about for so long and who, now he was back, just wanted to do nothing. I think it took quite a while for me to get back to normal and I must have been a bit of pain for others while I was doing it.

The nightmare continued for my parents. Peter, my younger brother, with the Parachute Engineer Squadron, had to stay for several more weeks down in the Falklands, clearing minefields – which the Argies had not mapped, in contravention of International Law.

My parents had been especially worried at the time of the Bluff Cove disaster as they knew Peter had gone out on the QE2 attached to the Welsh Guards. Then, in the *Daily Telegraph* on 12 June, they had read a despatch from correspondent A. J. McIlroy:

> "Lt Peter McManners, a Royal Engineer who has been dealing with mines for the Guards (the Scots Guards), said '…minefields should not be too big a hindrance to the advance. Mines are terrifying things but their aim is to demoralize rather than hinder…you need thousands of them to stop an advance…' Asked about reports that the Argentines were breaking the Geneva Conventions by not marking minefields, he said that this was done probably more by incompetence than malice."

This report had brought great relief at home – though the relief was tempered by a further worry about the mines. (Subsequently, A. J. McIlroy passed a personal message to Oxford through his newspaper, saying that he had met Peter in Port Stanley afterwards, and he was fine; the McManners family will always be grateful for this generous gesture.)

After a most enjoyable stay in Southampton I went back to Poole and spent two weeks getting all the kit handed in, serviced and ready to go again (heaven forbid) and then several days counting it all. The people we had left at Poole were a little shy, but very pleased to see us all again. There was the most marvellous unit party one evening (after a lunchtime drinking session to say goodbye to several people who were leaving – including me). Although it followed a very festive lunchtime, the evening was really excellent, with all our wives and girlfriends, finally establishing that our unit was all home and safe.

We had been miraculously lucky. Our only casualty had been Sergeant John Rycroft, on whose head the neon light had fallen during the air raid that so nearly killed Brigadier Julian and his commanding officers. The 'band-aid' was now off. However, we did not escape without tragedy. Back at Poole, our MT (Motor Transport) Sergeant 'Scouse' Graham, a very fit man who was a marathon runner, had been taken suddenly ill with a rare form of lung cancer and died.

There was a hectic round of celebrations to be fitted into the work, including dinner nights in Plymouth and Poole. Operation Corporate had caused a suspension of the normal process of postings, and so now it was over, there was an unprecedented changeover of officers in the unit. I discovered I was going off to something that was completely different – in London, working in the MOD. This would be a very great change in every aspect of my life, and caused me a certain amount of trepidation. It would mean a complete break from all my friends, and all the people in a very special world that I had come to know so very well.

But maybe, I thought, such a change was probably for the best, because going back to the old routine after such adventures would not be easy.

In the officers' mess at Poole, those who had been left behind anticipating our return had sewn a thick white line into the carpet in the bar. On one side they had written

'Falkland Vets Only'. On this side they hung a glass-cased electric lamp with 'Falkland Lantern' inscribed on it – with a ship's bell inside which would ring when pushed. In the amphibious operations business, there is a standard reaction when someone in a bar starts to tell a war story beginning with 'There I was'. The standard response is for someone to say, 'Pull up a sandbag', and make the gesture of pushing an imaginary lantern, to indicate the heaving of the ship and the magnitude of the storm about to be described. The new rule at Poole was that a 'non-vet' could cross the white line when a story was imminent and give the lantern a swing. This happened quite a bit in those first weeks and was a good antidote to out-of-hand war stories.

When I finally did get on leave I decided to cycle from Poole to Oxford via the Woodford valley and other picturesque routes, staying in pubs and seeing a bit of England. I had absolutely no desire at all to go abroad to the sun. Quietly meandering along the lanes, footpaths and towpaths of England for a week was marvellous, especially as the weather was warm and sunny. I wouldn't have minded if it had poured the whole time.

My bicycle tour ended in Oxford the day before my brother was due to fly into RAF Brize Norton from Ascension Island (he having sailed from the Falklands some three weeks after me). We got up very early to drive out to the airfield to meet him. It was another beautiful day and there was much anticipation at the airbase – a very much more intimate scene than Southampton with only the wives and families plus members of the media gathered, waiting to greet the men of Peter's small unit 9 Parachute Squadron RE. There was also the Royal Engineer band and several very senior Sapper officers to welcome the hundred or so men home again.

The VC 10 landed precisely on time (to the second) and after a short pause the door opened and the OC came out followed by his officers, the squadron sergeant major and then the soldiers. They were wearing, as we had done, combat kit and webbing, and their red berets. Peter was the fourth off the aircraft, walking past the band and across to our group. The McManners family were together again.

Cornwall was absolutely lovely. Nothing much seemed to have changed and I began to settle down and become normal again. The magic, elusive, almost fragile beauty of the Cornish countryside did the trick.

It was at this stage, about a month after I got back, that I rediscovered the complications of normal life. There had been none of the debilitating, trivial worries of ordinary life in the South Atlantic. One was either worried, scared stiff, completely tired out and pissed off, or tremendously relieved. Normal life is very bland and full of pathetic problems that are far more draining than the fundamental struggle to keep going. We had been living day by day, sometimes minute by minute, and we were now back to routine and safe, humdrum living. Life is far more intense and vital if you have to fight for it. I wish that I could always feel the way I felt sometimes when I realized that I had just survived – again. I haven't lost that feeling completely and it returns, diluted, to remind me of how lucky I am to be back. The events of one year ago seem to be a dream now. It is only when I remember the friends who didn't come home that the reality of it all returns.

The Falklands that I saw for a few short hours on 21 May, the most remote retreat in the world with its savage unspoiled beauty, which I shattered with 4.5-inch shells: it no longer exists, but might in the future. The Falklands that I knew too well, the combination of island paradise and war zone, is gone for ever – save the lonely graves at San Carlos and in particular that quiet hillside at Port Howard. Now that I'm back home, I would not have missed any of it, but I'm sorry it had to happen and so very glad to be home.

The debate over whether it was worth it – for only 1800 islanders who were not self-sufficient anyway…. and so on – will rage on and be dealt with in depth by future historians. The expense of maintaining a garrison there will ensure a regular airing to this discussion which like all political arguments where money is involved will be verbally bloody.

Our motivation when we were doing the fighting was very much simpler than the arguments that raged at the time, and which no doubt will continue. We did it for each other. In my team we all did our best and were mortified when we made mistakes and tried to be cheerful when we felt like crying. We chaffed each other when we were miserable and joked when we were wondering if we could carry on. We hid our fears, just as we showed them to each other so as to share them. We shared our letters when the postman had left one of us out. We did what was needed as firmly as we were able so that it could be finished quickly and we could all get back home to our families and friends. I do not know what I would have done if one of my team had been hurt. We were so lucky to have been spared that pain. We would certainly have carried on with the job – if only for the one that was no longer with us.

The most universal attitude of soldiers is the belief that whatever is going on around, they will not be the one to get hurt or killed. When others are killed the worry is short-circuited by saying 'If it's got your name written on it, then no matter what you do, it's going to get you'.

This optimistic fatalism is the only way to avoid becoming convinced of the inevitability of death, or worse – mutilation. It would be an impossibly brave man who carried on convinced that he was not going to survive. I suspect that such things as shell shock occur when the resilience of the individual has been taken too far and his optimism is destroyed. Probably then you are unable to carry on and simply crack. Des Nixon used to mutter to himself: 'I'm a rubber duck and you can't crack me', and he was right.

Of course you do have to anticipate and plan for as many eventualities as you can. You decide what you will do under these more desperate circumstances and then lock that train of thought away in a watertight box. Should that particular thing then happen you produce your plan and gain a reputation for being able to think fast on your feet. You cannot dwell on things, especially on what might have happened if… The mental discipline required to do this involves a very strict blinkering of your feelings, which is very hard to relax when you return home.

# HOME

I have tried to tell this story prosaically and in detail, as it happened, and with the tedious stuff as well as the excitement and the fear. I am happier recounting it all than recalling highlights; the trouble with adventure anecdotes is that they give a wholly misleading impression of war. The entire experience was so short and yet so profound that now, one year after returning, the shadow cast in my memory of those three and a half months seems disproportionately long. Strangely, these memories do not stand completely separate from those of earlier months spent (for instance) living in snow-holes in Norway or hacking through the jungle of Belize. The Falklands war was a sort of climax to all that. The hard training and experience gained over the years came into its own in those cold seas and on those windswept barren hills.

The media have pushed the Falklands at people to such an extent that I sympathize with those who are rather sick of the whole thing. It was however a remarkable venture, and this story is only one of the thousands that every member of the Task Force has to tell. It was a unique experience, personally and as an event in military history. That is why I have put all this to paper, and invited you to 'Pull up a sandbag, cross the white line, swing the lantern' and listen to my story – and spare a quiet thought for all those who did not return.

# Epilogue
## Christmas Day 2001

But not everybody lived happily ever after. It is unreasonable to assume that people who endure the fear and privations of war should, because they are soldiers, be unaffected by it. Military training gives you the skills for fighting effectively, but does not make the fighting easier, nor does it reduce its effect on you as a person. I have only met one person who declares himself to be completely unaffected by their Falklands experiences, and it is particularly true of him to say that he is an exceptional individual. Captain Hugo White was then the captain of HMS *Avenger*, and subsequently progressed rapidly to the very top of the Navy as an admiral, and only narrowly missed becoming Chief of the Defence Staff (in the opinion of several people who know what they are talking about) because it wasn't the Navy's turn to hold the top position. One of the other RN captains who I have particular reason to admire, got his ship's company safely back to the UK, but then once the reason for remaining strong was no longer there, suffered the collapse of his health, and was quite ill for some time. There were many other friends and colleagues who suffered ill health, marriage breakdowns and psychological problems.

Despite having greatly "enjoyed" the Falklands experience, I was also affected by it. In 1984, I suffered a strange and undiagnosable malaise, which lasted for several years. I left the Army in 1989 as a major, because I found I could no longer put up with the trivialities of peacetime military life. The medical doctor who saw me while I was working in the MoD, Dr Jean Peacy, who had become quite concerned at my uncategorisable illness, told me in later years that once she'd read a copy of "Falklands Commando", the reason for my condition had become immediately apparent to her, and she wished she'd read the book while I had been her patient. Several of the other people who appear in Falklands Commando suffered variously in their lives and health as the result of fighting in the war.

"I'm a rubber duck, you won't crack me," was Des Nixon's catchphrase. I hope you have remembered him as the older gunner in my reconnaissance team – a former commander of a parachute gun detachment. On Des' return from the Falklands, for reasons that have no logic and are not reasons at all, he was more sorely tested than any of us. His marriage collapsed. He remained with 148 Battery at Poole, and after a time he married again. Since the Falklands, unknown to anyone else, Des had been suffering sporadic bouts of depression, but had continued to pull his weight and do the job at Poole.

But then in November 1991 when his second wife left him for the third time, Des found he couldn't keep it together any more. Rather than admit that he couldn't cope, when it was certain his second marriage had gone the same way as the first and couldn't be saved, he decided to sort out his problems himself – for good. His legendary resilience had gone. One day deep in the New Forest, he took his own life. I wish I'd had the chance to speak with him.

# Chronology of Events

| Date | |
|------|--|
| 1 April | Rumours start concerning the Falklands. |
| | 148 Battery recalled from leave. |
| | Warning order for operations issued. |
| 2 April | Argentine invasion of the Falkland Islands. |
| 4 April | RFA *Sir Percivale* sails from Marchwood. |
| 5 April | *Hermes/Invincible* carrier group sails from Portsmouth and *Fearless* precedes them. |
| 9 April | 3 Commando Brigade sails on board *Canberra*. |
| 10 April | Haig arrives in Buenos Aires, having already been in London. |
| 12 April | Maritime Exclusion Zone comes into operation around Falkland Islands. |
| 15 April | Royal Navy destroyer group arrives on station in mid-Atlantic (submarine already on station in Falklands). |
| 17 April | Planning conferences at Ascension. |
| | Haig back in Buenos Aires, having been to London and Washington. |
| 18 April | Argentine aircraft-carrier returns to port for repairs. |

| 22 April | Pym to Washington |
| 24 April | Admiral Woodward's group RV with destroyer group |
| 25 April | South Georgia recaptured. |
| 29 April | Task force arrives at Exclusion Zone. |
| 30 April | Total Exclusion Zone comes in force. |
| | Reagan promises US support for Britain. |
| 1 May | Initial Vulcan bombing raid on Port Stanley, followed by Harrier and naval gunfire attacks. |
| 2 May | Argentine cruiser *General Belgrano* sunk. |
| 4 May | HMS *Sheffield* sunk. The first Sea Harrier shot down. |
| 7 May | Total Exclusion Zone extended to 12 miles of Argentine coast. |
| 12 May | QE2 sails from Southampton with 5 Infantry Brigade (and P.J. McManners) on board. |
| 14 May | Pebble Island raid – SAS. |
| 18 May | Landing force RV with Task Group, north-east of Falklands. |
| 19 May | War Cabinet gives order to land. |
| 21 May | San Carlos landings begin. |
| | *Ardent* sunk. |
| 23 May | *Antelope* sunk. |
| 25 May | *Coventry* and *Atlantic Conveyor* sunk. |

| | |
|---|---|
| 27 May | SAS move inland, SBS on to the flanks, 3 Para and 45 Cdo march toward Teal Inlet. |
| | 2 Para march toward Goose Green. |
| 28 May | 2 Para fight at Darwin and Goose Green. |
| | 5 Infantry brigade cross-deck from QE2 on to the Canberra at South Georgia. |
| 31 May | 42 Cdo land at Mt Kent. |
| 1 June | 5 Infantry Brigade begin disembarkation at San Carlos. |
| 2 June | 2 Para move to Bluff Cove. |
| 8 June | RFAs *Sir Galahad* and *Sir Tristram* bombed at Bluff Cove. |
| | The Welsh Guards bear the brunt. |
| 11 June | The main battle for Stanley begins. |
| 14 June | Argentine surrender. |

# Glossary

| | |
|---|---|
| AA | Anti-aircraft. |
| AB | AB Biscuits- ships style hard compo biscuits. |
| ADC | Aide-de camp. Personal staff officer. |
| AGI | Amphibious Gatherer Intelligence. |
| AOO | Amphibious Operations Officer. |
| AOR | Amphibious Operations Room.. |
| AP | Armour Piercing. |
| ASD | Anti-Submarine Duties. |
| Avgas | Aviation Gasoline. |
| | |
| BAOR | British Army of the Rhine. |
| Basha | Small hide area with poncho roof, where one or two soldiers live (more correctly a jungle version, but a general usage). |
| Bear | Russian high altitude reconnaissance aircraft. |
| Bergen | (also Bergen rucksack) – a large military rucksack back-pack with side pouches, made of waterproof material. |
| Binos | binoculars (abbrev). |
| Bite | as a fish bait. The reaction to a provocative comment may lead to commentator being 'goffa'd'. |
| Bivvie | from bivouas. See basha. |
| Blowpipe | Light shoulder launched point defence air defence missile. |
| BMA | Brigade Maintenance Area. (Mountains of stores, vehicles and a hive of activity). |
| Bombardier | A Royal Artillery soldier holding rank of corporal. |

# GLOSSARY

| | |
|---|---|
| Blue | small portable cooker. |
| Brew | a wet (*qv*) – a tea, coffee or similar hot drink |
| Brick | a man and his oppo (*qv*). |
| Burma Road | the main passage through a ship. |
| Buzz | a rumour (a gen buzz). |
| C130 (Hercules) | Heavy-lift transport aircraft, used by us and the Argentines. |
| Cache | hidden supply of ammunition, food, etc. |
| Cam cream | black camouflage cream, said to be very good for the complexion (Ed – or not!). To cam out or cam up with foliage. |
| CAP | Combat Air Patrol (Cap). Harriers. |
| Casevac | Casualty Evacuation. |
| Chaff | tin foil, used as a decoy on enemy radar screens. |
| Chairman Mao Suit | Quilted Arctic jacket & trousers. |
| Chatelaine | smaller hand-held thermal imager TI). |
| COMAW | Commodore Amphibious Warfare (Commodore Clapp). |
| Commando Snake | Single-file line of soldiers moving at night. |
| Comms | communications (abbrev). |
| Compo | combat rations (see rats). |
| Container | contraption of straps and clips with which a paratrooper jumps with his weapon and equipment secured to his body. (He releases it in the air once his parachute has safely opened and it drops below him, attached by a 15 foot rope to his harness). See also CSPEP. |
| CPO | Chief Petty Officer. |
| CSPEP | Carry Straps Parachutist Equipment (see container). |
| CW | Carrier Wave. (Used to transmit morse code). |

| | |
|---|---|
| DF | Defensive Fire or Direction Finding, depending on context. |
| DLG | Destroyer Light Guided. |
| DPMs | Disrupted Pattern Material, camouflage cotton uniforms. |
| Drop Zones | area of ground suitable for dropping paratroops. |
| First field dressing | |
| | vacuum-packed shell dressing with yards of crêpe bandage – for initial wound treatment. |
| Fives | measurement of satisfactory radio communications (out of ten). |
| Flick | verb meaning to rapidly change radio frequency. |
| Flyco | Flying Command running flying operations on a ship. |
| FO team | shortened version of NGFO team, Naval Gunfire Forward Observation team. (Also FO1, NGFO Team Number1.) |
| FOO | Forward Observation Officer (Artillery). |
| FPB | Fast Patrol Boat. |
| Gizzet | a spoil of war (from 'Give us that…') |
| Goffa | bread roll, large wave or a punch. (To be goffa'd is to be hit by a wave or a punch.) |
| GPMG | General Purpose Machine-Gun, 7.62 mm. |
| GPMG (SF) | GPMG in the sustained-fire role; on a tripod firing on fixed lines. |
| Green slug | sleeping bag (or maggot). |
| Gunner | a Royal Artillery private soldier (also the generic term for members of the Royal Artillery). |
| Hard | area of hard standing used to beach sea craft. |
| Harry | peculiar naval word added to anything to give emphasis (eg. Last night I was 'Harry crappers' meaning 'I was somewhat under the influence of alcohol'). |

# GLOSSARY

| | |
|---|---|
| Harry maskers | black plastic masking tape used for everthing. One item, without which military units would grind to a halt. |
| HDS | (see SDS) Helicopter Delivery Service. |
| Heavy weapons | Artillery guns, anti-tank guns, 130-mm mortars. |
| Helo | abbrev helicopter |
| Hercules | See C130 |
| Hexxy | Hexamine, tablets that burn to heat food. |
| HF | High Frequency Radio. |
| HLS | Helicopter Landing Site. |
| | |
| Jack | Jolly Jack; slang term for a sailor (Jolly Jack Tar). |
| | |
| Kelp | thick belts of seaweed that clog many Falkland inlets. |
| KMs | abbrev kilometres. |
| | |
| LAW | Light Anti-Tank Weapon. 66-mm rocket launcher. |
| LCM | Landing Craft Mechanized. |
| LCU | Landing Crafy Utility. |
| Light Gun | 105-mm artillery gun used by Commando, parachute and 'light'field artillery. |
| LPD | Landing Platform Dock (HMS *Fearless* and *Intrepid*). |
| LRO | RN rank. Leading Radio Operator. |
| LS | (helicopter) Landing Site. |
| Lynx | naval helicopter. |
| | |
| MASH | US army term for Mobile Army Surgical Hospital. (Also name of comedy film about Korean War). |
| MDS | Main Dressing Station – field hospital with rudimentary surgical facilities. |
| MT | Motor Transport. |
| | |
| Nav Bag | Navigation bag; carried by aviators. |

| | |
|---|---|
| NCO | Non-Commissioned Officer. |
| NGS | Naval Gunfire Support. |
| Nimrod | long range RAF reconnaissance aircraft based on the old Comet jet aircraft. |
| NOD | Night Observation Device. |
| NP8901 | Naval Party number 8901, garrisoned in the Falklands before the Argentine invasion. |
| Nutty | confectionery (nutty locker). |
| | |
| OC | Officer Commanding. |
| OGs | Olive Green lightweight trousers. |
| Once-only Suit | bright orange immersion suits to keep dry after abandoning ship (hopefully used once and discarded) |
| OP | Observation Post; Observation Position. |
| Oppo | partner. Everyone is paired up with a partner, and on operations they always stay close to each other. (See Brick). |
| Orbat | Order of Battle. |
| | |
| P Company | parachute selection company. Four gruelling weeks of long marches, assault courses and runs carrying heavy equipment and loads, to select soldiers for service with airborne forces. |
| Pipe | Tannoy announcement on a ship. |
| Pluto wave | exercise to strengthen arms, shoulders and back. Peculiar movements required reminiscent of canine olefactory investigation. |
| PNG | Passive Night Goggles. |
| PO | RN Petty Officer. |
| POL | Petrol, Oil and Lubricants. |
| Poncho | rectangular waterproof poncho, with hood for use as a raincoat. More commonly used as overhead shelter, stretched over a trench or a hide. |
| PoWs or PWs | Prisoners of War. |

| | |
|---|---|
| PT | Physical Training. |
| Proximity fuses | See VT. |
| Puri tabs | water purifying tablets. |
| Pusser | the purser. Term for anything official, eg pusser's issue rum – the 'tot'. |
| PWO | Prinicipal Warfare Officer. |
| | |
| RALONGS | Royal Artillery Liason Officer Naval Gunfire Support. (Lt.-Colonel Eve.) |
| Rapier | Short Range Air Defence Missile System (SHORADS). |
| Rat Pack; rats | rations. |
| RFA | Royal Fleet Auxiliary. |
| RIB | Rigid Inflatable Boat. |
| Rigid Raider | flat-bottomed fibreglass assault dory, very fast and very wet. |
| RO1 | RN rank, Radio Operator Class 1. |
| Roland | French-made anti-aircraft missile system used by the Argentines. |
| RS | RN rank, Radio Supervisor. |
| RTU'd | Returned to Unit (from a course). |
| RV | Rendezvous. |
| SACC | Supporting Arms Co-ordinating Centre. |
| Salvo | A round of Naval Gunfire Support. |
| SAS | Special Air Service. |
| SBS | Special Boat Squadron, Royal Marines; also SB, SB Squadron and The Squadron. |
| Schoolie | RN Education Officer. |
| Scout | light helicopter. |
| SDS | Sea King Delivery Service – also HDS (Helicopter Delivery Service) when RM or Army Gazelle helicopters were doing it. |
| Section | Smallest group of infantry, 6 to 10 men. |
| SHAR | Sea Harrier. |
| SIGINT | Signals Intelligence. |

| | |
|---|---|
| SLR | 7.62-mm Self-Loading Rifle. |
| Small arms | Hand Weapons, rifles, SMGs, pistols and GPMGs. |
| SMG | Sub-Machine-Gun. |
| Snake | see Commando Snake. |
| Spoof | joke. |
| Stickies | cakes eaten at tea-time in large quantities, by soldiers embarked on ships. |
| Stick Orbat | names of people to travel in groups in each helicopter, or to parachute, jumping together (see Orbat). |
| Stroppy | adjective meaning unco-operative and argumentative (can lead to *bites* and even *goffa's*.) |
| STUFT | Ships taken up from trade: merchant ships on charter. |
| Tabbing | parachute equivalent of 'yomping', ie head down, gun in hand, bergen as high as possible and you cover the ground steadily without pause. |
| Tail-end Charlie | could be a rear gunner in an aircraft. For commando purposes, the last man in a Commando Snake, or patrol. |
| Tank-deck | lower deck on any LPD. |
| Thunderbox | portable lavatory. |
| TI | Thermal Imager. |
| UHF | Ultra high Frequency. |
| VC10 | passenger-carrying RAF jet aircraft. |
| VHF | Very High Frequency. |
| VT | Variable Time naval shell fuses (similar to artillery proximity fuses). Operated by a sensor that explodes the shell a set height from the ground. |
| Watches | Royal Navy term for shift. |
| Webbing | (equipment) worn around the waist, with shoulder-straps and pouches (pronounced pooches by Royal |

|  | Marines at the time), for ammunition, food and medical kit (also belt order and fighting order). |
|---|---|
| Wessex | oldest but tried and trusted RN troop-carrying helicopter. |
| Wet | drink (a wet of tea of 'I've just made us a wet). |

\* I do now. AAF Mordey of Ferndown kindly wrote to tell me that Mexe stands for Military Engineering Experimental Establishment, at Christchurch, where they first built the Bailey Bridge.

\* It was essential to keep diaries in order that accurate post-operations report could eventually be written. My diary was left behind on HMS *Intrepid* and was written as soon as we recovered from operations.

\* Kelp – a floating seaweed, often hundreds of feet long, that clogs up many inlets in the Falklands. The islanders collect and use it for fertilizer and food, hence their nickname 'Kelpers'.

\* All this information as supplied by the Argentineans, with their spelling.

# Index

# INDEX

## B

*Bahia Paraiso* 248
Barfoot, Gunner 'Tich' 253
BBC World Service 67, 160-161, 216, 246, 270
Beagle Ridge **221-271**, 273-274, 281
Bedford, Captain Nigel 123, 293
Bedford, Gunner Tim 44-45, 82, 121, 123, 167, 196, 237, 241, 263
Bell, Captain Rod 132, 144, 145, 216, 269
Berkeley Sound 124, 232, 234, 245
Blanco Bay 261
Blowpipe missiles 227
Bluff Cove 205, 223, 228-230
Bold Point 183
bombs incorrectly fused 123, 160-161
Boner, Doreen 248-249
Booth, Radio Supervisor George 91
*Brilliant*, HMS 156
British armed forces 19-25
Brown, Captain Chris 122, 123, 124, 125, 151, 270, 278
Burrows, Pilot Bob 124

## C

Cameron, Major Peter 111-112
*Canberra*, SS 52, 90-91, 93-94, 154, 280-294
Cape Pembroke 124
Chairman Mao suit 192
Challenger tank 21
Chatelaine *see* thermal imaging camera

chronology 302-304
civilians killed and injured 247-251
Clapp, Commodore, Michael 125
Commando Logistics Regiment 98
Cortley Hill 236, 261, 265-267

## D

d'Appice, Captain Nick 258
Darwin 198, 202, 209
'dead ground' 237
Death Valley Hill 139
Defence, Ministry of
    author's transfer to 295
    civil servants 21
    High Court action 22-25
    media handling 15-17
dehydration 188-189
Delves, Major Cedric 254, 261, 266-267
departure 47-49
Dickie, Captain Roger 227
digestive system 190-191
Diggle, Flight Lieutenant Jeff 31
Doctor Point 265
Douglas 198, 209, 234
Dundonald Bombardment Units 34
Dutchman's Island 210

## E

Eagle Mount 210
Eales, Lieutenant Martin 231
*Endurance*, HMS 108, 134
equipment and kit 45-46, 116-117, 134-135, 191-193

# INDEX

# INDEX